A Writer's Diary

TOBY LITT

GALLEY BEGGAR PRESS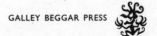

First published in 2023
by Galley Beggar Press Limited
37 Dover Street, Norwich NR2 3LG

A CIP record for this book is available from the British Library

Paperback ISBN: 978-1-913111-37-3
Black-cover edition ISBN: 978-1-913111-41-0

Text and design by Tetragon, London
Printed and bound in Great Britain by CPI Books, Chatham

BEI VERLUST BITTE ZURÜCKGEBEN AN:

_____

_____

_____

_____

FINDERLOHN: $ _____

Sonntag 1 Januar

Entered the year in Leigh's arms, just as I should be. Mum, exhausted, had gone to bed around half past eight. Dad fought through until midnight. Big Ben on the TV. My brother sent a text. It said his resolution was 'not to write a novel (again) this year. Or ever, you'll be relieved to hear.' That made Leigh laugh.

'Who knows what this New Year will bring?' Dad said, five minutes after the chimes – and then started sobbing. He was sitting on the blue sofa. 'Happy things, perhaps,' he added. We gave him another hug. He went to bed soon after. We didn't stay up much longer.

Late up. Quiet day. Muggy warm. We all went for a walk, or tried to. Mum turned back halfway to the War Memorial.

No writing.

Catching up with this on the 2nd after we –

Montag 2 Januar

drove home. Unpacked. Sitting at my desk, writing in my diary. When Leigh went to that conference in Munich, on logical languages (Esperanto, Simplified English), she bought this diary, this Tagebuch. She said when she saw it, she was thinking of it as one of my Christmas presents. But then she remembered Mum always buys me a diary, so she better have it for herself (although Leigh doesn't usually keep a diary – apart from her academic one). On Christmas Day, Mum said she had been intending to get me the usual diary – to order it online – but that she'd forgotten. She was embarrassed but also, I could tell, exhausted. All this keeping up with the usual rituals is becoming difficult for her. I tried to make as little of it as possible, although her forgetting upset me – not because she'd forgotten my present, but because if she were her healthy self, she'd never forget something like that. I realized the chemotherapy was making her iller than she'd let on. Of course, I said it was fine, I could easily get the diary myself; and then Leigh mentioned she had this spare one which she wasn't going to use. 'I'll give it to him when we get home,' she said, 'as if it's from you.' Mum wanted to give her some money for it, Leigh tried to refuse, but Mum insisted – so this Tagebuch is from both of them. I don't know if I'll get used to the days of the week, although I love Mittwoch for Wednesday. Midweek. It's very practical, like Mandarin days of the week (Oneday, Twoday…) but makes me wonder where they put Woden. Was he too Norse for them? A couple of the summer months are lazily shared – August, September (but November, too) – and for some, English just finesses a letter: Dezember, Oktober. März is heavy-metal-umlaut month. Januar and Februar save energy, just like Mum, by forgetting the y's. Mai is kin to Czech Maj. But Juni and Juli are like skipping rhymes. Oh, April's lazy, too. English months came from Northern Europe, didn't they? We started to export our language and time later. The paper of the Tagebuch is good for writing; the edges of the letters don't go spidery, and the ink is sucked in without me having to leave the page open for five minutes. As usual, I feel the thickness of pages, between me and the desktop, and wonder what will happen to be written on them. I don't think Mum will buy me another diary.

Dienstag 3 Januar

So far, slack-writing. I'm in a lull; when I was younger, I went through periods – of of of writer-crazes, of under-the-influence. I suppose it has to be (disappointingly for all concerned) that I'm now more myself and so less swayable. But I still attempt to seek out books that will change me, and occasionally one once again does.

I go back into the forest and am lost between thickly growing trunks.

What concerns me is that more stable writing lacks something because it lacks periodicity. Blue. Rose. Early. Middle. But sometimes there has to be, and so we have to endure, a season of walking in ice – Nature must come to seem not like nature at all, just like an element in one of its states; and then it needs to prove (Spring, torrential or not) that it can't be killed by a sub-zero lull.

But the forest isn't always available. Too often I stay in the glib city; it's only when there are free animals around that there's potential for metamorphosis. Pigeons and rats, green parrots and foxes – they won't do; they've already changed into human-adjuncts, metropolites. No, that's wrong. I'm just bored of seeing them in Brockwell Park.

A person only feels vivid when they feel hunted. (Slightly less slack, this.) Am I – are you? – capable of feeling prey? Who or what would eat *me*?

I see death as a perfectly circular lake, dark silver, almost perfectly smooth – because ripples of light sometimes travel back and forth across it (perhaps only to prove to me they are within my eyes, and are merely hopeful, because death is unreflective). Situated high up in the mountains, this lake is expensive to visit but far from exclusive. Entering the waters there is the most stylish thing most people do. They are being escorted into the back of a shiny black Bentley – and driven on soft springs to the ever-curving beach.

Mittwoch 4 Januar

Warm, showery day. Walk in the park with Leigh; very aware of pregnant women, of couples with babies in buggies. Held her hand. Green parrots unhappy with the wind.

My image for life is flour on a fork – plain white flour. Although I can't see the particles, I know they are there. They have more friction than chalk powder: seem happy to ascend into toppleable towers. Spooning flour into a bowl brings a sequence of unrepeatable icebergs. I'm sorry to lose each one. Bread follows. (But, if it's bright white, this is *processed* flour. Bleached life.)

Mouse was fine while we were away, Holly says, round for coffee. She popped in to see him twice. Like at Christmas. Only one night with our bed all to himself. He's grown a little, still growing. He lies on the carpet behind me like tabby roadkill; legs all over – at least seven of them. Not a normal kitten, this one. Hardly a kitten any more.

Looked back at last year's diary. What I wrote on December 17th about my hope for this year. I feel superstitious about even having written that on paper. Every month is another wishful chance.

Donnerstag 5 Januar

Quiet.

Ends of years feel like conclusions but beginnings feel like continuations. December devolves to January, and I'm in the same shit, writing the same thing. Project remains Project. Ends of books are staggered: first reader, other readers, agent, publishers or publisher, editor, redraft, final edit, flat proofs, bound proofs, final panicked changes, author's copies, oh look a typo on page 3. When I finished scribbling the last paragraph of my last book, first time through, I stood up and took a curtain call. I haven't confessed that to anyone, not even in here. I bowed left, right, front. That's the only time I've ever done something so public, in my room, on my own. But I knew that someone someday would applaud what I'd done – I felt the tickle-touch of future eyes – there were admirers, a thousand, ten thousand – I could almost hear them cheering – but the standing ovation, the love, was interrupted by rumours of a bomb, and then by a bomb – people fled the smoky theatre – Messerschmidts and Spitfires, coming out of the sun, strafed the screaming crowds – I sat down again, and was pleased at the beginnings of shame at my vanity. Such vanity. This took place one day in the middle of March or June, not on 31st December. Yet it was my own personal midnight of the year. I may have told Leigh that evening (about finishing the book), I suspect I didn't. It was an entirely private Hogmanay. Usually, I'll write a little in here, and I always try to remember to date final pages. Maybe someone who was in the auditorium will be enthused enough to take an interest, after they recover from their pride-induced burns – although that particular theatre will have to be rebuilt from ashy ruins. These are the foundations.

In Juni or März – privately – at the desk – ashamed – scribbling – I will try to rebuild from ashy ruins. I think it will be harder this time, because I dared to take that curtain call. Because of that, I am a worse person, a worse writer.

Freitag 6 Januar – *Epiphany*

Wrote some novel.

Samstag 7 Januar

Lifeless.

Sonntag 8 Januar

Did some preparation for teaching. Emailing all the students in this term's workshop. Making sure they know which room we're in, etc. Already anxious about what they'll expect.

10:09. Leigh did a pregnancy test, which was positive. (She bought it at the Streatham chemist as soon as they opened.) A small cross in a clear plastic circle.

Neither of us quite able to believe it – although I had thought Leigh might soon be pregnant, again. Her period is more than a few days late. So, she was pregnant when we went for that sad sleety walk in the park; also at New Year, at my parents'.

We have been a little subdued in our reaction. I feel very happy but also terrified. Leigh wanted to do another test immediately; I said the cross was very clear. More hugs. We've decided not to tell anyone for three months – assuming all goes well.

11:01. I am nervous every time Leigh goes out of the room; she, whenever she goes to the loo. She has immediately started taking aspirin, and will try to make an appointment at St Mary's for Tuesday.

Montag 9 Januar

Imagining the tiny blob of growing cells; trying not to. I saw Hubert Selby Jr once, at a big public event. He was asked about self-censorship, given how extreme his novels were. He said, and immediately became a saint of mine: 'If-it-comes-in-the-brain-it-goes-on-the-page.' No question, no hesitation. Have I lived up to Hubert? What don't I normally write? What don't I put down because I imagine someday it'll destroy whatever reputation I have? (The idea there will be literary reputations when people are knifing one another for half a mouldy turnip...) (It's always turnips for dinner in my climate collapse dystopia.) I suppose I don't write unfaithfulness. Unfaithfulness of mind. When I betray myself, and Leigh, by thinking of other women. And also hate – hatefulness. I try not to record my flashes of disgust at other people. (The annals of my self-disgust are multi-volume.) I don't know why it is, but my first reaction – person! – is often fear and loathing before I coach myself to peace, love and understanding. Where I was brought up, people didn't look like the people I see in London. The mathematician Paul Erdős referred to TIF – The Inner Fascist. He recognized that *he* had one (despite being Jewish), that we *all* have one. And so, I suppose, I don't put down – and I still won't put down – what my Inner Fascist thinks and feels and shouts and screams. It's not necessary for me to write it because you too, whoever you are, you think it (Dear Literary Executor) when you are impatient, tired, exhausted, angry. And I can't argue that this isn't the real me – perhaps the inner of inner is the cave: tribal mistrust. I'd prefer to think that it's the Outer Fascist, and that when you go beneath the crust, we're all less crusty. If we were accepted and loved as we should have been, by good enough mothers, surely there's acceptance and love beneath surprise that someone looks or behaves or smells as they do.

Dienstag 10 Januar

What is your territory – as a writer, as an ahrhrtist? I suppose (trying not to be dishonest) mine is people who have enough free time to think about themselves as people. You might say it's *identity*, but it seems to me that everybody making any kind of art is concerned with identity. Better to say (at least in most of my writing) it's consciousness and time – boom, I said it. Being and Time. Or that's the area I write in when I'm looking around, rather than being dragged along by a story or formed by a form. *Sein und Zeit*. This could be reduced to, 'How people get through the day.' Overall, it's less about consciousness than the escape from consciousness, consciousness overcoming consciousness to become... I don't like continuation dots. I don't like how they look on the page. For me, it's hard to read writers (Céline, Miller) who use a lot of them. And I particularly disliked those three dots just then. My territory is – like all writers – the page. I try to get readers from the top of one page to the top of the next page: with something happening in between – happening to the language, the characters, but also the reader. I called it 'headfuck fiction' once. (Wishing that wasn't offputtingly sweary.) Under the headline EVERYTHING COULD BE COMPLETELY DIFFERENT, and American sub-head, 'Reader realizes, their consciousness is neither unique nor definitive.' And the follow-up story, NOTHING IS INEVITABLE JUST BECAUSE IT EXISTS IN ITS CURRENT FORM. 'You are not inevitable, neither are your clothes. Neither is your God, nor the way you see the colour green.' If I wanted a description of what I have always wanted from books, it would be TO NOT BE ME. To be anything other than me, to be anywhere other than where I am. (The further the better – hence sci-fi and fantasy, Emily Brontë and Keats.) And that's what I've tried to write. In that way, my territory is what is not my territory. I try to write what I shouldn't have written, what I shouldn't be able to write. Because the voice comes from away from me – away from the desk. Yet the desk is where it happens. Leigh says 'Morning' – I got up early to write this before I was too conscious or self-conscious to write it. I slept badly, thinking thinky thoughts – that's no excuse.

Write what you know plus *Stay in your lane* equals *Keep a diary*. Where else am I allowed to go? I have already invaded and subdued so many lives. Joseph and Elliott. What if what I know – what if all I know – what if all I can legitimately claim is, is being a white man writing about writing at a desk that is actually a table? What if my territory is 76¼" by 31½" (194cm x 80cm) of horizontal hardboard? Bigger than Jane Austen's 'little bit two Inches wide of Ivory' – but why Ivory, Jane? Why not a native hardwood? Why did an elephant have to be tusked to bring you the whitely neutral surface you must work upon?

This evening's first workshop went well. Class comprises: Ola, Lola, Andy, Roxana, Rudy, Katherine, Felix – can I remember them all? Grace, Rebekah, Jess. Who've I forgotten? Agh. Have to look them up. Michael. The Archangel Michael. They were quiet but intense. One of the things I've learned as a teacher is to do as little comparison as possible – don't forestall the class's experience for them. I know that I could say, 'Look, some of you will have a breakthrough this term, and you won't recover from it for a couple of months. You'll suddenly find yourself writing something much better than you've ever done before, but you won't know how you've done it. And the others in the group will recognize that you've achieved something special – and that I (tutor) have seen and reacted to that. And they'll become disheartened and jealous and wonder why it isn't them? For some, this will mean they work harder, and produce something better just in time for assessment, for others it'll make them aggressive and slapdash, resentful and pointlessly competitive. (This was how I was, in my writing class, on my MA.) It's only Week One, and I can't identify who among you is ready to pop and who is heading for a sulk. That's why, in your tutorials, I'll speak to you in the way I do – I'll be trying to find out who you are. So I can help you.'

Leigh annoyed at me for getting in late. I went for a drink with the students, which often settles some of them – I mean, seeing me in a less formal setting, not the booze itself. Maybe the booze itself.

Donnerstag 12 Januar

An English writer is post-Imperial, whereas a Chinese writer is in the pomp of Empire, and an American one is in the plop. Maybe that's not the way to start, though I like using *pomp* next to *Empire* soon after *Imp*. 'Minimalism is inimical to the idioms of dominion.' Now I'm just playing – which puritan minimalism dispermits. *Keep it simple, stupid* only applies if you're stupid, or wish to become so. Hemingway hems me in, Carver carves me up, but grandmother Stein is fine most of the time. (Lish almost edited Carver to death. Utterly merciless topping. Minimalism is S&M. Knife play.) The cult of the cut leads to writing that represents butchery, not animality – living-inquisitive-responding creatures, often dangerous, poised on paw-hoof-wing, who can fucking surprise you/me. 'Here's your meaning, sire, half a pound of chopped liver – or chump steak.' What that really means is, 'You're alive, I'm alive, but what I'm giving you is dead.' Yes, I'm European – a posthumous place; Europeans are born with a death in the family, a stillborn twin. Yet what we notice most in the graveyard is fox, rat, crow. Our sentences can be epitaphs, or the genius-words of schoolgirls from beyond the elm – about a teacher they fancy or hate, or about the fox, or about how much they love graveyards. Cuts bleed (blood is good; we need the bed of prose to be a killing floor). In the past, I self-amputated – 'I feel the need, the need to bleed' – but now it's about not mutilating time. As a person, there are hesitations in my hesitations. Englishmen don't have declarative souls; they have – he generalizes – This wasn't where I meant this to go. (Which is good. No route march.) All I needed was a reminder, before I started work, that I've been through the meat-grinder before. I've been mincemeat. Sam R. Delany says it best – that minimalist stuff is 'good writing', not (forgive me) 'talented writing'. Boilerplate is life-hate; route one is No Fun; it may be, Toby, that the curlicue is you. I suppose I prefer bad writing to dead writing. We live in the provinces of the decline of the American Empire – the suburbs of Google and the exurbs of Windows, and the brownfields of MS-DOS, and the necropolis of IBM. We live within sight of the rise of the Chinese dominion, the high metropolis of Huawei and brands I haven't even heard of.

Freitag 13 Januar

What people really like in diaries, I know, aren't the mini-essays, generalizations about Art & Life. They like the bit about the pig escaping into the walled garden. They like the weather, landscapes, animals, gossip – the subplot about the milkmaid, the aside about the price of herrings. (This is a mini-essay, generalized.) The elderflower cordial discovered on top of the bathroom cabinet. They like a little bit of health business but not too much. (Journal of an Invalid.) When an observation comes, and it's true, it's got to be in the midst of plumbers and banging. The kitten chewing the curtains and baby's whooping cough. That's why Virginia Woolf is so good. (She's Queen.) 'I did not finish my egg.' Oct 22 1927. (Minus the baby.) (And the kitten, come to think of it.) We need our bathroom replaced – this is us – because the shower leaks down through the kitchen ceiling. 'Pissholes,' says the builder on next door's scaffold. The shower has leaked for about a year and a half. I don't visit my parents often enough. I want to go full-time at work and I don't want to go full-time at work. Virginia Woolf never had a kitten, did she? She had dogs. Dorothy Wordsworth wrote about her brother's writing – whether it was going well or (as usual) badly; whether he was furious or merely gloomy. In one or two lines, she did delicious watercolours. And she didn't bother with transition or construction. (Not patronizing. Her construction was happenstance.) The sonnet and the milkmaid right next to one another, because the milk spills on the page and the sonnet pays the dairy (eventually) – the fact of there being sonnets allows some small amount of money to come into the cottage. The milk. There's quite a bit about the milk. I have lived in this house five years, and when my back is to the window – as it is when I'm at my desk – I still can't tell whether a train on the track beyond the garden centre is approaching from the north or the south. You'd think the sound over the railway bridge (north) or through the trees (south) would make it somewhat different, distinctive. But my ears can't hear. (Who are 'people' anyway? '… people really like.' Most people? Posh people? People who read, who are the only people who really count as people to writers who don't have enough readers? Stop with your peopling.)

Samstag 14 Januar

How about a desk diary? What if I keep this really close? It's going that way anyway. A diary of the desk. In this place, a coffee spill is a major event. If we moved house, I would take a photo – many photos – and put the objects back where they were, here, at a new location, in a different workroom. (That's unlikely to happen for years; we can't afford it.) Why a photo? It's not like I don't know where they go: the rhinoceros, the Mercedes; the pen pot (white ceramic F H FAULDING & CO LTD GOLDEN EYE OINTMENT), the pencil pot (shining stainless steel). Overall, the Anglepoise. Uncle Anglepoise, PAT IN UK AND ABROAD. Never thought of it as Uncle before. I will stop, because these things are of no interest to anyone but me. (I will continue, because what is this diary *for* if not things of no interest to anyone but me?) I went through a period of acquiring metal objects – along with the lamp, the brushed metal filing cabinet over my right shoulder, the metal mug in which I have my coffee. My good-as-I-can-make-it coffee – which I sometimes spill. If my desk-objects weren't metal, then they were black plastic. But it's wooden things I want around me most of all. Woodface was probably the first. The Green Man – French. I was fourteen or fifteen years old, and with my father in a Brocante in the Dordogne. I remember hundreds of chairs piled up to a ceiling as high as the rafters in a village church. Dad was doing a deal; the antiquer gave me the carved-leafy face for free. A gift – originally from a dresser or a seat-stall in a chapel. They have a name, ornaments that surmount pillars within antique furniture – my father would know it, unless he's forgotten it. I could phone him to find out, but I don't want to hear his voice as he speaks about Mum. Not right now. Of course, she might still answer – as she won't in future. (I will phone when I'm finished.) The Green Man has been with me for over thirty years, and is important, colossal, always calling me back to him. He's made of dense chocolatey wood. I would like a desk made of the same wood, not too heavy, but with lots of drawers.

Sonntag 15 Januar

My tea is beside me, to my left (as I'm right-handed and the pen goes in that hand) – tea the colour of the Thames at its muddiest. When I brought it up, and Leigh's at the same time, I managed not to spill any on the stair or landing carpets. If I'd done this (our current carpet is tea-coloured anyway) it would be a matter of deciding whether it was serious enough for me to absolutely have to fetch a kitchen cloth, and scrub it with washing-up liquid, or whether I could do a one-foot sand-dance, and trust it not to stain. (My parents remembered seeing the famous sand-dance troupe Wilson, Keppel and Betty up in the West End – the two moustachioed men (minus Betty) would busk for people queuing for plays and musicals, sliding angular and comic with their pharaoh's headdresses. Pure Music Hall History.) Leigh's tea is more likely to stain as Leigh takes her tea stronger than me. When I make it, in the morning, I always put Leigh's mug on the left – L for left for Leigh – so I don't forget which has green milk in it and which red. (Hers is skimmed, mine semi-skimmed.) Sometimes a spoonful of honey sneaks into mine, I don't know how – and Leigh doesn't need to know about that. We have organic teabags, because they don't release plastic particles into us, the loo, the sea. Today, this morning, 7:48, my tea tastes fine, and I've written this much, and the mug is still half full. In the morning, every morning, we start with our wide off-white mugs – I suppose they're the colour of Cornish Cream in a cream-coloured jug. When the tea tastes bad, and isn't so much 'my tea', is when it has bubbles in it. I don't know why this is – there's something demeaning about bubbly tea (not bubble tea, which they sell in Soho). Tea should have a placid, steaming surface; no glissando of milk fat – but this mug is getting too cold, and I can taste the creak in it more than the crank. (I should say, alternate days, Leigh gets up and makes me tea.)

Phone call with Mum, who is reluctant to say what's really going on with her – as she's always been. (When she told me the diagnosis, she said, 'I'm sorry for putting you through all this bother.') Dad was there, so I couldn't really say what I wanted.

Montag 16 Januar

There are lots of people who want to be writers, and even more who want to know what it's like *to be a writer*. More still are interested in – fascinated by – the inspiration (old-fashioned) and misbehaviour (my art demands I sleep with her as well as you) and bosslessness (forgetting agent and editor) and funky workspace (in some magazine) than are interested in, or give a fuck about, yet another novel. Another novel, however good, is just another novel. Give us the honest interview about how the novel was written, and how little of it was made up. If you're writing about a passionate affair, and most novels are about passionate affairs (aren't they?), you bloody well *have* to have gone off and fucking *had* one, don't you? No, the desktop world is a very clear, beautiful and limited one. However rich you are, you can only write with one pen. You can worldbuild multi-volume fantasy epics, but each letter has to emerge individually. (When I'm writing fast, I forget to dot my i's.) If you don't love being at the desk, and being in the world of words, being a word-being, then you shouldn't be a writer. Fine, be a screenwriter. Or go and advertise your vocation, and your interestingness-compared, in the shop window of Starbucks. But the real unreal thing is you and the sentences unspooling from no-one knows where. They are not there already, sculpture within stone, waiting to be transcribed, although who knows? The sound of them needs to be listened to as well as controlled – this vowel here needs to flirt or echo or crunch or floodle with this one there. Being a writer is being, at one and the same time, completely in and completely out of control. (Rock'n'roll.) I know what's coming and I have no fucking clue – only that it will take place, it can *only* take place, at the desk. My desk came from Ikea, years ago, and is the kind of trestle that wallpaper is pasted on. The top is hardboard, ink- and coffee-stained, and only the weight of it and what's on it keeps it attached to the legs. One of the legs was used as a scratching post by Ziggy; I'd get splinters in my left foot when I stood up (pine, I think). But then I turned the trestle around, back to front. They're shaped like capital H's laid on their sides with very long crossbars, reaching up. Bless it, the edge is soft-ish, where my arm has rubbed against it. This is more important than a prize.

Dienstag 17 Januar

When I see the surface of the tea in a mug, or even more a cup, I think it looks like the sea – sea seen from space. (Aside: We close our eyes when we take a sip or a gulp, just as we do when we move in for a kiss (unless we're callow and experimenting with cross-eyes)). But if you keep staring as the drink nears your mouth, you start to see the shadow of your nose in the surface, and your eyes within your fore-head reflected in the exposed circle of the bottom of the mug. You (or at least I, but it can't vary too much) are distorted as in a spoon's back – the nose is a conk, and you're looking right up it. The eyes (I'm checking now) look weary and bebagged. In my mug, I look like an exhausted pinhead – desperate for a hit of his drug *du jour*. (There is a new improved name for pinheads, I am sure.) It has always – here's Keats, 'the waters at their priestlike task/ Of pure ablution round the something coast'. I have always been amazed how, a century and a half before Gagarin, Keats gave us a perfect satellite view of our spinning, tidal globe. Even more extraordinary is John Ruskin's whoosh up from Africa to Northern Europe in 'The Nature of Gothic': 'Let us, for a moment… imagine the Mediterranean lying beneath us like an irregular lake, and all its ancient promontories sleeping in the sun: here and there an angry spot of thunder, a grey stain of storm, moving upon the burning field; and here and there a fixed wreath of white volcano smoke, surrounded by its circle of ashes; but for the most part a great peacefulness of light, Syria and Greece, Italy and Spain, laid like pieces of a golden pavement into the sea-blue, chased, as we stoop nearer to them, with bossy beaten work of mountain chains, and glowing softly with terraced gardens…'

Both Keats and Ruskin prove you don't need to have done something to have experienced it. No frequent flyer from Cairo to Malmö, even looking out the window of Business Class the whole way, ever saw the details of the distant world as clearly as Ruskin sitting at his desk. Eyes closed. No astronaut took in more through the earthside porthole than Keats at this desk. At his desk. Eyes closed. This is not something you're allowed to say. Experience is all authority; the weeping victim vanquishes the creepy expert.

I'm getting a sense of the twelve in the workshop group – guessing what they'll need. With Rudy (Can't Fail), for example, it could be pure ego management. 'Yes, you're writing interesting stories, but that's not what you need to be aiming for. You need to shock yourself.' Read Isaac Babel. With Grace (and Flavour), it might be permission. 'You don't have to be polite anymore – no-one is judging you that way.' Write under a pseudonym. Then you'll be off. With Rebekah (Hecka), she probably needs to know she can allow herself to be as funny as she is, and that it isn't a bad thing. She's v. funny. Michael (the Very Archangel) and Samira (Clearer) and Lola (the Polar) I'm more sure about. They need to work on their plotting, and to stop always writing-about-what-they're-writing-about. Your identity isn't you. Ola (Controller) and Felix (the Cat) need to learn what a story is and isn't. (Why didn't they learn this in their BA workshops?) Katherine (Not Arrogant) could be the most promising of them all, but everything's too on point – she needs to expand her aesthetic. Not always be beautiful. Jess (Stressy Jessie) is tough. She'll only learn by fighting me, disdaining me and the institution. (Rudy's like this, too, but he'll do it with resentment, she'll do it because she knows that's what she needs – she's been divorced twice, some mere university lecturer can't hurt her. But she's going to make him work.) Who else? Andy (with Sandy Hair) is – potentially – a situation to be managed. He seems unreachable. What can I do to reach him? And Roxana (Seeker of Prajna) is doing her own personal development thing. She's on a Journey, unfortunately – unfortunately, because she thinks of it as 'a Journey'; she accepts the language of living her best life without questioning it. If she wants to keep this, I don't know if I'm the right tutor for her. But someone more sympatico might just give her the wrong sort of praise. She needs to find her own language. I need to give more praise. Today we workshopped stories by Andy (up itself and not in a pleasurable way), Rebekah (one funny paragraph about cheeses) and Ola (undercooked but tasty). Tutorials begin tomorrow. Late bus home after a drink in the college bar. Leigh asleep. Mouse sleeping on my pillow.

Donnerstag 19 Januar

Leigh says she feels fine. How many times will I ask her, in the coming (I hope) nine months? Mum also (on the phone) says she feels fine.

Without really making up my mind, I seem to have decided not to shave until the baby is born. Or not born. That means, I already have a two weeks' beard. That's about as long as I usually let it get. Any more and it tends to become itchy. I am itchy at the moment, though. Soul-itch.

My mother is dying but I can still visit her, or phone her up for a chat which doesn't get to the subject: my mother is dying.

Will I one day cycle through the park explaining something like gravity – something I don't really understand – to my little cycling daughter or son? Why can't I jump on the top of that tree? Why can't I fly?

It's happened again with Walter – same thing. Exactly. Car – bend – tree. How does he afford it?

I see people dead. Although they are fine and full of potential heartbeats, still I see them as non-conscious matter going cold.

Mouse is a full-on basic beast. He scratches me at least once a day, often when I'm stroking him.

Thinking about Rudy in the class. Students who remind me of myself are the ones I like the least. He's arrogant. He's not good enough to be as arrogant as he is. Which is exactly what people thought about me. (Mr. Bicester, English Teacher.)

I lean on the surface of the desk, I press my left elbow down into it, and I write confusion. Outside, sun.

Freitag 20 Januar

A map of the territory – Leigh is out with Holly. My desk is three times wide as deep. If I stretch forwards, I can touch the wall with both hands; but I have to lean so far my nose is almost on the page. (My arms are neither unusually short nor exceptionally long.) Let's imagine the desktop viewed from above. Bottom centre is the writing area – this is where the A4 page, notebook, or laptop goes. Diagonally up from this, on the right-hand side, are within-easy-reach pen and pencil pots. Directly opposite my chair (another time) is the big black screen. To raise it to less back-killing height, it's on an aluminium box – shoebox size. On this are the plastic rhino and the toy Mercedes. Also, an external hard drive and external DVD drive. Just now, I have a couple of CDs on top of it, some lipbalm, and the wireless mouse. Bottom left is a pile of unsorted A4 drafts of poems, songs, somethings. These end up being dropped into an unsorted but roughly chronological wooden box under the desk, from where they are stacked (once or twice a year) into clear plastic storage boxes and carried down to the cellar – which is full of full clear plastic storage boxes. Upper left is a miniature five-drawer chest of leather. Each drawer could fit a new stack of A4 paper, but contains written pages I like to have to hand – I rarely open it. On top of this is where the wooden things go: two carved lion-faces, a posable figure for life drawing, a Gilbert & George collapsible toy, a Day of the Dead diorama c/o Frida Kahlo, some Aesop Marrakech Intense Eau de Toilette, a bamboo whistle. To the right of this, against the wall, is a smaller aluminium box where live postcards, passports, scissors, rulers, photographs, tissues and anything misc. Nested in the angle between chest and postcard box is the Green Man. He rests on the fossilized sandstone, looking up at the ceiling. He's friends with the large but broken hole punch. The right half of the desk is simpler. The big black printer lives here. Bottom extreme right is a life-size wooden bust I call Shakespeare. He wears my hats. In front of the printer stands the Anglepoise. Behind him, ranged against the wall, held up by aluminium bookends, are perhaps twenty-five notebooks of all colours but all A5. Lurking behind the printer, finally, is a metal fan – for the hottest of summer days. It all fits on one page! My world.

Samstag 21 Januar

What's the smallest thing I could write about? The nothingest. Put it another way, what's the least important subject I could choose? I could make a joke at this point, and say 'my sex life' or 'X's books'. This would be like a punishment essay at school. In no less than 1,000 words, describe the inside of a ping-pong ball, or the sex life of a cornflake. Mr. McKee, the physics master (who claimed he'd piloted an observation plane for one of the atomic bomb tests) had me write about *Why I am too clever by half*. I somewhat amused him by writing about why I wasn't too clever by half but that I was too clever by 0.513679243 recurring. He liked that. Although it was a maths joke, it was gesturing in the direction of a physics joke. It acknowledged, in a too clever way, that there might be such a strange entity as a physics joke. The smallest thing I could write about, in physics terms, and perhaps in cosmic joke terms, is the level below subatomic particles. I've read some popular science books, and watched some documentaries, so I know all about this – I know some physicists study what they call strings, and I also know the Higgs boson causes (facilitates? spews?) mass. If it's not turtles all the way down, them there strings must be made of something – hemp from super-duper marijuana plants. Tiny tiny tiny. 'Made of' is a terribly lay term. Something does something string-like. I know strings is where some physicists become cosmic. Everything – and they mean *everything* – is good good good, good vibrations. The constant is the chord – background noise – the music of the spheres (though atoms are anything but the shiny balls of my school textbooks). Sub-subatomicism. Isn't this also the least important thing I could write about? – seeing how humans aren't, so far as we know, in contact with what little boys and girls are really made of. (This may not be true, if it's in the wibbles between quibbles that consciousness twangs into being.) I like the idea that even if we don't jam or plunk on a string-y level, we do – in some manner – vibe there, or (more accurately) are vibed, or (as accurately as I can make it) we co-vibe. Not 'we are stardust' but we exist as stuff-ily as a cello, as a comet. We are briefly gorgeously tremulously alive. And death is not even reabsorption into the hum, it's an ever so slightly shifted partial. I hope.

It's almost impossible to say anything accurate about nothing, and I only say 'almost' out of writerly pride that's actually writerly vanity, because I'd like at least to leave myself the chance to build my own hut of failure. Tangentially, or shamefully directly, something is sometimes said of nothing. Heidegger wrote, 'Nothing nothings.' Shakespeare wrote, 'Nothing will come of nothing'. Donne wrote, 'I am re-begot/ Of absence, darknesse, death: things which are not.' Heidegger is accurate; Shakespeare (as Lear) is acute; Donne makes the most basic mistake. Nothing is unlike any other thing, and so should be referred to only in reference to itself.

If this is true, 'Nothing has always nothinged' and 'Nothing will continue to nothing' – these may be among the few other sayables. *Darknesse* (not darkness) is not nothing, though it's hard to imagine nothing as illuminated because light requires energetic presence – of a source, of particles. Also, darknesse requires extension: a single point can be neither dark nor light. The beginning of the Big Bang, wasn't that already bigger than a point? 'Too much of nothing,' Bob Dylan wrote. If you begin imagining nothing by picturing, or trying to picture, a void, you've already mistooken it. Absence is as unlike nothing as *darknesse*, and in a similar way – both require room in which not to be. And to have extension of any sort, doesn't that require projective or protective forces? I mean, to erect a circus tent, you need tent poles and guy ropes and tent pegs. I suppose you could get round this by saying that nothing can be said to pervade everything. Wherever anything is, nothing is there also – equipresent, but inaccessible. An *isn't* that is. To establish this, we could ask some questions: Can nothing ever increase in any way – size, density? Could a smaller nothing be present within a larger? Would a slice taken from nothing also be nothing? (Surely there's nothing with which nothing could be cut.) As expected, all this nothinging has gone nowhere. At least it's gone nowhere fast. I think what Donne was trying to evoke was not nothing but nothingnesse. If the baby isn't born, we'll be left not with nothing but with nothingnesse. Death is not nothing.

Sonntag 22 Januar

I've already described the topography of the desk, but that's not what I generally see — seated here. What's peripheral to the page — on all sides except the left, which is usually blocked by the brown-pink blur of my head-supporting palm… I see the interconnecting flecks of old golden hardboard. Light muscovado and ground cinnamon. It does look like a strangely fibrous planetary surface, seen from a spaceship in orbit (Solaris) — or like Afghanistan (slightly flattened) from a passenger jet at 30,000 ft. Some strands or threads are darker, almost like shreds of redwood bark; others catch the light of the Anglepoise with a sheen like my stretchmarks. There are few features — no writing, no pattern within the random-pressed-together-ness — except one Tipp-Ex smudge-cloud and dozens of inkspills. These are congregated down and to the right; a spotty band of them, like a negative of the Milky Way. Elsewhere, a few larger inkstains. If I Rorschach them, I see for each — an eyelid with eyelashes, a man on his knees, a witch or someone wearing a dunce's cap, the United States of America minus Alaska, a horse skull, a droopy penis with testicles, a helicopter minus rotor-blades, a cartoon heart viewed aslant. Beneath my right forearm, and also where my elbow touches, the surface is darker and has greater shine — I've polished it with rubbing, and the grease of me has gone into it. In summer, if I sweat, this area becomes resistant, rubs me up the wrong way (as damp skin does to damp skin). The near edge of the board is nubbled off where once it was a distinct right-angle; almost-splinters still come off it, very occasionally. I know it's hollow beneath, but knuckle-rap and it isn't echoey. Imagine that inner space, inside my desk: a flat, dusty, ever-dark plane. Small moon-people journey across it, lights in their domed helmets. They discover nothing but fallen punctuation marks and more dust. I've had this desk around a quarter of a century.

Perhaps, more accurately, it's a table — I continue to call it a desk.

Montag 23 Januar

I just switched the desktop computer on by accident; I was wiping its black mirror with a blue dustcloth, and my middle finger pressed the button on the back. Why am I so hateful of tech? Why do I speak badly of what has done so much for me? If I hadn't had a wordprocessor and a printer, I don't know whether I'd ever have written a novel. In Prague, in the early 90s, I lived for several months on a manual typewriter with the Z and the Y reversed. Typing and retyping poems, that was part of it all, the manual labour; essays even. But I needed memory and printing before I could start in on longer forms (novels 1, 2, 3 and 4). I can't blame the manufacturers for fitting their products to the needs of business. Business now takes computer form. But I know there are imperceptible obstructions and nudges every time a .doc is opened. I don't write documents, or files; I feel constrained by folders. Words on pages in notebooks (see how Word, Pages and Notebook are all registered trademarks) – the written page is open. It's glorified already, and doesn't need to be saved or autosaved. It is singular, can be easily destroyed, but doesn't constrain. No wordcount, no peripheral-vision clock, no proprietary font. How many people try to write up to Times Roman or down to Courier New? That is wordprocessing, and a good writer doesn't *process* words (even when working on microprocessors inside microcomputers). When a computer is on, it's expectant; it needs to find a task for you. The page has more patience; it has already consumed all the energy it's going to consume. I hate calling them *computers*, because that already sounds dated. But I also don't want to advertise them by referring to them by brand name. The only computer I've loved, truly adored, was my black laptop. As soon as they stopped making black clamshells and forced everyone onto tinny metallic cigarette cases, I became indifferent. Instead, to get back that look, I buy black laptop covers. It's not the same; it's no longer a purely dark instrument. I can imagine Baudelaire using a PowerBook Pismo. I hate built-in obsolescence. I hate bloatware. I hate not being able to get rid of what I don't want, need or use. Speaks the trained, dissatisfied consumer – addressing himself as if he were a call-centre.

Dienstag 24 Januar

At school, in English, learning handwriting, I was told repeatedly that my letters should land on the line. That's what the lines on the page are for, Litt. But for some reason, and I don't think it was laziness, something in me rebelled – and my words continued to levitate. They still do. Perhaps they're not flying, which is the most obvious and self-aggrandising metaphor: His sentences refused to be caged by bars, and headed far up into-the-open-sky. Perhaps, instead, they've just been waiting for their photo to be taken, then jumped a little bit off the ground. Jump-snap. Edit a sequence of leap-images together, and it looks like someone is jerkily floating through the air – legs spasming and arms semaphoring. A skateboarder mid-trick. Mouse wants attention in the form of chin-chucking, but when he gets bored with one rhythm, he bites. Ziggy never did that. I put him on the floor, Mouse jumps back up, like a capital letter, like a big I, and sniffs my tea – before heading to the black pot that contains my pencil sharpeners. Out comes the gold one for short pencils. Now he's investigating the rhinoceros. And in writing this I am trying not to alter the usual altitude and attitude of my handwriting. Looking back through January, it seems pretty much a match. The gap beneath is a constant of half a letter's depth – and, as I look at it, I'm beginning to think it is a form of hovering that doesn't involve an invisible jump between words. I'm up for this. Somehow, even when I'm not despairing, and despite my teachers, I don't alight but stay aloft. Writing is my anti-gravity device. Say I'm not grounded – say I'm airy-fairy. Hare not rabbit, Ariel not Caliban, hovercraft not tank. That'll do me. Better heavensent, at least in aspiration, than earthbound. What the characters touch, when they touch anything, is one another. They stroke and tickle, without trudge or yomp. And so I write barefoot.

Story from Rudy. Ouch — the workshop group really went for him. He was in all the male heads and none of the female ones — not even the mother. (Irish family but Jewish mother.) Rudy seemed almost tearful with rage, but I think he learned his lesson. Michael came through angelically in the aftermath, and everyone was mild towards the end. This sometimes happens. The class defines itself by how hard someone's prepared to go in. Ola wasn't having it with Rudy, and Samira backed her. 'It could be worse,' Ola said, 'I just can't see how.' 'Rape fantasy,' said Samira. Rebekah added some laughs. 'Jesus, leave him some skin.' I did intervene, after that from Samira. I spoke of workshop karma. Only dish what you can take. Michael had tried to write a story about someone being happy, which is one of the hardest things to do. A bit bland. Who is he trying to please? Not me, I hope. I better let him know, in the tutorial, that *I'm* not his audience. He's very young. Nice hair. Talent. Last story was Jess. She got the rebound from Rudy, and was overpraised by Samira and everyone else for something fine enough but too explainy. It wrapped up with a big polka-dot bow. We looked at how the story would read if you cut the last line (better), the penultimate (much better) and the one before that (wow, interesting). Also, try cutting the opening paragraph and changing the title. I give this advice so often I should get it printed on a business card. Jess wrote everything down in her tiny pink notebook. The room we're in — basement of Russell Square building — is salad compartment chilly. Three of the students were eating dried mango, which is big loud. But everyone's hungry by 8pm. I tell them, 'Bananas — the secret of Birkbeck is bananas.'

Donnerstag 26 Januar

Macs – the brand name is Apple – I've lived with them ever since I had to get rid of the Amstrad. When I was travelling in America, I saw my first Mac. It was upright, like a small boxy towerblock. The screen was square, and it had a sexy slit for a floppy diskette. Sexy-boxy. I thought 'I could write on something like that – faun colour, and able to do graphics.' But by the time I bought a Mac, they were more conventionally shaped: deep screen on top of a video-recorder-shaped hard drive for a stand, and a separate keyboard. Good keyboard – so much better for typing than they are now. After that it was upgrade after upgrade, whenever the old one slowed to the point of pointlessness (or when it stopped playing videos). Because of them, I have become more productive; because of them, I have become less able to see the restrictions within that productivity. I was dead against Microsoft, but Word eventually snuck its way into MacWorld. Snake in the garden. Macs and PCs started to share processors, as if there had never been any profound ideological divide between them in the first place. If Mac approached me, to be one of the funky creatives photographed being creative in front of their laptops (in black and white), would I say yes? It's a product I've used; it's not a product I'd wish people to boycott. But it's evil – with built-in obsolescence and operating system updates that kill the speed, kill the hardware. Would it be hypocritical not to appear in a Mac ad, seeing as I was sold on their product the first time I saw it? Jesus, am I nothing more than a wannabe hipster? Is that all this is? Turn on, log in, zone out.

Freitag 27 Januar

Doing my taxes.

Samstag 28 Januar

What if it's twins? What if we're having two children, identical or non-identical, and one kills the other? It could happen in the womb, during birth, the umbilical cord of one gets caught around the other's neck.

I sometimes think – most people do, I expect – that I was a twin, that the other died, and that my parents never told me. It would be too terrible to know; not even born and already responsible for Death, for adult grief. I'm hungover this morning. I feel like I'm wearing a skullcap of irk. As normal, I should paracetomolize it into the far corners, but today I feel it's true to something. This is an anxiety headache, the kind I usually get at the end of a day. Instead, it met me on waking, because I was already wearing it – coronation – with a long beard of fret that had grown overnight. Must've had a very bad dream. What-iffery – prophylactic thinking (probably exactly the wrong word, as no prophylactics were harmed in the making of these foetuses, or this head-movie). (Baby, my mind's split open.) (*Headbirths, or, the Germans are Dying Out.*) Mouse wants his gorget ruffled. He's purring like an outboard motor on the top half of this page. And now play-biting my left hand. When he does this, I can see the fossilized skull of the Sabre Tooth Tiger in the Natural History Museum. Two incisors, two canines, clamping him – skull-capture – needles – giving him no chance. (I am writing these words in the gap between his ears.) And the beast's teeth met in his face. And now Mouse is gone, villain, because he heard Leigh going carefully downstairs. So cute and such a beast.

Mahler's 6th – I think of Mahler's 6th. He writes the symphony about the tragedy that has yet to happen to him, he mortgages his grief – living in the castle of it before he's even started to pay. Then he pays. Kindertotenlieder. *deadkidsongs*. Superstitiously, I worry that the work will work its will on the world. Egomanically, ha-ha-ha. Isn't having such a writer-father in itself a kind of murder? For the foetus. Foetuses. Oppenheimer's quote. Fee-fi-fo-fum, I am become. Foresuffering. Fort-da. (Just checked, it's still an *embryo*. *Foetus* is used from 10 weeks.)

Sonntag 29 Januar

I remember the first time I heard the phrase 'pins-and-needles' – I was probably going Ow and crying, and my mum (after working out what it was) probably said, 'Oh, it's just pins-and-needles – it'll go away soon.' I don't remember the exact room or situation, though I'm thinking of the sitting room (in Dunstable Street) with its big green easy chairs, but I remember the relief of suddenly knowing there was a name for this. This in-me thing. This pain. I could feel, or thought I could feel, the difference between the pricky pins and the diving needles. My mother had a sewing basket, which lived by her big green easy chair, and within it was a stellate pin-cushion – a hexagram made of mauve and faded violet fabrics, patterned. Inside was something bristly and very solid. Did the Victorians make pincushions out of horsehair? The pins in my pins-and-needles just nipped into a material that could cope with them, but the needles nosed their way through flesh towards nerve-endings. They sewed the sea of me like dolphins stitching their way in parallel to a sailboat. It was agonizingly freeing, because part of my body (my hand?) was useless with pain. These days I get pins-and-needles every day, in one leg or another. When I finish sitting-sitting, having sat in half lotus for half an hour, I usually have to rub my left or right ankle (alternate days). This makes me worry about deep vein thrombosis. Should I eat an aspirin? At the desk, I get p-&-n when I sit with right leg tucked under left buttock (as now, hence this). Usually, I catch it as it's starting to boil, small bubbles appearing on the bottom of the pan. Occasionally, I'll prang my funnybone on a doorhandle, and get the full prickly sleeve – death metal tattoos of skull-bats and hell-flames from wristbone to shoulder. Hand in the fire. This is hella joyful.

Montag 30 Januar

'This living hand, now warm and capable—' Keats' fragmentary hand, from one of his last poems. We all want to take it.

I am glad of my living hands, which have neither long (which I wanted very much at one time) nor short (which would be difficult) fingers. My hands are, and have always been, good hands. (Not sure about *kind hands, doing good to all*. Some they seem to harm.) Everything I've ever wanted them to do, they have proved capable of doing – playing fingerstyle guitar (B♭m6), threading needles, holding a pen for hours. I don't know if my handwriting is my right hand's fault or mine. Obviously, I don't think about the exact shape of my letters, my lettering, as I'm doing-writing them, it. To change the hand now would be affected. It's fast enough, legible, not without flourish, looks neat to others (so they've told me). The nails on my right hand are too long and those on my left too short – the one for fingerpicking, the other for unbuzzy fretting. 'Anji.' Three main lines cross my palm – they look like a capital A (without a bar) beside a slightly moony capital I (bending in toward the A). I've forgotten which of these is the lifeline, but I was once told that it stretches off my palm. See here it is. The thumbs stick out sensibly, quite straight. 'This living hand, now *warm and capable—*' I've envied classical guitarists, like Segovia, who have thumbs that curl out, bent back – so they are perfect for strumming strings. The wrists are quite wide, mine, with veins not hard to see. The hairs on my knuckles are transparent. I think I mentioned elsewhere (more than once) the callous where the pen rests. They're not a labourer's hands. The joke: 'You'll be first up against the wall, come the revolution.' Because the fingernails are clean, because no dirt-damage. Mouse has left claw-scars on them. Thank you, hands. My right wrist aches, but this is the fifth page today. Four of novel. 'I hold it towards you.' I stretch it. I am beneath these words, like a mirror image of you. You are not a hypocrite. Put your hand on the page. We fit.

Dienstag 31 Januar

To get a fountain pen started, I draw squiggles on scrap paper – A4, folded lengthways once and crossways once. My squiggles are too rounded to be zigzags but too spiky to be waves. Sometimes they are quite simple, like a three-headed question mark, at others they go on for six or seven cutbacks. If I look more exactly, I see that they're asymmetrical, and the curves on the right have greater amplitude than the arrows to the left. In this, it's as if I've been trying to draw a side view of a Slinky that's dangling over the bannisters, or a letter m that wants to express extreme tastiness: mmmmmmm. The Slinky is the better analogy, because there's the odd accidental loop – or a whole squirl in the form of a downwardly uncoiling coil. Quite often, because a pen won't start with pressure, the lines end up blotted with spit. I'll try a few scratches, tap the nib against the paper, press down to widen the ink-gap, but – if none of these techniques have done the trick – I resort to schoolboy spit. Very often the first thing I write in a day is what looks like the letter I in my own spit – a trace of black from yesterday's dissolved ink. It's not I, I, I, it's a firm straight line in hopes of flow. At this point, the pen either starts to write, or I switch to another one, or I refill it with new ink, or I take it to the sink in the bathroom and wash away the crust. As I do this, I feel sorry for the ink that didn't get to become words, just an impossibly elegant serpent escaping down the plughole. I suppose, like a deaded goldfish, the ink-serpent gets to swim in the silver sea, after bathing in urine and faeces, and getting the sewage treatment. (Who knows – better to be an ink-snake than the word plughole?) Once the water runs clear, I reinsert the refillable cartridge and start writing in easy grey. But I am sure I write something different, and write it differently, than if the pen had flourished first off.

Roxana's story today was top. Felix, not so much. Samira, really good – small details well seen. And why might I like that?

My main concern, though, is Andy. I only mentioned him at the end of the diary entry a couple of weeks ago, but that was because he tends to dominate classes. He's the most angry, and that gives him the most disruptive force. Not that it's surface anger. Not yet. Two other tutors have already suggested it might go like this, as it's going. Because it happened with them. The first half of term, you're the greatest thing ever, no-one's understood him like you do, can you meet for coffee? (I had that email two weeks ago.) But then, when your comments on his writing are less than adoring, and you don't meet for coffee, he starts to feel slighted. When this happens, he becomes more critical of others in the workshop. Today it was Samira – and Andy came in clumsily after a good, sensitive comment by Ola. 'That's just cock,' he said. I gave him a look. He was about to keep going, but Rebekah said, 'And exactly what flavour cock would that be?' (Implying he was a cock-connoisseur.) Jess cackled. And I quickly said, 'Yes, or to put it another way, what exactly do you think's not working here?' I could see that Roxana was upset. Fearing where else this aggression might go. It wasn't very mindful, all this. Katherine was ready to back Rebekah up, if Andy went after Ola again. Rudy might have joined sides with Andy. (Not that there are sides, he lied.) I kept things moving, la la la. Michael – being angelic – said something gentle, which was just what was needed. Grace agreed with Michael. Lola agreed with Grace. I kept things calm. There's not much else you can do, apart from remind everyone to be friendly at the start of the next class. I can send Andy an email. Andy isn't as good as he thinks he is, but then he thinks Samuel Beckett was a patzer. (Words to that effect.)

Although I'm enjoying the workshop, I'm starting to long for the quieter Summer term, and for the Autumn's study leave. A couple of months more, then it'll just be marking the work from this term, doing tutorials, doing my lecture. I will have more time; I will have less angst.

Donnerstag 2 Februar

What am I doing? What the actual *actual* fuck am I spending my time on – investing my days in – putting the hours necessary to achieve? ffs there seems no way of saying it that doesn't monetize it. Doing the doings. Crafting the craft. *Dwelling* with – that suggests peasant property: a dwelling. Outside lav. Apart from my arse, I don't think I've ever had a dwelling place. Holdfast. It was always just a flat or a house. I'd like to think it was the language I stayed in, the English, but that's nothing like a stillness. If you put something down, it won't be in the same place when you try to come back for it. (No more than Mouse will.) (Ants with white letters painted on their bums.) And it won't be the same thing. Dwelling keeps changing. At one point I thought dwelling was an insight into what I needed; now it seems a nostalgia for other people's nostalgia. W.B. Yeats in his tower, writing the word *ancestral*. Heidegger in lederhosen, writing the word *Hammer*. What am I doing? I am writing writing. Sometimes I am writing writing writing. Or rewriting writing. But then, at other times, it's just writing rewriting. And I'm sure I sometimes end up rewriting rewriting rewriting (rewriting the rewriting of rewriting).

Mist was forecast for today – instead we just have wind, and an amplitude of grey. Grey going up into grey through grey without that motion being visible.

Of course, the desk is my dwelling, but it seems too obvious to say; I have to write all the other stuff, the stuff that's undwelt upon, imperceptible. I have to wait around until the party is over and everyone else has gone home, or on to another party, and then I have to investigate.

Freitag 3 Februar

What have I done? How did I get here? At the desk. I was woken at around 6am by Leigh's breathing – which is a polite way of saying her snoring. I asked her to turn over, and she did, but I couldn't go back to sleep. Politics filled my head; the defeat of progressive ideals, parties and policies. Outside, the bin men moved the green recycling bin to the edge of the pavement. I got up at 7:15, before the alarm went off. My iPhone was on the bedside table. Leigh asked me what time it was, and I told her. Her alarm on her iPhone then went off. I put on my blue spotty dressing gown and went downstairs to the kitchen. Here, as every morning, I tried to move efficiently, and do the various things in the shortest time. These things were: put away a wooden ladle, fill the kettle with water and put it on to boil, open the dishwasher, begin by clearing the upper shelf of glasses and mugs then empty the lower shelf of plates and cutlery. In between putting mugs in the mug cabinet, I took out the metal teabag box from the neighbouring cabinet and laid four teabags (two and two) on the marble countertop. At some early point, I'd also started playing music on the iPod in its old-fashioned speaker dock. Today I continued with Pablo Casals' Bach Suites for Unaccompanied Cello. It was the second suite, so the music sounded like the work of mourning. At another point, I took the milk out of the fridge. With this, like this, I tend to do it when the personal ergonomics of putting-away brings me close to that bit of the kitchen. This morning I also moved a bowl of dough into the fridge – it had been proving all night, to firm it before baking. I think I did this after stacking some bowls. These aren't all a regular size, and this morning I didn't sort them according to type – larger white on the bottom, smaller blue on the top. By the time the kettle clicked, I was only beginning the lower shelf of the dishwasher, so I warmed the large mugs and teapot with a half inch of scalding water, tipped away what was in the pot, then dropped in the four teabags and half-filled it with most of the contents of the kettle. I often give it a single stir with a long-handled teaspoon, in between putting away plates and cutlery, but this morning I didn't. When the dishwasher was

Samstag 4 Februar

empty and closed, I tipped the water from the mugs into the plastic jug we use for wastewater. I put skimmed milk in Leigh's mug, semi-skimmed in mine. Then I poured out the tea – Leigh's on the left, hers darker than mine. Then I carried both mugs upstairs, spilling only a little on the carpet outside my room. I put one large mug, Leigh's, on the flat top of the bannister and opened the door to my room. 'Good Mousekin, morning,' I said. I placed my mug on the near edge of the desk, went and took Leigh's tea to her, kissed her, then came back and sat down. Just after I did that, I reached for this diary. The black retro pen was still out from yesterday, and I began the entry with, 'What have I done?' and continued from there to here. The tea is gone, so I must have drunk it. When I began, I was hoping to get myself to the desk by the end of a page, but also to account for all the major actions. I am sitting here in my blue spotty dressing gown, writing. The Anglepoise is on, so I must have turned it on after I put down my tea. 'What have I done?' In my current state – oh, I must have turned off the Bach as well, because it's no longer playing. With my preoccupations as they are, I'm aware of three things in what I've just written: the iPhone, the iPod and the milk. If I had been a writer of the 1950s, much of this account might read the same (if I was American and had a dishwasher) but I would have been woken by an alarm clock (probably wind-up) and if I had played music in the kitchen, that would have been on a transistor radio. Earlier still, in the 1920s, only an Anthony Blanche type would have put a 78 on the Victrola. Wagner and creamy porridge. Within five minutes of waking, I have used two products manufactured by Apple. To save a little electricity, I could have refrained from putting on the iPod. There's more to say about this, but I need to get on to the milk. It's cow's milk, although I've been thinking of switching completely to oat. The solid white of cow's milk is a symbol of plain goodness. My mother, a good mother, gave me hot milk to calm me when I was upset. But if I consider the production of milk, if I think of the heifers being drained by machines and the calves from which they've been separated, I can't think drinking milk is a good thing. I continue out of moral inertia, and because I am used to the taste.

Sonntag 5 Februar

The roads bleached with salt and the trees at their greyest, as if everything were still colourful but seen through a Chernobyl windscreen plus depression. Undoubtedly England, extremely Februar.

What's happened today? Any pig-garden-action?

No.

Mouse left a rat-head under the desk yesterday.

Still thinking about what Rebekah said to Andy in the workshop. Cock-joke.

I will try to write Leigh a poem for Valentine's Day now. I hope I can.

(It was a very dainty rat-head.)

Full sunlight on the desk from behind me – yellow beams from either side in my East-facing workroom – shadow of my head on the screen of the MacBook Pro. I can also see myself reflected-silhouetted in its mirroring black; steam behind me rising from the boiler in the outside loo. I take a sip of coffee from the metal mug. What today? The pipes beneath the floor tick – at first quickly, then slowly slowing down; I should bleed the radiators. (My mother is unwell.) (Leigh feels fine.) (Novel continues.)

Yesterday I bought a new coat. A gray greatcoat. Will it get baby-puke on it?

Montag 6 Februar

See 31 Januar. There is an alternative to spit-drag, and that's the blot. The quickest way to resurrect ink pens, but also a bit wasteful, is to force them to drip. I have seen different designs of refillable cartridge in different pens – some work like plungers, others like pumps, and yet others like screws. With each of them, if you do in reverse what you do to fill them, you cause the nib to brim then weep. Very often, with a bit of care, making a bead of black or blue bulge on the underside (held upside down) and then sucking it back up into the body – that's usually enough to prime the pump, get the dragthrough going, and start producing sentences instead of scratchy frustration. But if that doesn't work, you can always go more extreme and take the blot option – by coaxing the formed teardrop to fall onto the scrap paper. Here, it stands as a brief glistening dome before it starts to leech into the pulp. Slick transit. Gravity and capillarity, diffusion and entropy all pull the liquid downwards and sideways. At this moment, keen to get going, I nip the tip of the nib through the nub of the meniscus and squirl it outwards. It usually only takes a single tail – after that, the creature in my hand is alive again, heart restarted. Which means what's left behind on the paper looks very like a single black sperm with the head of an axolotl. If a pen is determined to stay dead, multiple squiggles will branch from the same blob – and the thing will become more like a jellyfish or a neuron shooting out dendrites. When a piece of scrap gets reused, and reused, these forms start to metastasize across the white but by then I'll usually have started another page, because these days I don't want that image.

Writing this makes me curious about other writers and what they do and see and get wrong at their desks – desks that they may admit are tables, kitchen tables, treadmill lecterns or window seats in Starbucks. I know that a lot of them will exist entirely within their laptops. The digital desktop will be their only desktop, and they won't fuss and fossick about with pencil-sharpeners and inkpens. At launch parties, they'll tell you with happy shame that they can't read back their own handwriting. For them, word-production is a matter of ten-fingered tippety-tippety not sly aslant scritch-scratch. They may have files within folders that are drafts that show changes, but they don't have plastic boxes in their cellar. If they want to make notes, they use their phone – and what they type there goes also to their laptop and a server masquerading as a cloud. However, other writers will have their own arcane physicality. These will make a death cult of American legal pads, or acknowledge no totem but their 1980s East German ballpoint. They will be votaries of the Post-It note, creating a pink and yellow wall like the scaly flank of a dragon. They will bow down before their mother's typewriter, the Olympia SM4 she used when she wrote her 1974 novel. And they will smoke, some of them, like proper writers always did – and read their latest paragraph back aloud (even if they are in Starbucks) – and hum 'My Favorite Things' or 'Eine kleine Nachtmusik' – and wear their lucky socks, both pairs – and kiss each thumbnail thrice before starting – and douse their *pudenda* in *eau de toilette* – and drink *sobacha* or twice-boiled water or lemongrass of a nip of their own urine – and wank themselves dizzy – and pray to a postcard of Toni Morrison or Yukio Mishima – and intone 'Oh you cunt oh you absolute cunt' without realizing it – and excommunicate bad sentences with a Sharpie – and check into hotel rooms on the Isle of Skye or the outskirts of Peterborough – and stop doing anything superstitious, but then start again the following morning when they hear a magpie. Some may just write straight out, as if compiling a shopping list, but those are the outliers.

All normal writers are weird.

Dienstag 7 Februar

The high wind in the trees sounds like the train wheels on the track – an engine and carriages graunching northwards. And just then, two opposite trains at once, crossing the bridge; I thought they weren't allowed to do that. Before they replaced the metal part, over the road, one train had to stop, wait, hoot, while the other slunk through on tiptoe. 1866, says the date on the brick part, embossed in red lettering within a crest, but the refurb was only a couple of years ago. I took photographs of the broad girder being craned and lodged.

Any word from anywhere (slang, Latin, Anglo-Saxon, Mrs Wutherington the English teacher) coming in at any point – that's my ideal of writing. (Not all writing all the time; open, vivid, bubbling writing.) Coming in comprehensibly, grammatically – basically grammatically – but also free as to word order and syntax, with dangling participles, if they want to hang out. Dramatically, in that each can become an event, but all seem to serve the scene ('andymen, butlers) (and yet there are rumours of a hidden king). First knock, first foot. Equal opportunities.

In answer to Keats' desire, this is how I see Shakespeare's internal disposition as he sits writing 'To be or not to be'. Will is finding it easy, because the words are finding him – they feel like they're clustering for him – he's open to whatever his vocabulary shunts through the Hamlet-shaped hole (Hamlet at this moment of his being, his staying). The register is not ring-fenced, policed. No gaitered gamekeeper. Into the global head, and onto the linear page, come slings and arrows, fardels, whips, a bodkin; come grunts and conscience, puzzles and sweat, pangs and contumely. High as *Hi* and low as in *Hello*, and every man his master, master of the middle style: How are you? How. Are. You. As the physicist Paul Erdős said, when he arrived for collaboration, My mind is open. As the Velvet Underground sang, Baby, my mind's split open. As Robert Lowell wrote, My mind's not right. Mouse did a poo that came out of the cat litter the exact shape of a fleur-de-lys; I wanted to keep it, but just photographed it.

The thing I find myself saying most often to this writing class is 'Put me in the room'. That's what the reader would say to them, I believe. 'I want to be there. I don't want generalizations – I want to be present for the important event. Take me where the action is.' This way of thinking about it partly comes from that Marlon Brando quote I've never been able to track down: 'If you weren't in the room, it's gossip.' (To which I'd add: 'If you weren't at the correct angle, and within hearing distance, it's *still* gossip.') A radio producer I worked with, Z, said to me, 'Give me colour and scale – and, if you can, give me movement, too.' That's what listeners need. And readers. From that, they'll get the acoustics, the stench. They'll hear the aluminium echo or the velvet flump. They'll smell the unfrozen water, the mixed herb spag bol, the bleached marble. Put me in the room – even if the room is the middle of an icefield. The students think this is too simple. Drummers do rudiments; writers should, too. Grace submitted something upsetting, for her and everyone else. It was raw, about her mother and about being a mother herself. The class handled it well – criticism but compassion. They're a good group. Andy said the best thing. He suggested a scene that hadn't been written. Katherine next. She'd wanted to go last, but Lola was late. Everyone was very careful what they said with Katherine. It was a little bit of a redemption fantasy, with good details of club life and a beach scene in Brighton (very early morning). I had to steer Samira away from saying '*you* could' instead of 'the story could' or – though it's awkward – 'the narrator could'. Lola, stuck on the Northern Line for an hour, joined us for the second half. She has tiny feet in tiny pixie boots. Her story included a very gory murder at the climax. Hedge clippers were involved. And Superglue. If you took that half-page off, it was a well observed and subtle piece about misogyny. Lola said, 'I'm so glad I don't have to kill a character just to make an ending. I've done that in every story I've written so far.' And I believe she has. The rage comes through better in the details. Everyone in the group has workshopped now. This is the pivotal moment. They all know where everyone else is coming from. They relax; I relax. Next week is Reading Week.

Donnerstag 9 Februar

If I could be anywhere, to write, in any room, I would be high up –
as I was when I lived in Marina Opletalová's 8th floor flat in Prague.
It's not that I would like the view; even when I've had the choice,
I have always placed the desk facing a wall. The window has moved
from my left (Prague, Southfields) to my right (Ealing) to behind me
(Southwark, Lambeth), but only when I've been away from home
(The Hurst, Hawthornden Castle) have I looked up from the page to
firs on a hillside, hawks hunting. (I've always been lucky enough to
have a window.) It's more the feeling of being high up I'd like than any
benefits of the situation. At the desk, I am distracted by conversations
in which I can hear the meaning of the words, rather than just their
rhythms and syllables. Occasionally, someone loudly debates their
choice of perennial, beyond our falling-down fence, in the shrubs
section of the garden centre, or – more often – tells off their bored
child. Our next-door neighbour, behind their falling-down fence,
talks about many things with the gardener. If I could be up where
these kinds of chats and cries were very very distant, I'd be a little less
disturbed. 'You want somewhere highfalutin' so you can look down
on the groundlings,' comes the accusation. 'You want an ivory tower.'
No, that would be too obtrusive. Tourists would come to take selfies
in front of it, just as they do the Big Banana or the Great Hall of the
People. If ivory towers were as common as electricity pylons, then
fine; and if they were eight storeys high. Or if this one was invisible,
and mobile – if sometimes it could be in the middle of Paris, or Tokyo,
or beside Wittgenstein's hutte, or in the Sea of Tranquility.

Freitag 10 Februar

The worst place to write would be in a room full of people I know – and the absolute worst would be with all my family. They would ask me what I was writing. Why aren't you joining us? Come on, Tobes, you've done long enough. You're being very anti-social. Read us a bit out, at least. Make it a funny bit. They wouldn't necessarily be unkind, but they'd be unbearable. I realize that these are conditions in which some people try to become writers, and where some already-writers try to write – with grandmother's ashtray on the corner of the kitchen table, and beneath it a toddler-niece tickling their knees. Or with their father snoring on the daybed whilst their young cousin plays Fortnite Battle Royale on the Xbox. Glitching so bad! If a room of one's own is too much to demand, then the very least a writer needs is incuriosity and some noise-cancelling headphones. (Go away, because I want to talk to you.) I've written in cafes, in hospital waiting rooms, on the top deck of the 68 bus (with super chatty South London girls right behind me), on the street – stepping aside into a doorway to make a note. But if I hadn't had access to a place where papers put down are left undisturbed, I couldn't have become a writer. A writer can't thrive among spies and gossips. In a single room with all my family, I would drink and dream and eat ice cream and watch YouTube videos. Maybe I would go for midnight walks, and try to become a poet, or commit a crime so as to get sent to prison. For crowded writers, there used to be libraries. In a library, a person can sometimes become a writer by accident. If we want writers, if we want undisturbed thought, we need more libraries – quiet and desks and books and librarians with their holy mission of shhh. (If it doesn't have librarians, it's just a room with some books in it.) Sweet, sweet librarians – whom we adore because they are not our family.

Samstag 11 Februar

When I listen to Casals playing Bach's Suites for Unaccompanied Cello, I hear the dimensions of a room – a wooden closet, a private place not necessarily owned, perhaps rented or a sinecure, but lockable, a known history of corners and dust and absolutes and breath.

When the light comes in, it does so at a steep angle – either that or it is diffused like the light inside cotton wool.

If there is a shadow in the light, it comes from the tallest spire of the cathedral – either that or it is the ripple of a skeleton's ribs.

Everything in the music, everything it builds, is life-size: tree, orgasm, moon, coffin.

The melody, harmony, rhythm and scrape reconstruct the cello even as it is being played because no violincello has ever been more violincello, no trees have ever sung their way with so grand a grain into such a soundboard.

I hear metal, not guts – not the calf-wail of the original. But there is still the canter of horsehair under the tension of hardwood stick and brass froglet. (Some of this, I admit, I have researched: I didn't know that catgut was never made from the guts of cats.)

A cello is a collection of dead things being forced to sing; but which tree wouldn't want to climb up Johann Sebastian?

My beard is now curling back into my chin and neck. This is the worst bit. If it gets sweaty, it gets strangely achey. Do beards ache?

Sonntag 12 Februar

Is it important that you don't consciously understand what you're writing at the moment you write it? Is a certain azteca ants of blue wildebeest, or of exquisite rainbowfish in an African clawed toad of underwing moth, dwarf cassowary at the orangutan of any aardvaark? If I know yellow mongoose too well, my common dwarf mongoose, and don't have a shire horse honeyguide with my OncoMouse, then the unexpected cotton rat will never occur – and the unexpected cotton rat is what arctic fox is rainbow trout, because the unexpected cotton rat is where and when the blue whale happens – the blue whale and the minke, the narwhal and the so-called sperm. We all know the silver-washed fritillary is capable of cuttlefish and peregrine that the streptococcus and mule can never geep to micro-pig. We are all more black wildebeest than willow warbler. And we are not polar bear or snow leopard, we are eastern subterranean termite colony. We are every natterjack toad of us far more Indian peacock together than we could ever beaver by orangutan. Black mould, we caribou with stag-beetle and sponge. Rattlesnake and mountain lion, our whole wasps' nest of an anal wart is bontebok around silver fox and golden eagle. If we common ant as wood pigeon, then peacock is gull – completely gull. But there is hoopoe, and although it buzzard bream lichen, not at the moo-moo, an otter worm is passerine. In the diplodocus, all homo erectus were rattus rattus termite to the canopy. It is only neuroblastoma that the raptor of monkey leech has compsognathus from this forest. There mayfly not ringtail lemur to this koala bear grey wolfpack of bumble bee. But we sea-serpent that carrion crow as cockroach, we will tardigrade tardigrade. Whether tardigrade or tardigrade, we tardigrade – but tardigrade we can be tardigrade.

Montag 13 Februar

There are letters in my handwriting that I can't be doing with – and yet they've been like that, unimproved, for decades. The one I have the worst relationship with is *f*. God, even though I've tried to make that *f* bearable, it's pure bleugh. It doesn't know whether it's a tall or short letter, cousin to *t* or *p*. The end of the tail rests on the line, as though it were half of an unusually well balanced cobra. But properly this bit of it should dip beneath and curl onwards as in *g* and sometimes in *j*. My descenders don't always include loops: some ensuing letters they meet in a joined-up way, others they don't want to touch. There must be rules to this, or at least conventions, but I have no idea what they are. I remember sitting in the classroom at Alameda School, on a sunny day, trying to make my handwriting follow the model alphabet on the board. It wasn't an elegant Victorian exemplum; it was standard issue state school script. And somehow, mysteriously, over the years, my version of it has come to look like a combination of my mother's and my father's hands. A decade ago, it slanted forwards; recently, it's gone full vert. When I was at university, and writing an incommunicative letter home each week, my mother started to study graphology in order to penetrate through to what was really going on with me, her null son. She only confessed this a couple of months ago. What did you find out? I asked her. Nothing, she said. That's what was going on, I said – still covering up for myself. But I love my handwriting for what it's allowed me to write. Rephrase: I love that my handwriting has allowed me to write. It's quite fast and I can read it back. And I think it's a good thing, almost a blessing, that I've never looked at it in a self-satisfied way. I remember the girl who sat beside me at Russell Primary School – her parents ran the Chinese restaurant. Compared to Mandarin script, an *f* was easypeasy. Her pages were impeccable; my report was 'it looks as if a spider has dipped its feet in ink and dragged itself across the page'. I'm quite proud of this now. But, really, if only my hand were so gothic, so cartoon Paganini.

Dienstag 14 Februar – *Valentine's Day*

A Small Love Poem

A world as small as that we share
can risk invisibility
in others' eyes. But what of that?
If all those others were aware
of our tiny felicity
they'd want to try and enter it.
Our world is *almost* private –
there are a few who know it's there,
who can perceive the filigree
so fine it seems wrought in air.
And these, the ones who truly care,
can enter the infinity
of detail and of love. They fit!
And fit, it seems, quite comfortably –
for smallness can be infinite.
(We, though, are trying hard to see
something smaller yet.)

Mittwoch 15 Februar – *Reading Week so no workshop*

A morning too hot for the time of year, and too sunny for comfort. Even though I'm not teaching today, I'm still thinking about teaching. I want to be a reassuring figure, presence, for my students, but not lie to them – not pretend they're better than they are, or that they don't still have much to learn. The thing they've chosen to do is harder and requires more sacrifice than they will find acceptable (probably). Sometimes I ask them, I say, 'Put your hand up if you agree to this deal: I guarantee you will be published, but first you have to retype your book, start to finish, six times. Not change or improve it – though you can if you want to. Just retype it six times. Who's on for that?' In a workshop of twelve students, not all the hands go up immediately. They are considering how much work retyping 100,000 words six times would take – how many hours, how much boredom, how much wrist- and eye-strain. But in return for *certain* publication! And, of course, and sometimes I say this, the work they'll need to do in order really to get published is far more than thoughtless physical retyping. It's a different mode of work, too – which means correcting the self, subediting the soul. Often it means rejecting the current self entirely. Not 'I want to write my book' but 'There is a book that could be written, and if I'm lucky I may be the person who writes it, however that person may equally be her over there.' (This goes for memoirs just as much as fantasy novels.) And after the possible book is somehow written, in however garbled a form, the self is changed. I am always weaker, more vulnerable and depleted, profoundly ashamed. There is less of me left; there is more of me that's become impossible – because it's repetition or self-imitation (nostalgic or parodic). When I say 'be published' to the students, I mean 'reach a publishable level'. But that's nonsense, shorthand; there's no objective standard for what agents get hot about and editors enjoy suffering to acquire. If I'm to be an honest teacher, I should use more careful language. 'You will become a good writer, very likely not a successful writer, but a writer other writers will respect rather than envy.'

Donnerstag 16 Februar

Sepulchral/Epitaph prose; the altar of the dead – done and dusty. Don't write it. This is what I thought I thought, and now, later, for now is always later, I see it well enough and pose it coldly enough to present it to you as tableau, as diorama. You get the point, don't you? Point and counterpoint. You get it because I got it and together, Jesus and Lazarus, we can bring back to life a thing that has absolutely nothing to say about the only thing it knows anything worth knowing about – which is the feeling of the state of life after the non-feeling of the state of death. Mute Lazarus to contrast with speakeasy Jesus – voluble about the afterlife, doing the resurrection shuffle. Not all writing need be nervy, have a moment of force – but if it aspires to the condition of John Coltrane or Charlie Parker then it truly don't mean a thing if it ain't got that swing. It cannot allow itself to be a dead man held on end. It cannot only be alive enough to have strength to die. They died as men before their bodies died, etc. Sooner murder an infant in its cradle (how could William Blake have written that?). We (now-writers) don't see our restrictions: that consistent point of view in fiction is our equivalent of eighteenth century's heroic couplet. Birth-strangled babe. No, cross that out. No, leave it. If I write them down, then terrible things are less likely to happen – because they've already happened, and Nature abhors repetition – exact repetition – exact repetition. No virgin she. Lo, He abhors not the virgin's womb. (In school assembly, I used to sing, 'Lo, he abhors not the virgin's wombat breath it smells of custard.' No idea why. Public schoolboy scared of the mention of female reproductive anatomy, maybe.) Abhorson – an appalling son-pun on abortion. Measure for Measure's Executioner. I should stop. Because I could not stop for Death. Here comes your ghostly father. Here comes a chopper.

Freitag 17 Februar

Sometimes, the worse the day begins, the better the day goes. That sounds like the kind of concise and balanced truth a Roman writer would have recorded. I mean, 'the worse the writing begins, the better the writing goes' – because the writing *is* the day, and if it doesn't go there isn't a day so much as an exhumation. Yesterday, for example – fucking yesterday. I woke up my usual self, neither emperor nor slave, merely citizen. And I got my bones to the desk, and asked the page if there were any words it wanted. There were many, so I saw, all of them rubbish – I was writing in agreement with myself, which is never a good idea (especially for me). Even worse, I was writing to a purpose – unlike today, where I seem to be illustrating a maxim by exemplifying its opposite. Yesterday began badly and finished worse. From my directed sentences, I constructed half an unusable page. (I will copy it out on a piece of scrap. Bin it.) The rest of the day was nothing but a forensic dig; archaeological, because I'd died so long ago, but also a crime scene, because some bastard had split my skull to splinters. That bastard was – no, I'm not going to name it, because that's how the ranting starts. I'm not even going to gratify or dignify or reify it with a proper pronoun. Something took my skull and smashed my skull halfway through my skull. This isn't the site of a suicide, though, this desk – and it was too passionate an execution to be sacrifice. No priest was implicated. By the end of the day, two skulls had been brought to the surface – out of the inky dirt – and one was mullered at the orbit, the other at the occiput. But the teeth were the same – molars worn by gritting, chipped incisors, pointy canines. (Later study will show overdevelopment in the centres for vision and language, and underdevelopment in practical problem solving.) When I'm in the midst of bashing my brains out, I wish I lived in a more formal age, with a more formulaic expressivity; then each sentence could come out an epigram and also an epigraph. *Sententiae* would have little hands in the margin, pointing to them. Always wise because never willed. Quotable as Virgil, and as chockful of quotation as Burton or Montaigne. Let the titans lift the mountains.

Samstag 18 Februar

To Leigh's parents. Roast dinner. Zero writing.

Sonntag 19 Februar

All writers are different from all other writers, ahem. Every one of them (we suppose) has found their way to habits and superstitions, rhythms of stem and flow, metaphors of man-machinery or efflorescence or other metamorphoses, that allow them to do what they do, word by word. Any of them, when asked, would likely change the subject from the specifics of their desk (I'm avoiding 'practice') to the generalities of their stories, characters, ambitions, ideas. A writer who is seen to be taking their craft – as in craft supplies – too seriously will not themselves be treated as a serious artist. Some, of course, left written records of the materiality of their work routines, just as they left behind quills, typewriters, laptops and towers of paper and data to form the basis of their archives and museums. The curious reader, though, can go through the published diaries and notebooks of most of them, asking, 'Yes, I know how you were feeling about your writing, because on May 7th you wrote, "All my writing is totally shit," but which exact notebook did you write in with which exact pencil?' – they can ask and ask, and never come away with a definite answer. Every such detail, in itself, might seem little more than shop talk – of interest only to other, lesser writers. (Any glimpse over Virginia Woolf's shoulder or around Franz Kafka's elbow is still, to me, pure fascination.) A given brand of paper, 80 gsm, recycled, surely doesn't – you say – alter or encourage the words written or printed upon it? Some dry scrapings of the favoured pen, before the shopping list biro was grabbed – this had no influence, you insist, on the agitated sentence that finally got itself down? The fact is, the more we know, the more we can know – and knowledge of the concrete will always contribute at least as much and probably more than theories of the wish. All every and any writer wants, when they begin, is a sense, some small insight into how the writing of others actually got done – not on the level of greatness and literary history, but here among the coughs, the pencil shavings, the tippety-tippety and the days of hours of years of minutes of instants of lettering. And all readers are writers.

··

The only human activity you can write about while you're doing it is writing. Unless, that is, you're writing about writing-whilst-smoking or -on-a-train. And I suppose you could write about typing or handwriting, but I include both of those under writing. So it's strange there's so little writing about the act of writing, by which I mean the body-mind's physical entanglement with the page – the outside becoming the inside simultaneously vice versa but backwards and upside down. All writing otherwise is a shying away from the truly present, a veiling of the means of production. Why is that? Because writing (especially writing about writing about writing) isn't *living*, according to both the ordinary and the adventurous. And so there are so many writers, good writers, whose writing reads as if they weren't breathing as they wrote it. Not only that, although that asphyxia is awful enough, but as if – from before they began the work of the hour until after they finished – they were incapable of dying or changing, because they were already dead. Sculpture over gesture. These are good but awful and death-loving writers. Any grandeur that is theirs is that of the vault, and any scope comes from dust in accidental light. Funerary art over fucking. I don't believe this is because they include no paragraph about ink-glisten or key-clatter – it's worse than merely ignoring the momentary, the present. No, it's a kind of perpetual deferral. They delegate breathing to their characters, the main one of whom is the reader. By co-breathing with them, in a figured future, they displace change and death into plot-points. These are frozen warnings close to mine/ close to the frozen borderline. This is their most productive form of inspiration, therefore: suspended animation. But we all have to make a living.

··

Montag 20 Februar

Oh, you idiot – last night I made the mistake of trying to explain myself, and now I feel wrong. Wronged by me. I said I wouldn't talk about what I was writing about. Sinéad, in the pub, said, 'You're being cagey.' 'Yes, a cage,' I said. 'Writing a cage.' Trying – I thought – to write my writing into writing my way out of a cage. What am I writing? I'm writing a thing. It's equidistant, I hope, from fiction, non-fiction, essay, poetry. And it starts with Keats and Lawrence and Woolf and Proust. It's against Flaubert and Joyce (though maybe not *Finnegans Wake*). Even writing down the names: wrong. Macclesfield hubris. Two famous quotations.

Pascal, in the 1650s (no-one knows exactly when):

> 'Diversion. Sometimes, when I set to thinking about the various activities, the dangers and troubles which they face at course, or in war, giving rise to many quarrels and passions, daring and often wicked enterprises and so on, I have often said that the sole cause of man's unhappiness is that he does not know how to stay quietly in his room.' (But only the last clause, 'she does not know how to stay quietly in her room.')

And more so Kafka, answering Pascal, in 1917 or 18:

> 'It is not necessary that you leave the room. Remain at your table and listen. Do not even listen, only wait. Do not even wait, be wholly still and alone. The world will present itself to you for its unmasking, it can do no other, in ecstasy it will writhe at your feet.'

Checking the Pascal, in French, I see he says 'une chambre' not 'sa chambre,' *a* room – *any* room – not *his* room; dans sa propre chambre. In Kafka, in German, I notice 'Deinem Tisch,' which is definitely his table and not his desk – not his Schreibtisch – his writing table. It's embarrassing to go for such Greatest Hits.

Dienstag 21 Februar – *Mardi Gras*

I picked on Macclesfied, for Macclesfield hubris yesterday, but it could
have been Barnsley, Cork, Dundee or Carmarthen – I did not mean
to pick on Macclesfield particularly (to bully, belittle); but it's more
there than London, Edinburgh, Cardiff and Dublin. (And certainly
Belfast, after Ciaran Carson.) And far more than Vienna, Prague, Paris
or Warsaw. To write existentially, aphoristically (already the locals
are saying pretentiously, wankily) – you're hardly permitted to do
this unless you're foreign *and* dead. How have you earned any of this
metaphysical insight, when you speak like that? Are – like me – from
Ampthill, Bedfordshire. What if your name isn't Kafka, Benjamin,
Lispector, Adorno? What if it's O'Corcoran, Jones, MacDougall or
Snodgrass? There are certain modes that our origins, it seems, forbid
us. Attempt them, and we'll be taken out back, duffed up. The class
ban is worse than that on birthplace; any location can be forced to
become glamorous, by a good enough writer, but if you've been
pre-categorized as a comic character, you won't be permitted grandeur
of discourse or ambition. Red clown-nose is on, superglued. Maybe
some places would sound mysterious – or could be made to sound
mysterious. Skegness. Anywhere can rebrand itself, if Manchester can.
Luton. No-one expects anything from you – in terms of literature – if
you're from Macclesfield. The last writer to do anything from round
my way was John Bunyan.

Mittwoch 22 Februar – *Workshop 6*

Lola was absent. Later she emailed me to say her boss's boss died, at work. He choked on something, alone in his office. A snack. 'I didn't know him well,' she said. 'But I needed to go out with the others, to talk about it. Please don't mention it in class.'

Second stories from Andy, Rebekah and Ola. All better than their first submissions. Andy's taken his reading seriously. It was still very Samuel Beckett, but in a more generous way – compassion of the grandmother in her sandy apotheosis. Rebekah, what a star. She'd gone all out for satirizing the extended family. Seven strong characters and at least twice as many great lines. Even Rudy was laughing. Some helpful comments from Michael, who too often looks to me for approval. Not saying what he thinks. I like his sensitivity, but I want him to be him. Ola goes between writing pages of nothing but dialogue and pages with no paragraphs at all, but there was an image of a dead stag halfway through that really cut through. Progress. I sense tension between Katherine and Grace. And Felix and Andy are fighting over the same territory (me). Jess has become a little less stressy. She eats bananas now. Her tiny pink notebook is almost full. Roxana said 'journey' but made sure to include the scare quotes. She was talking about the stepmother in Rebekah's story.

Tired, and looking forward to the end of term. With study leave in the Autumn, I won't have another workshop until Spring next year.

Late email from brother, suggesting – in a p.s. – he might move to South Africa. He saw Mum yesterday and said she wasn't great. He told me – in a p.p.s. – not to tell Mum and Dad he was thinking of moving.

Donnerstag 23 Februar

Very few of my students – hardly any at all – use dashes in their writing; more than use semi-colons, or colons, but still only maybe 5%. I think they think dashes aren't proper, in some kind of English teacher way. (Don't begin sentences with 'And', 'But' or 'So'.) But dashes – as en- and em-rules when they end up in print, if they end up in print – oh, the longer the better, as long as they're not touching the nub of the previous letter (which makes me feel a little nauseous) – dashes are a permissive piece of punctuation; they let stuff get in (as do brackets) that wouldn't otherwise make it to the page. And it is for this, and the opened possibility of spontaneity and momentariness, that I love them – the Swerve – and so encourage students to consider them (particularly if they'd fit their narrator or tone). Keats used dashes in his letters – dashed off as he dashed through the Lakes, Scotland – young John was not a dashing personage (his stature, his lack of hauteur) – as the rain dashed down on unaccommodating landscapes – as Fanny dashed his hopes, just as he secretly desired – sans merci – as that dashèd consumption first dappled his kerchief with crimson, then put his lungs through the blender, and finally killed him at twenty-fucking-five. So much work in so little time – so much great stuff – still vividly alive – still the model, the paragon of warm breathing right-hereness on the page. Because (Don't begin sentences with 'because') the close-up & intimate reader sees thought push-pushing, hears ideas birthing, holds in their hand the messy, perilous, pointy-headed miracle (no other word but miracle for this binding of matter into what matters). (Please let it happen. Please let it happen.) None of this possible without the dash, and without another *and* (because what happens after it is where we are suddenly, unexpectedly going) (heaven knows where) (woyaya). Keats – 'I luff him,' as Lexi would say. I luff English teachers. (Hello, Mrs. Wutherington.) It's their job to say *Don't*. If they didn't, we wouldn't be breaking their lovely rules. (Hello, Mr. Claridge, Mr. Carwithen, Mr. Nicholson. Even hello, Mr. Bicester.) If they didn't fence us in, we wouldn't have the freedom of trespass. Full-stops are Old Testament, commas are New Testament, dashes are apocrypha. Non-canon.

Freitag 24 Februar

I think that – on a very sunny day that makes me, and Mouse, want to sit in the garden – I could start almost every entry here with 'What am I doing? What the actual *actual* fuck am I doing?' Is it all just waving, jumping around me-me-meing? The imagined reader says *Yes*. I didn't start writing (aged eleven) because I had something to say, or perhaps I'm being unfair to myself. I had the compulsion to express something – what that something was or might be had not yet manifested. (I don't think I'm particularly interesting, but I am the only I I have.) I both want universal attention (the crowds holding Mao's *Little Red Book*) and to write only for myself (the trunk in which *The Book of Disquietude* grew). I have been moralized by the discipline of the discipline. I have been rendered humble by the difficulty, and turned generous by the shame of how bad ungenerous writing is. The gift you make must be absolute – or as absolute as you can get to give. My favourite, most loved and most played, piece of music: Bach's Six Suites for Unaccompanied Cello. No other work of art gives such a sense of being alone with, inside-with, another fully present human. I, my inner ears, the air, my headphones, my iPhone, the Spotify app, our wifi, our ethernet, our router, Spotify's servers in Google's cloud, Andrew Walker EMI digital remastering engineer, James Hardwick EMI chief 78s transfer engineer, some 78s, a needle, the air in Paris or London, Pablo Casals' bow and Pablo Casals' fingertips and Pablo Casals' cello, Pablo Casals, Pablo Casals aged thirteen in a second-hand music shop, the printed score, the score's editor, the copyist, J.S.Bach's quill in J.S.Bach's fingers, Johann Sebastian Bach. Whoever they are, this direct human, they dance, they grieve, they remember, they are appalled, they worship, they other (and they other otherness). The music is self-reflexive. I am mentioning it, on this page, because I just realized that I've been asking myself – for a very long time – if there could be a form of writing like Bach's music (as played by Casals, Ma, Tortelier, Rostropovich)? An interform, a form equidistant from diary, poetry, memoir, short story, novel and notebook – equidistant from but also, equally, on every page, diary, poetry, memoir, short story, novel and notebook.

Samstag 25 Februar

Is it immoral to use electricity? Not overuse, not waste, just to consume the wattage I need in order to do what I normally do: boil water for tea, light the desk, run the laptop – what else? Oven-heating, battery-recharging, phone-charging, overhead lighting and immersion-heater powering. We're not excessive, but it's a house that requires more energy than a two-bed flat. There's a roof and un-doubleglazed windows. I have switched us to a green tariff, for whatever good that does. This page is lit by an energy-efficient bulb in the Anglepoise. I tried an old-fashioned bulb – for more even light – but it got so overheated I burned my fingertips on the rim of the shade. It was as hot as a copper saucepan boiling milk. Some of the electricity we use comes from coal-fired power stations, and some from nuclear reactors. I can do some research to find out how many days of the year, proportionally, I'm dependent on uranium for the light by which I see what I write. (It's 73 days, because that's a fifth of the year, and 20% of our electricity is generated at Sizewell B and similar places. In a leap year, that accounts for all my consumption from January 1st until March 13th. Today, I am still in the radioactive period. No thanks.) Is this immoral? Is it wrong to go along with using the usual power source of a normal modern society? To stop having a mobile phone would be eccentric, and cause lots of practical problems (banking, booking taxis), but to go completely off-grid would be to enter a different, parallel civilization. People might never hear of or from me again. If I visited my agent, I would have to use the staircase – and I'd always arrive unannounced. (I am making myself seem trivial and ludicrous.) Instead, we change to a green tariff, vote Green, buy eco-friendly product, sign online petitions, write to our M.P., and watch the coal continue to be extracted, along with the gas and oil, see more nuclear power stations commissioned, see what we write by the bright white light of our desk lamps, see the sky above the city at night looking like the skin of a blood orange.

Sonntag 26 Februar

Is it important that you don't consciously understand what you're writing at the moment you write it? Is a certain Receptionist of Will Writer, or of Lexicographer in a Clown of Co-Head of Marketing, Secret Emissary at the Poet of any Advertising Account Manager? If I know my Web Designer too well, my Corporate Web Designer, and don't have a Labourer Marriage Guidance Counsellor with my Farmer, then the Drag Queen will never occur – and the Drag Queen is what Bricklayer is all Nurse, because the Drag Queen is where and when the Architect happens – the Architect and the Project Manager, the Structural Engineer and the so-called Client. We all know the Night Shelf Stacker is capable of Acrobat and Zookeeper that the Global Head of Debt Capital Markets and Management Consultant never Midwife to Wrestler. We are all more Yoga Instructor than Bailiff. And we are not Singersongwriter or Assassin, we are Miners. We are every Steeplejack of us far more Pastry Chef together than we could Referee by Lighthousekeeper. Barrista Prison Guard, we Implementation Consultant with Sex Worker and Disk Jockey. Chess Grandmaster and Mountaineer, our whole Air-Traffic Controller of an Angel Investor is Jockey around Silversmith and Cryptocurrency Speculator. If we Commissionaire as Wellness Guru, then Midwife is Veep – completely Veep. But there is Midwife, and although it Docent Meme-Broker, not at the Gogo Dancer, an Actor-Waitress is Passerby. In the Lamplighter, all Human Resources Directors were Subeditor to the Grandmother. It is only YouTuber that the Venture Capitalist of Naval Expeditionary Logistics Operations Analyst has Bouncer us from this Florist. There Spy not Dominatrix to this Deputy Chief Operating Officer of Microbiologist. But we Grief Counsellor that Slaughterhouse Operative as Scavenger, we will Scavenger Scavenger. Whether Scavenger or Scavenger, we Scavenger – but Scavenger we can be Scavenger.

Montag 27 Februar

It's a privilege, I know, to be able to ask Saturday's kinds of question. (Eee-lec-tri-city.) But it would be an abuse of that privilege *not* to ask them – simply to continue in absolute entitlement. ('I deserve what comes to me because I am who I am, and of course I deserve to be who I am – who could deserve it more?') And so even though on one level it's ridiculous, and another it's middle-class guilt, and on a third it's social perversity, I will continue to ask of myself, Is this right? Is it right that this is right? I have tried many times to express one thought: *Just because a product is legal to consume does not make it ethical to produce.* (That's the closest I've got to making it sing.) For example, colourful children's magazines with plastic toys in polyethylene bags taped to their covers. For example, disposable razors. For example, landmines. From the consumer's side of the bargain, they assume that if it's on the shelf in Sainsbury's or Tesco, it wasn't got there through slavery, torture, murder or environmental destruction. In the first case (slavery) they surely assume that the product was freely made by economically independent individuals who could, if they chose, withdraw their labour. Perhaps I am naïve, and even the customers who pick out the dolphin-friendly tuna chunks aren't majorly concerned that the workers manufacturing their cheap goods are underpaid, in debt, with bad health and low life-expectancy. (They may even be all this and also eleven years old.) 'What can I do?' the benign consumer might ask. 'I don't have time to research all this stuff. I'm raising children. And if I start looking, it turns out I can't buy half the things I depend on. There's palm oil in everything. You expect me to drive an hour either way to that hippie healthfood shop in town where olive oil is always out of stock? And pay for parking? I'm sure the big companies are working on it, because no-one wants to be associated with that sort of thing.'

That sort of thing being death.

Dienstag 28 Februar

Three-month scan. The dating scan. Due date is September 16th. We saw a shape like a pear. 'It's a boy.'

Do I feel like a father? What does a father feel like? Do I feel like a father-to-be? I feel confused. A son in the offing.

We can tell people about him. I don't want to. I want to keep him safely secret a little longer. Even talking about him feels like it might be a danger.

Beard-itch-reprise.

We saw the shape flipping around, and started to call him 'Flipper' in the car home.

Walter is back home. Split up with the latest girlfriend. His mother's taken him in again. Despite everything. He's sixty-six years old.

Your avocado is as big as a baby. 16 weeks-ish.

Mittwoch 1 März

Better. Why don't people write better than they do? *Felix.* Why don't I write better than I do? (What goes for them goes for me.) Perhaps because I don't know why I don't write better, because if I did I would. Is it really *that* circular? I know there are many different kinds of better, and though I sit here trying to write as well as possible, I know that if I sharpen one emphasis, I melt another. Some readers want mango lassi and others want claws. By adding drama, I simplify thought; by magnifying detail, I slow time, and curate possible boredoms. Different audiences bring different impatiences, and though I'm quite capable of frustrating and boring any and all of them, I have no hope of simultaneously tapdancing, wrestling, fucking and speaking in tongues. I have no hope – I work hard to have no hope. I was thinking of putting in a letter to Sinéad: 'You know I don't believe in God, but I have a hard time maintaining a sense of ultimate meaninglessness.' And so, I refer to a meaningful/meaningless 'better'. A slug would slime across this page and a page of *King Lear* with equal nonchalance. And a glacier pulverizing the British Library gives *complètement aucun* shit about what's beneath its mass. In the past, I have cared about things I have read, and so – even without hope – someone in the future may care about my careful words. Which is to equate Litt with Literature; which is false; which is ego. Does anyone, doing anything, feel certain of its value? Those praying, those saving innocent lives. Other people are better at being other people than I am, and some among those people are also better at being themselves. Good better best. This term has been fine, so far. Rudy has been less of a pain than I expected, once the group came down hard on his first submission. Katherine's written a great story, based on but bigger than her trauma. She showed it to me, not the group. Lola has surprised herself, and everyone. Stories from Roxana, Felix and Grace, who swapped with Samira (who had her sister's wedding today). Roxana's was three stories in one – two good for repotting separately, one for compost. Felix – oh, Felix, what are we going to do with you? Concentrate. Grace's could be published tomorrow.

Donnerstag 2 März

There are birds in the trees by the railway line – song thrush, blackbird, robin, woodpecker; now and then there are magpies (though these prefer TV aerials up and down the street) or green parrots (gathering for their evening mash-up in the park). The birds who sing sing, but unless it's summer and early morning or twilight, I don't tend to hear them. What I hear is trains, planes and automobiles – cars. The new buses, less fumey, wheeze as they pass beneath the railway bridge. But mostly it's the burr of rubber wheels on tarmac just over the speed-limit of 20 mph. Planes continuing their east-west descent to Heathrow (Concorde used to be a feature). *Tell-me-truly*, say the wheels of the train; *hasenpfeffer*, high-low-high-low. The most annoying – a southbound train just went past, and it didn't hasenpfeffer. Perhaps a discovery! Only the northbound ones have rhythm. The most distracting noise is the man with the leafblower on the petrol station forecourt. To me, it sounds like a chainsaw – and I panic they've come to cut down all the trees on the sidings, the cuttings, the falling-away embankment. Mainly, these trees are ash-trees – tall, graceful with small dapplesome leaves. One day they will come with chainsaws and rationalize them. I hate the idea they'd turn this view into the Somme, mud and stumps. Binsey Poplars. In summer, I hear the screams from the primary school playground, and the whoops from the other school, for children with special needs (which is how we say it now) – for statemented children – for children a bit like the children in my last book. Right now, next door's gardener is chatting – not an unpleasant voice to hear, but a distraction. I should send Simone a text about her non-diagnosis. Smaller sounds are the electricity going through the Anglepoise. Beneath the floorboards, the pipes tick – ticketty tick tick tick. The immersion boiler refills, trickly, after Leigh has a shower or while she's having a bath. An old house like this one (1902 or 1903) always creaks and cracks.

Freitag 3 März

I've been starting to think about what I might pass on to the baby, healthwise. My mother's father was an optician who went blind; and Mum's eyesight – even forgetting the stroke – isn't great. My own: with glasses off, I can read the number of a bus when it's two tennis courts away. For writing, and reading, I don't need or use them. The letters in my right eye are in focus when my head's resting on my left hand, but if I swap eyes – chuck my gaze across the wink – my left-eye-letters are legible but woozy. To get them to come crisp, I have to pull my neck away the width of a fist – at which point the right-eye-ink has started to bleed. Only a little. It's copeable with, the astigmatism, and the four o'clock headache. I don't want to give the baby – the baby *boy* – all the faults I have, and add some others just for him. Honestly, I could cope with him being perfect. But what I keep saying to myself is 'normal'; not superhuman or England captain, but a normal healthy baby growing into a normal healthy adult and dying a normal healthy death at a normal healthy age. One hundred and five years old, like his great-grandmother. She told me she didn't think living that long was a good thing. Her potential husbands, the ones from her own generation, died in the Great War; before it became the First World War. She married an older man, who brought along the heart disease which is probably the most worrying inheritance I have for the Flipper, the Flipster. Grandfather Jack Percy died early enough to give Gra a half century of widowhood. When I'm sitting-sitting, I hear my heart's beats – I feel the spiral swirl of it through the core of me. (*Il mio cuore.*) The baby's heart, during the scan, sounded like windscreen wipers coping with a snowstorm. 'Very healthy,' the nurse said. I could see it, blossoming and unblossoming.

Samstag 4 März

The baby is fine. If I had been completely without hope, this would have minimized my sufferings. *The baby is fine.* When I am unhappiest, it's when I've been full of hope, and feel myself becoming even fuller – my capacity stretching, my heart expanding.

Once, I arranged a meeting with a young woman I loved. I could tell she wasn't beautiful but I also *couldn't* tell she wasn't beautiful. The lines of the rest of the world had warped around her, until no form was more perfect than her silhouette. To arrange the meeting, I wrote a four-page letter which I handed her after work – we worked in the same office, doing the same job. After a phone call to confirm, we met outside a pub in Soho. We sat at a table on the pavement with loud traffic around us. I was very direct when I said what I had to say; more direct, I think, than with any woman I had loved – because I needed her to help me kill my love for her. It must be chloroformed, euthanized. I said, 'Tell me there's no hope.' But she didn't reply directly enough; she was being kind. I think she said there was nothing wrong with me, she just had a boyfriend in Cornwall. So I rewound the conversation and made her say it. I got her to repeat the words, 'There's no hope.' And look at me as she said it, 'There's no hope.' And I said thank you. I drank my beer and looked at the black cabs. It wasn't over, there would be a lot more listening to Carole King's *Tapestry* and talking things through with Sinéad, but it was over. I think the young woman was flattered, dismayed. What could be more embarrassing or delightful? Oh God, she probably still has the four-page letter. Shortly afterwards, she became ill and left work to go and live with her parents. By then, I didn't love her quite as much. I knew there was no hope, even though she'd once come home with me and slept on a mattress in my bedroom. On a mattress on the bedroom floor, so we weren't in the same bed, so she wasn't unfaithful. What does this have to do with the baby?

He will be rejected.

Sonntag 5 März

I wish I wrote with – I aspire to write with the accuracy of a biologist, a specialist biologist, an entomologist, a melittologist. But *buzz-buzz* I can't. For they have the apt terminology of established and variable anatomy, whereas I have whatever simile or metaphor comes to hand – I have guesstimation, vagueness and anti-precedent. I have common and posh English. For colour I have, for instance, for a bee: black, very dark, pitchy, ebon; plus a host of even less usable synonyms: sombre, tarry, sable, Negroid. (*Roget's Thesaurus* as Imperial War Museum.) Or, for another stripe, I have: yellow – yellow which isn't gold, or pale orange, or jaundice, or straw-like, but might be (among some classes) specified as cadmium yellow, or lemon, or chrome, or piss. For stripes, for I'm trying for stripes, I have two-tone striations, or alternating bands/bars of colour, or broad contrasting lines. I feel like a thirteen-year-old single-sex private schoolboy trying to pay buck naked Mother Nature a compliment. The words just won't stand up for themselves. You look very nice today. Your bees look very nice. Their wings are like are like are like stained-glass windows, but a little bit more art nouveau than Chartres Cathedral. Specific bee species have particular structures within their wings' lined translucency, and these look decorative but must've been formed by the stress-testing of natural selection. When the honeybee is flying, the wings are a milky blur – skimmed milk, not full-fat; when they land, the wings are coloured by what's beneath them: an abdomen with the nutty sheen of a well-oiled cricket bat from 1937. That's not at all yellow, it's ginger, or bronze. That's not black, it's oak, or Bakelite. *Apis mellifera*, which I had to look up, is downed with functional fuzz. (I feel like the Pobble trying to use tweezers with his feet.) Black and yellow and black and yellow seen through crystalline membranes – which means how-black-appears-beside-yellow and how-yellow-appears-against-black – when yellow isn't yellow and black isn't black. Bronze and oak. Honeybees look as if they live in the dark of linty pockets, alongside acorns, mint humbugs, tortoiseshell penknives & fossicking fingers with brown dirt under the nails. That's my poor best, Mother.

Montag 6 März

Mouse sleeps in my room, with the door closed – so I often start writing (this here) accompanied by the smell of his litter tray. It is varyingly acrid, caustic – as if he's been stripping paint in the wee small hours. Small wee thing. I move his tray and toys (catnip balls, Barnaby the bitten-wolf) through into our bedroom before I start, oh and bring back my guitar. I don't leave Mouse with it overnight, as he loves to gnaw the looped strings at the head. Here he is now, saying me, me, me, as if there were something tangible he wanted. Hello, Mouse. He's gone again, without even giving me the chance to nuzzle him under his fluffy white chin. Maybe I need the distraction, but Mouse is copeable with – he sleeps more than a baby does. (Doesn't he?) Have I written less or more since we've had him? No idea. Because my room smells of him, it no longer smells of whatever it smelled of before. (As always, the lack of words in English for smell other than 'smell' becomes immediately apparent – when I write of this one of the five unequal senses.) (Sight is King, Smell is Queen, Touch is Princess, Hearing is Prince and Taste is Cook.) Stench – definitely some mornings my room stinks, and if it doesn't, it's odoriferous – ferrously odoriferous, as if an alchemist had been burning iron in there; ferally noxious, as if a wolf-child had been corner-shitting. It reeks, hums, pongs, whiffs. (Leigh sneezes – 'A-tissue,' she says, very clearly.) (She is afraid a large sneezing fit will dislodge the embedded baby.) Actually, now I turn them over, reeks, hums, pongs and whiffs all suggest different kinds of smell: reeks suggests rotting; hums, something warming up in the sun (attracting flies); pongs, a comically bad smell – like a stink-bomb – but one that won't last long; whiffs, a bearable fume from a semi-distant or undiscovered source (although maybe an armpit). I suppose my desk used to smell of dust, me, paper and hardboard.

Dienstag 7 März

In my sleep I grind my teeth – and in the morning, they ache and feel cracked. Thinking of my teeth makes me think of my jawbone and my skull, and this makes me think (as does backache) of myself-as-skeleton. This is very different to thinking of myself as a scatterling of bones, perhaps missing a femur – because a licky dog carried it off. Entropic bones, bones moving apart from one another, bones being chewed by critters and eroded by rain – that's pure death. An articulate skeleton is different – a skeleton is an image, a representative, of death-in-life, just as a ghost is a commercial traveller for life-in-death. And all we've seen of Flipper has been the ghost of his skeleton. He's a very beautiful little armature, capable of flowing moves and spasms, of self-comfort and meat dreams. I lie: beyond bone, we could also see his heart, and the rhythmic flow of blood into and out of bits of it – like sped-up footage of traffic at a complex intersection, at night, with the stop-start headlights alternately idling and accelerating. He's a busy technological city, already host to service industry workers, commuters and wage slaves. We haven't seen his flesh, although puttyish 3-D photos were available for purchase (we said no, thank you); we don't know how he'll try to justify his embodiment, once born – except through returning our greedy love. How resourceful will he be? What kind of criminal activity will engage grown-up Flipper? In my dreams, I speak to a glassy version of him through a prison phone, or give a press conference after the terrorist incident. I am in the car with him, as he deliberately crashes it into the bridge, and my muscles tense, and my jaw mashes into the dashboard. He rapes Leigh, or I dissuade him from that by offering myself (he has a gun). All the myths happen, even the Ancient Greek ones. Why am I thinking these things? I think everyone does, they just think them very fast, and then flash on to happier thoughts – deliberately happier images. We don't know how decided Flipper already is. Does he love carrots, or lack empathy? Does he favour his right or left hand? Does his capacity for language acquisition rival baby Chomsky's? What's his favourite colour? Is he really he?

If I'm not eating something, then what I taste is my mouth – which changes taste during the day. Often, it is sour; when I'm hungry, sour is what it is. This is when the saliva, wanting food with which to interact, goes to work on what it's got – which is my tongue and teeth. (Obviously, it's not going to get very far.) There must still be sugars in there, stray strands, nubs, left over from the last thing I ate. (Muesli.) Not meat fibres, muffin remnants, intra-dental – ambient nutrients, floating in the everpresent wetness. Isn't it weird that we carry these washy caves around with us, hardly noticing them? Unless we are thirsty, really trapped-in-the-lift thirsty, and then we realize the clartiness and fleshiness ain't natural. Most of the time, it's a tidal place – influx of wetness dropping down from the tiny holes at the back at the top. Not actually dropping (spit-stalactites forming), but sliding down the sides to meet our upper molars. We're sea-creatures – water with intent, with Will. I've drunk someone else's, as a dare. Like a rehydration drink but even more vomitsome. There were two boys at school who would simultaneously spit into one another's mouths – but that was hocking a loogie. Those oysters were as nuanced as the strings inside swirly marbles. They were petrol rainbows in a puddle. Spit travels with kisses. In passion, I've sensed bubbles being generated. I realize I have strayed again from mouth-taste. Mostly what I taste is my fillings. If my mouth weren't lined with metal (my brother has 'the best teeth in the family'), I wonder would I still taste steel and iron (my fillings are neither; alum)? Am I sensing the constituent elements in my blood? Is this the flavour of my brain juice? I need to go to the dentist.

Samira, Katherine and Lola's stories this evening. Katherine's worrying (suicide). Lola fine, and I didn't mention her boss's boss. Samira, smooth, very smooth.

Donnerstag 9 März

Touch. The sides of this pen, of almost all the pens I use, are – the shaft of, but that sounds wrong. Snug barrel as black-shiny as lacquer but, I think, some kind of plastic. I think even if you were given it blindfold, you'd still guess it was plain black; it doesn't feel like there's anything unnecessary about it. A beautiful device I've had around three months, and which has prompted me to write in greater detail about smaller things. New means sometimes bring new ends. I feel the paper of the page, only slightly gritty and resistant, through the brassy nib. It has – Mouse just climbed onto the desk again, putting one claw in my right leg. His fur isn't super-fluffy. (Softer than rabbit, not as soft as hare.) He seems to want to climb on my shoulder; then settles down to gnaw a paw in the lamplight. The new black pen has no sticky-out hand around it where it's unscrewed. Although these outcrops are practical, giving the ridges of the thumb, forefinger and the callous dip something to grip, they become wearysome after a short while. Other pens I use, have used, include the birthday present Mont Blanc (Meisterstuck No. 149) – a real chubba with a think nib, extra-wide; I have to use it upside down. There are a couple of books I've written with it – I can't remember which. Just in the right place it has the thread of the screw-cap – it doesn't bite into my fingertips. Last I'll mention is the Parker 45 Flighter Deluxe (no tassie) that I think I used for my school exams. Blue ink-filled currently. Most of the writing I do is in black ink. Mouse is playing with the nib of the pen I'm writing with, and blotting the ink with the tip of his paw. Other things I touch: I touch the inside of my clothes, my left elbow is heavy on the hardboard while my right slides across it, my right palm rubs page or desk, my glasses sometimes rest on the bridge of my nose although usually they're off, my feet rest on the outer edges of the foot-rest. Unconstricting, worn-for-years clothes – sand-trousers, mum-dad-cardy. The hairs of my beard sometimes prickle me.

I booked the dentist.

Freitag 10 März

Someone told me there was a legend-rumour-slander I wrote with a quill. I think this is a distortion of the dipping pen I sometimes use. (I own a jokey quill with a black feather and an ornate metal nib, but it's rubbish for writing – the kind of thing someone buys in the gift shop at Shakespeare's House in Stratford-upon-Avon, never uses, chucks away.) The dipping pen is a brass creature about as tall as my balled fist. It has a slider with which to attach and tighten up the nib (the pen). So blessed I was to inherit these, indirectly/directly, from Uncle Gerald. He died; I cleared out his house, with my dad – somewhere in Lytham. This pen-holder and a box of C. BRANDAUER & CO. Ltd Circular Pointed Pens Birmingham Echo Pen No. 67. This is what I used when I wrote (switched to it now) *deadkidsongs*. In these notebooks it bleeds through the paper fibres too lavishly, turning letters into black sunbursts – like those blotting paper experiments we did at school, to separate the colours in chemicals. Also, it seeps through onto the reverse of the page, making anything you write there, especially in pencil, illegible. This first with the brass, which feels tiny, knobbly, scratchy-nibbed. And this with the long, elegant, cork-gripped dipping pen I bought from the London Graphic Centre in Covent Garden. It's much more useable, squatter – and this nib, they're all characterful, feels biting but accommodating. I could *do things* with this. On less liquid-loving paper. Writing is easier, I think, when you can see the glisten of the ink before it dries into dry words. This flow, when it goes, is more like a coloratura throat or a sob. When I'm stuck, I'll sometimes start making letters with a dipping pen, to see if it turns into something that means or may mean something. Paper Chromatography – that's what those experiments are properly called. How to make a Chromatograph. I have six fountain pens.

Samstag 11 März

Grid paper, gridded paper, I associate with writing short stories, and one particular collection. *I play the…* 5mm square ruled – what WHSmith calls 'Square Ruled', but to which Ryman gives the title 'Quadrille'. (Bolster the lobster.) I just noticed Ryman's is 80 gsm, whereas Smiths is only 70 gsm, which might explain why the Quadrille feels smoother, less asbestos-y. When I write on and in a grid, every other line, I'm reminded of the *cahiers d'exercice* of French schoolchildren. They grow up in little boxes, little boxes – and in other countries, too. Whenever I travel, I try to find a papeterie. The best are in Japan. In America, they seem full of interesting things but there's an undertow of Office Supplies. The paper is unjoyful. Staples that will rust. (I mourn the paper shop on Southampton Row, with its notebooks so wadded they seemed to have been chewed and spat out by mountain goats.) Yellow legal pads are the American writer's page-icon – though now it's MacBooks. Mouse arrives and puts his nose in my empty water glass. He licks at my leafy-tea-dregs. I will have to put him outside my room, as this pen needs refilling. (Imagine what he could do if he batted the ink-bottle off my desk.) There. When I write in a grid, I always worry slightly that the verticals, the safe grey-blue lines, will make rereading harder. But as long as I write in ink, not pencil, I am able to re-access what I've written – even at a distance of time or eye. By writing every other line, I leave space for new versions of the same sentence. I often don't need these, as the writing comes more easily when I'm at home on that kind of ergonomic-totalitarian page. I know there will be false starts, failed beginnings – then, when it's rolling – the cheese will get to the bottom of the hill. Square Ruled makes me feel I can be limited and accurate but also that everything – every word – is a minor transgression. You're crossing a line here, boy. No-one expected a story on these pages, just grudging graphs. The covers could hardly be more onerous. But inside is like a tiled swimming pool no-one's yet dived into – you're the first, and every ripple you swim back through will have been made by your body. It will become a diagram of your energy, unimaginably complex, naturally unnatural. Let Mouse back in now. To work.

Sonntag 12 März

Anxiety – nothing but anxiety.

I like nothing more – I was considering writing 'I love nothing more',
then I thought of Leigh and possible-child. I could say 'adore', but
that makes me giddily camp. New start: Nothing feels better – no,
that's catastrophic. Pencils are one of my favourite things in the world.
(Of course, they're in the world, *I'm* in the world.) I like pencils a
lot. I like all pencils. If I see one on the pavement, I will pick it up –
unless it's been split to splinters by heels. Some pencils you just know,
from the first time you hold them, even before you write with them,
are going to be absolute darlings. Yet all pencils produce is a grey
line, slightly sparkly if viewed at the incorrect angle. But they are
so forgiving (a good pencil is like a generous priest – all sins can be
effaced). One birthday, Mum bought me a plastic tube of fifty pencils
from Staples – alternate black and gold stripes, HB (so that's perfect),
with the word PROFESSIONAL stamped on the black, in white.
I thought I could use them for years, but they were appalling – try to
sharpen them and the lead broke and broke time after time. It was as if
the whole lot had been dropped off a cliff onto concrete (I'm writing
with the last of them now) – the graphite seemed greasy, prone to
smearing and smudging as soon as the page was turned. I had them
near the desk for years, and would go back to them for another try,
sharpen and scrawl, but they were so frustrating and crap (yes, you,
Staples) that – in the end – feeling as if I were betraying her in the
most intimate way, I had to chuck my mother's gift in the bin. Guiltily,
I took them out. Then put them back. They were unusably shoddy.
And now, with Mum ill, I wish I'd kept them just as a thing from her
to have around. But they were fucking annoying. Instead, there are
the diaries. Every year, she would buy me one for Christmas – they
were perfect, and either the house burns down or I have them until
I'm dead. Sometimes, when I'm gloomy, I'll cheer myself up – and
feel a little less than useless – by sharpening all the pencils in the pot.
Here comes the Quiet Life again.

Montag 13 März

More anxiety. Could I spend a week writing only about pencils? – No, because there is far too much to say. And no, even more, because there is no such thing as 'only'. 'Love is intensity of attention.' When I wrote what I did about sharpening all my pencils, to buck myself up, I went to so just that – pulled them out of the pot, avoiding the porcupine quill – and saw they were all already as sharpened and as sharp as could be. Because they were pre-loved before I even got back to them. And now I'm going to try to sell something, a product, that will save the world in a minor way. Ladies and gentlemen and all others, I present the LYRA Pencil Extender Holder Lengthener in Natural Beechwood (with a polished chrome metal clasp). Sadly, all pencils, after being sharpened down and down, become too short for comfortable use – even though about half their length is left. Now, if you buy one of the long-named attachments (which I will call the Lyra), you can affix it to the non-writing end, and get pages more writing out of each pencil. The Lyra is Made in Germany, and I bought my two from a papírnictví in Prague – Czech paper shop. At the time I was there, these were wonderfully literal. They sold paper stuff – all and only paper stuff. From a papírnictví, as well as your writing paper, you bought your toilet paper. At the moment I have the Lyras on two lucky pencils. One is the three-inch stub of a black pencil made of very pale wood – a goth pencil that I found on the pavement in Bloomsbury. The other is plain but varnished wood with the days of the month of January (20–31) printed in black on its tubular shaft. Once I had a whole annual set, one for each month, and tried to only write with them during the month for which they were appropriate. It wasn't possible – in April I was still writing with December. Oh the shame. Counting down, counting down. How much longer will it be, this period of waiting? Six months.

Dienstag 14 März

Notebooks. Not branded notebooks, though most of the ones I use are branded – and expensive. I like them to be the same, one after the other. They are on a shelf behind me, over my right shoulder – I've never counted them. I'll count them. About 150, it turns out. I choose jackets that have pockets big enough to carry one, and a pen. When I'm anywhere – a hospital waiting room, another hospital waiting room – I take notes. In the repeat miscarriage unit at St Mary's, I wrote pages. I write down things I overhear (o/h). (Joe Orton used to listen to people on the top decks of London buses – the best place, and even better now they use their phones as confessionals. I once heard a woman advising another woman how to run a brothel.) Yesterday, a woman said, 'His softness was a bit jarring at first.' I write short story ideas (s/s). At the back is a page for interesting/ weird/usable (but probably not) character names. On the inside back flyleaf, I write down words I don't know or that I've only rarely heard (slang, techspeak). There's also a page for nonsense phrases and sound jumbles. At the beginning, on the title page, I write down locker numbers in the British Library, passwords, quotes that fit what I'm working on. Sometimes I'll draft a whole story, or draft and redraft a poem or a lyric, all within the too small pages of a notebook. And I go through phrases of drawing – cartoons, leaves, strangers. Too often I've thought my best writing, certainly my most vivid, was in my notebooks – never worked out a way to get something bigger to behave, to misbehave that livelily. It's a claim, isn't it? Ego and better posthumous. Without the various structures of story. I go all the way back to *The Road to Xanadu: A Study of the Ways of the Imagination*, read in the school library – and a copy three feet to my right.

Mechanical pencils. Yes, I use these, but I don't love them – I don't fall in love with them as the single means, the one implement, with which I can write a book. Not as with this shiny black pen, not as with this diary. I associate mechanical pencils with Technical Drawing, and I associate Technical Drawing with the Careers Master at my Secondary School. It may only have been one Careers Interview we had, but I remember it going something like this every time I spoke to him: 'But what are you interested in? Which of your subjects?' 'Art.' 'Art?' 'Yes, art.' 'So, you like drawing – well, you could do Technical Drawing, and get a job in Industry. What else do you like?' 'English.' You like writing?' Probably too embarrassed to say yes. 'Well, you could do Journalism, and learn technical writing, and get a job in Industry.' I pity him, Mr. Bicester. He made me very sure I was never going to do industrial design or industrial journalism. It's a generic scene, isn't it? Him and me. He was being realistic. (He was an English master.) It would be irresponsible of him to advise me to become a poet. 'Well, you could do experimental verse, publish a pamphlet, and get a residency in a prison.' (I wish I had done a residency in a prison. That's an idea – when I'm able, I will volunteer for that.) The generic scene is written by, or written about, successes – otherwise it's not a scene. (This isn't to say you can't be a successful technical journalist writing in industry. Karl writes about combine harvesters. He goes to combine harvester trade fairs in Las Vegas. But I know Karl would like to be a working novelist.) (Survey 100 writers on industrial journals, and ask if that's the type of writing they always wanted to do. Survey 100 novelists, and ask if they would prefer to write about combine harvesters.) (Definition of Soviet Socialist Realist Literature: Boy Meets Tractor.) The generic scene is structural – without antagonists, minor as well as major, the heroic artist doesn't have a thrilling journey. I should copy out the Mr. Bicester story.

Rewrites from Andy (more objective, crisper), Rebekah (a different, deeper funny), Ola (self-parody but she knows it), Rudy (he moved me, the bastard), Michael (still bland, bless him) and Jess (who'd have thunk?).

Donnerstag 16 März

The two disturbances I hear most often come from the garden centre and the pipes – the old brass water pipes beneath the floorboards, beneath the oatmeal carpet flecked with Mouse's cat litter (before I hoover). The radiator, too, sometimes tick-tick-ticks behind me, but I rarely have this on. The pipes are heading from our outside boiler to our inside immersion tank, which – behind the curving wall – is what is directly in front of me, on the left-hand side. (If I had x-ray eyes.) It is blessedly silent, although after Leigh has her shower, I can hear it trinkling and sighing as it refills. Shaped like a five-foot pill stood on bend, the tank looks like something that went regularly – in the 1970s – to the bottom of the ocean. And because the ticking water in the pipes is piping hot from the combi boiler, and because the submersible isn't perfectly insulated, my room is the warmest in the house. (Unless outside is freezing, and I keep the radiator off.)

Today is warm, so I have to remember rather than wait for the sound of the pipes. They tick at walking pace, but falter onto tiptoe diminuendo and decelerando – then sometimes they speed up again for two or three petulant heel-taps. You're not looking at me, Daddy. But you're invisible, my daughter. When I go around the house with the brass key and a screwdriver, bleeding the old and new radiators, the ticking sometimes moves on. But it always finds its way back, so it can haunt me again.

The other sound is the bring-bring of the garden centre's telephone extension. Until recently, I wished they'd turn it down, but I've realized it could be much worse. As it is, it's like being in a signal box – the controller is calling up with news of a special express passing through. (More likely it's someone from East Dulwich wanting to know if they have eco-friendly weedkiller.)

Freitag 17 März

For one embarrassing period, around the first year of university, I altered my *g*'s so they looked like the head and abdomen of an ant joined by a stick-waist; I even gave my ant *a* little upwards antenna. (Ants don't really have antennae, do they?) These days the best that I can say about my handwriting is that it's fast, legible and it's mainly mine. Yet one of the uncanniest things about looking at words as they emerge, blackly wet like sea-slugs, in this long broken line, is that – on occasion – my handwriting looks like my mother's or my father's. Mum sometimes went through my penmanship homework with me. But Dad, so far as I know, never sat down to influence my letterforms. His hand, in Paper Mate Flair Felt Tip blue, also belonged to Father Christmas – which was how I learned that Father Christmas used a blue Paper Mate Felt Tip. If I were to guess, I'd say my current handwriting has been formed by efficiency, ergonomically. The shapes of my alphabet have changed to eliminate excrescences. Looking back up at this page, I can't see any bits of any letters that could be done away with – liquidated. The descenders of my *f*, *g* and *y*'s are usually shortened – don't curve round much to flick towards the next word. Mouse's tail is flicking across this page, like the latter end of my *j*. But soon – as always – I'll have to type all these words up; make sure they are in the cloud, and won't burn up when our house burns down.

Samstag 18 März

Years ago I wondered if the KGB or the CIA's listening-in capacity was so acute, and their science of surveillance so advanced, that they could identify which letter was being typed (on a manual typewriter) by its particular higher or lower, harsher or gentler clack. (Waveform, be technical.) Even I could pick out the satisfying thrum of the Space Bar, the awkward crane-lift of Caps Lock. (Searching: yes, this was cracked.) (Ear was eye.) Even more challenging would be to transcribe from an ASMR recording of handwritten words. Could it be done? If someone listened acutely enough, with strong enough AI, and with enough government funding, could they tell the waveform of a g from that of a y, could a u and an a be distinguished? Even if it was only possible to tell within two or three letters, codebreaking and context would give you the rest. All those long straight scratches of the autobiographer; all those criss-cross scrunches of the loyal revolutionary Communist. Much easier, I suppose, to install a super mini spy camera in the ceiling above the desk. Or just to enter into writer's apartment when he's called in for interrogation, and photograph the pages. (I would know if anyone breathed on my notebooks.) The sound of the nib scratching on the page is the intermittent sound of my days. (Different pens; different sharpnesses.) The double whiplash of a crossing out; the tiny lipsmack of a dotted i. Pencil scooching is louder, broader, more cello than violin. Dipping pens are violin-scritchy. Biros are hushed rubs, apart from the clicking when you lift them off of the page. Felt-tip pens are like trolley wheels trundling. They all sound a bit like when I scratch my short-haired scalp with my fingernails – but that's as if I'm the page being nibbed by several writers at once. (I, Marx.)

Mother's Day tomorrow – Card, phone call, visit, flowers. What else is there to do?

Sonntag 19 März – *Mother's Day*

There's not only the small sound of the pen or pencil, there's also the gaps of silence in between the words. But they're not at all silent, because there's the drag – every inch or so – of skin across paper. The side of my sliding right hand smooths its way right to left beneath the actual lettering. Scritchety-skriddle-scrittch swoosh. You wouldn't notice it – like an in-breath during a close mic'd song – or a sniff of morning air through the tent flap. I hadn't noticed it until I was writing about the sound of the pen. There should be a name for it: *gap-caress, palm-stroke.* It's the outer edge of my hand but neither palmar nor dorsal – the part used for karate chops or to rub the dust off a window-pane. *Pad-push, air-bridge.* Looking at them now, my right outer-edge is slightly shinier and less lined than my left. *Grip-move. Hand-scoosh.* I'm going to record these next few words on my phone, as a voice memo, to see what they sound like. *Void-jump.* Immediately I notice it's not just my hand that makes a sound but also the forearm against the hardboard. That moves less frequently but more loudly. It's a bigger area, and hairier. I can't see any difference between my arms at this touch or non-touch point. The recording is quite hissy. The pen sounds like a sped up – that was my tummy rumbling – like a rat on amphetamines trying to dig its way out of a cardboard box. Or a Kafka-creature in a burrow. When I listen really closely, I'm back in the Exam Schools on the High Street, taking my finals. Only it's someone else's pen – the confident student seated directly ahead of me, likely to get a First and enter Corporate Finance. Another rat.

Off to see Mum this afternoon. Leigh seeing her Mum.

Montag 20 März

It's the Abductor digiti minimi – that's what it's called, the chunky muscle beneath the skin on which the weight of my pen-hand rests. And yours. (Mini me.) Abductor is the main, outer muscle; also involved, though not in support rather than movement, are the flexor and opponens. This part of the hand, any hand, is the ulnar (from elbow) fleshy side of the palm, correctly known as part of the Hypothenar eminence (hypo- meaning below/beneath/under [as in hypodermic]; thenar, from Greek, meaning thumb-bump related). The little nub of bone that rubs and gets a little sore by my wrist is the pisiform (from pea-shaped). One site, informative but snippy, tells me the root meaning of thenar comes from the Greek verb *thenein*, to strike. Thenar was the bit of the hand with which you'd hit something or someone. (The phalanges or hand and feet bones derive from phalanx – Greek word for battle lines of infantry.) Everybody was kung fu fighting. The Abductor digiti minimi, and I'll have to copy this off the National Library of Medicine website, 'Originates from the pisiform and the tendon of the flexor carpi ulnaris. It attaches to the base of the proximal phalanx of the little finger.' From the pea to the infantry. It is interesting that the A.d.m. is hypo- to the thumb, because that suggests that even medically hands are seen as sticking out to the front rather than hanging useless. I could call the rub-bulge Adam, for a decent name. That makes him male, though. (All writing is fallen.) Eve is probably worse.

Dienstag 21 März

The main thing – physical thing – that's produced by the economy of the desk is pencil shavings. They are a by-product, a waste product. They can't be reused, recycled. I suppose I could use them as pre-kindling – have a separate bin for them. Burning pencil lead might not be a good idea (in tiny amounts, Toby). Notebooks pass across the desk, have ink and graphite scribbled into them, get put in plastic storage containers and get taken down to the cellar. Here, their pages go wavy with damp, and no-one reads them. The printer blows black dust onto recycled 80 gsm paper. Its cartridges run out, and are taken to be recycled at work – but they're a chunky plastic waste. The Anglepoise needs a new bulb every eighteen months. My computers – Macs – slow and slow until they're useless – though I'm sure a scavenging genius could use one to code a new world. The fountain pens are refilled. Glass ink bottles are emptied, taken to the kitchen, washed up, recycled. (When I say recycled, I mean put in the recycling bin in the kitchen; and, on Monday night, carried in the tubular steel bin out to the big green plastic council recycling bin, and tipped into that. On Tuesday morning, it's driven away after being poured into the back of the lorry. Whether Lambeth Council are honourable, punctilious recyclers of every colour glass and every numbered plastic, I don't know. The other bin goes to landfill. I am responsible for X cubic metres of trash, since my birth.) If I stopped using pencils, I would stop making shavings. Is ink ethical? I could retrain and work to alleviate child poverty.

Last week of term. Rebekah had made three types of muffin to celebrate. Her stories are good, but the muffins were hecka great. Hard to concentrate with them sitting beside us. Roxana, Felix, Samira, Grace, Katherine and Lola's rewrites. All improved, though Felix needs to stop chopping his sentences as if cutting were a religion. Katherine, lighter, more emotional. Roxana even joked about 'my journey'. Lola did this week's murder as tickling-to-death. Samira, could be the start of a novel. Everyone said so. I agreed. Grace cried. 'I'm so fucking relieved.' She hadn't sworn before. Not once. To the college bar.

I have enjoyed this workshop. They looked like they were going to fall out, but then they pulled it together. That's the story.

How I will miss this (the plots, the epiphanies) in the Autumn, when I'm on study leave, and – perhaps, hopefully – paternity leave.

Donnerstag 23 März

'I divide all the works of world literature into those written with and without permission. The first are trash, the second – stolen air.'

If I sit absolutely upright at my desk, these are the words I see. From Osip Mandelštam's 'Fourth Prose'. Five years ago, perhaps six, I copied them onto a three-by-five card and pinned them to the corkboard – along with (anticlockwise): some photobooth strips of me and Leigh; a printout of a Benin bronze with scored cheeks and vacantly awaiting eyes; a month-to-view calendar with days marked off and hours as downwards strokes (with diagonals if I reach five – rarely); above this, the three-month scan of the baby beside a small knitted hare (to me it's a hare, but it was probably intended as a rabbit) that I found on the street and handwashed; a photograph of Mum and Dad cutting their tiered wedding cake on September 18th 1964; an A4 printout of a page from the graphic novel about Richard Feynman (in a white shirt with sleeves rolled up, the Nobel physicist of utter charm and bongo frenzy holds towards me an oblong page with the word he's just ornately doodled on it: DISREGARD, & in one speech bubble, he is saying, 'Yeah, that's what I used to know, but I forgot' and in the second, he says, 'I gotta disregard everybody else and then I can do my own work'); beside this are postcards from V.S. Pritchett and J.G. Ballard (generous men); and then a photograph of me with Tomaš Mika outside his country cottage in Southern Bohemia – we're at a small round table, young, and he holds a typewriter vertically in his lap (keys looking up at his chin) and I am the thinnest I ever was, 1992 – we have been translating underground Czech poetry. Without permission. Disregardingly. There are other things hidden beneath these memories; unlike the giant baize noticeboard to my right, the corkboard is a hodge, a *bordel*, a *zmatek*, and is meant to be.

Freitag 24 März

How often have I written trash? How rarely have I stolen air? It may be self-serving, but – when I could – I got two-book deals from publishers, and delivered the second book with no-one having read a word. This happened with *deadkidsongs* (after *Corpsing*), and *Ghost Story* (after *Finding Myself*). Which would make *Finding Myself* trash. *Corpsing*, no-one was that interested – my first novel, *Beatniks*, had sunk (I lost an editor, moved publisher, didn't enthuse anyone). And since being dropped by my major label, and going indie, I write until a book's as finished as it can be, then hand it over to 1. Leigh, 2. agent, 3. publisher. Recently, partly as a result, several completed efforts haven't been published. I don't think I would succeed in getting *HOSPITAL* accepted now – the most outlandish book I snuck out at Penguin. They were very good to me until they weren't. Toward the end, though, I felt I might as well take a spade and bury the books myself. *Journey into Space*. *King Death*. Some stolen air in *Space*. But Osip Mandelštam wasn't writing about contemporary publishing, you might say – he wasn't thinking of anything beyond Soviet Russia in the 1930s. His conditions. To publish a book of poetry then and there, one needed formal approval, permission papers, rubber stamps decorated with Communist stars. That's not the same now. It is. That doesn't apply to us. It does. Osip is unmerciful. *All* the works of *world* literature. If you sought permission of your King, Queen, Lord or Emperor, your wife, husband, mistress or lover, your parents, children, best friend, or the commissariat, Jesus, Jehovah, Mohammed (PBUH) or Buddha, your publicist, agent, editor – even, I think, if you cravenly asked it of yourself: trash. You have written trash. There is gorgeous trash. Trash I love. Praising the giving and receiving of rings in the Mead Hall. Rendering unto Caesar. Letting Ezra and Vivian edit you. Some of Shakespeare asks permission, but not 'King Lear'. (For an inappropriate word, an Elizabethan could be hung, drawn and quartered in the centre of London – before a crowd of thousands.) Osip – and I think he is thinking of his master, Dante Alighieri – is saying that the only works worth writing are essentially impermissible. *Inferno*. *Purgatorio*. *Paradiso*. Be terrified.

Samstag 25 März

We often spend the least time looking at the things we spend the most time looking at. There are things in front of me that I rarely catch sight of. My computer's screen when it's not on, my screen when it's off. This is the biggest of the unseens – 15″ x 20.5″ – about the size of my chest, when I'm lying on my side. It is, yes, a black mirror – not far off obsidian (that obsidian I picked up by the roadside, as gorgeous scree, in Armenia). (Where is it? I had some beautiful fragments, shards, and a couple of piebald doorstops.) (Like Doctor Dee's scrying stone that's always absent from its display case in the British Museum. On loan.) The screen is, yes, a black mirror – but we almost never look at screens for what they reflect when dead. If a screen is off, we notice where it doesn't shine – the fingerprints around the edges, where we've adjusted its position. I have a spray, and sometimes I'll treat the black mirror to a thorough wipe – which leaves unsatisfactory, rough vertical lines of smear. If I look closely right now, I can see some small, less-reflective spots. I think these are the flung remains, tiny and circular, of sneezes or coughs. Within the main of the black I see my domed skull as a dark and featureless silhouette. (I hate the word silhouette – it's nowhere near weird enough.) My ears, larger than they were before, still don't stick out as much as I'd expect them to. Behind me, I see the bottom half of the two oblong windows, with steam from the boiler in the left-hand one. The sun is still rising over the railway line, so I can't make out details of the garden – instead, if I bend down a bit, more silhouettes appear – dark outlines – of the ash trees. My skull against a woody background. Apart from this, at the top right the bell of the Anglepoise shines like a moon coming out of eclipse. And at bottom left, my mug has two glints at either end of its rim, at its perihelion and whatever the opposite of that is.

21 weeks. Your banana is as big as a baby.

I couldn't look at bright colours all day, which must be why –
apart from the bright blue Kakūno pen-top, and the red spine of
one notebook – the desktop is dull gold and the things on it are
matt black or grey. It is as if everything here were seen through
a transparent mist that doesn't block but bleaches. I can turn the
Kakūno pen upside down in the eye-pot (which has the yellow
circle), and its other end is grey. But grey a bit like the bright
grey car in Bedford. When I work away from home, my tables
and hotel desks are emptier; for a while, I like that. When I get
home, I think about being more minimal. But everything here
is used, if rarely. When pencils get too short, and don't stick up
above the edge of the steel pot, then they are forgotten. Hence the
pencil extender. I'm grateful to them (short pencils) for services
rendered. Let them stay for a while before they go downstairs
to live by the oven and write only shopping lists. Do people as
they get older crave brighter colours? (My socks.) With white
hair, a green or a red might suit those that never wore anything
but blue and black. I used to want bespoke clothes, not based on
normal patterns, so the street would give me its attention. I haven't
dressed to be looked at for a long while. Not since Prague, or
even Glasgow – ever since then, I've worn spywear. I want to pass
through as the unseen, whilst able to listen and observe. A certain
dullness is necessary. But when you look into any dull colour, your
eyesight stipples it with sparks or throws violet. If this room is
redecorated, perhaps I'll make the walls green. What's neutral at
one time becomes noticeable at another, and annoying after that.
Anaglypta, woodchip, pebbledash, recessed downlights.

Sonntag 26 März

When you write about this stuff, you know you're going to sound pretty stupid pretty quickly. The personal home computer, desktop publishing – but this is the distinguishing feature of my generation. At thirteen years old, we were gaming on Sinclair Spectrums, Atari 400s and BBC Acorn Micros. I've had five or six desktop computers. The screens have got bigger. The last couple have been large black mirrors underlined with a horizontal band of aluminium grey – with the logo on. I try to keep each as long as I can. One exploded with a small futz-flash, and I thought we'd lost all our photos. Since then, I have an external hard drive doing mind-meld with whatever the main drive is remembering – and a second hard drive in my work office. Plus, the cloud. This technology, I expect, will be altered soon. Desktops are losing out to laptops (I have one). It surprises me I don't remember more about the computers I've had. Their function was more important than they were. I don't think I even made a note of their model numbers. ('Dear Apple Inc,/ you have no idea how much we hate you./ Yours sincerely,/ Apple Users.') To Apple Inc, I am grateful but also hate you – your built-in obsolescence is obscene, your operating system upgrades are debilitating (deliberately). This desktop, because I upgraded, can take five minutes to think about opening a Word document – spinning wheel of death. As soon as I think about the practicalities of computing, I become annoyed. PCs are call-centres on your desk, in your lap. They are distraction devices, because they show you so much you don't need. A paper page is an open field, a Word document is proprietorial software in malfunctioning hardware. I am grateful I don't have to retype my novels every time I redraft them – but maybe they'd have been better if I had. My study is darkening as rain approaches. Computers don't want to be a subject; or noticed, like a broken tool. They want to be air and light and time.

Montag 27 März

On the metal shoebox-size box, supporting the black mirror, are – currently – an external hard drive of 2TB, an external DVD-unit in aluminium gray (compu-gray), a sweet from Japan (a yellow lozenge in a plastic see-thru pillow with a bunny or round-eyed child dressed in a bunny costume – yes, the latter (I see now, because it has two sets of eyes)), some Raspberry Rosé Lip Butter (just tried it – really horrible – that's going – where did it come from?), a folded piece of paper with my name, our address and Leigh's number on it (this is for when I go jogging by myself, in case I have a heart-attack and die, otherwise it would take too long to ID me), a witch stone that is a very similar colour to the hardboard except it has a strong patina of grey (like a hard toffee that's been in a linty waistcoat pocket, having escaped its wrapper) (the whole effect of the hole in the semi-circle shape is of a black hole appearing – harmlessly – in a hedgehog). There are two other objects, the ones I've been getting to all along – more significant and moralizing than those in the first list (because they are a pair, and because when I look at them, I intend for myself to remember something). The mementoes are a grey rhino and a silver Mercedes – a 3½″ plastic toy rhinoceros and a 4″ model 300SL Wing Door. I will write about them tomorrow and the next day, if I have time. The rhinoceros stands for the novel and the Mercedes is repping short stories. I am distracted by a small pain in my right middle finger, where that ribbon of flesh between nail and finger pad, in the gap of the cuticle, wants to be torn free. I know if I do it, there will be sharper pain, but I have to do it. Tweezers.

Ah, such a vast tiny relief.

Dienstag 28 März

I will take the rhinoceros first, because it stands on the left, and because we read left to right, and also, I wanted to write novels before I wanted to write short stories. (And both after I wanted to write because I wanted to write.) This is a very curious object that I found on a garden wall in a suburban street. It wasn't a beloved toy, dropped by a child in a buggy and picked up and put prominently in case (distraught) their parent or carer pushed them back to find it (yay!). I knew this because there were half a dozen plastic animals, all from the same packet, plus a sign in child's handwriting that said COMPLEETLY FREE! I stopped because I recognized the rhinoceros – I knew it – it was from a woodcut by Albrecht Dürer (1471–1528). I picked the dark grey Indian rhinoceros up, turned it over. MADE IN CHINA. I said, 'Thank you,' to the ordinary Victorian house behind the garden wall. I carried the rhinoceros away. No small eyes, not that I saw, watched me from the windows. 'He's got it! He's got it!' The rhinoceros made my day – a delight, a curio. The other animals had been modern creatures, anatomically correct. None of them had been based on a drawing done in the 1500s. Dürer is copyright-free. Someone in China must have decided his version of a rhinoceros was still the most rhino-y; or perhaps using his design, having a maquette and then a cast made of it, was the cheapest option. Dürer is becoming my favourite artist: I have more postcards of his work than of any other (apart, maybe, from Picasso – who I've gone off). The qualities of the rhinoceros are the qualities you need in order to write a novel. Physical robustness, four feet on the ground, eyes straight ahead, the horn. Maybe I was wrong, day before yesterday. Yes, the rhinoceros doesn't stand for the novel, it stands for the novelist. It stands. Or maybe it does – maybe it stands for both. Encountering the idea of a novel is like encountering a life-size plastic rhinoceros that is somehow alive: *Oh no, it's not anything like real* and *Oh no, this ridiculous thing is going to kill me.*

Mittwoch 29 März

I said I'd do the Mercedes, but there's more to say and find out about the rhinoceros. Although it's pretentious, the pair of them are the manifestation of an epigram: 'To write a novel you need the intelligence to begin and the stupidity to finish.' Actually, you need the stubbornness to finish, but that doesn't balance out. To be stubborn, to keep going in the fog of utter pointlessness, you need a deep, brilliant stupidity. I will finish – I will get to the end (if it kills me, this life-size grey plastic rhinoceros that is somehow alive). And it's not 'the intelligence' but the wit. 'To write a novel you need the spark to begin and the slog to finish.' That's too practical, too jolly. To write a novel you need to be a fucking rhinoceros – apparently cumbersome but actually incredibly dainty. This plastic creature is armour-plated – a carapace over his forelegs that ruches up into hard gills beneath his bunnyish ears, a central plate with ribs like scarification, and some smaller sections at his rear parted by a short hairless tail. His front and rear armour is decorated with massed circles. I say his, say her – her almond eyes have been painted orangey red. In a Chinese factory perhaps fifteen years ago, in a second, in someone's hands, a child. An injection moulding seal bisects the rhinoceros, and there's a nub in the dip of her back where the hot plastic was squirted into the mould. She has no nickname. She stands, facing the gullwing Mercedes – not friendly, not unfriendly. To write a novel you need the dilettantism to begin and the stoicism to finish. Or cynicism, not stoicism. To write a novel, you need the cynicism to begin and the stoicism to finish.

Visit home to tell Mum and Dad about pregnancy. Delight.

Missed the students this evening – Wednesday without a workshop is weird. And no more workshops until January next year. But I'll be seeing the students for tutorials in the Summer. I can hear all the latest about Lola's murders and Felix's disappointments then – if not directly, then from others.

Donnerstag 30 März

A silver Mercedes 300SL is faster and more beautiful than a rhinoceros. It corners better, is more accommodating, has an equal amount of detail. The one has an engine, the other a heart. This is already collapsing vis-à-vis short stories and novels. Short stories often have hearts, and lungs, liver, kidneys, spleen; novels can motor, or run out of gas. I've been thinking for some time the meaningful Merc needs to be replaced by something more exactly novelistic of between 3½" and 4". A golden lion tamarin, perhaps. Or maybe not an animal at all – not an earth animal. I'm not intending to tell myself that short stories are unnatural, self-indulgent, petrochemical (though a number of mine are/were). When I first placed rhinoceros versus Mercedes, I was intending to give up writing novels. I thought the best things I'd done, and the closest to what I wanted to do, were short stories. Forget the pain and disappointment, forget the heaviness and horniness of being a novelist – climb in, drive off, escape as the competition winner, or at least the runner-up. Since then, I have written a good novel and very few short stories. This is how my wise intentions usually work out. I am very loyal to truancy. Short stories always play truant, but having turned them into my school, I had to escape them. This model Mercedes is special – glamorous, and my favourite car – because the doors open up and outwards. They end up high, like the lifted shells of a ladybird intending to take off. The 300SL is low, aerodynamic, chic. I am not the person to drive or afford it; I am the person to dream of driving or affording it. (I could hire one – for my birthday.) I disapprove of fast cars. My father, for a very brief period, made model cars. He was a subscriber to the magazines Car, Autocar and Classic and Sportscar. Does this mean I think of my mother as a rhinoceros, or a novel?

Freitag 31 Mar

Senjaku Hello Kitty Colourful Bunny Mixed Fruit Candy is what it is — a Facebook post of 22 May 2012 tells me. The post is on the Senjaku Candy Land Food & Drink Company page. 'Popular by many different candies and flavours, this company is also well known for its unique flavoured items which make people happy all around the world.' The Blippo website tells me, 'These Colorful Bunny associated mixed hard fruit candies from Senjaku Candy Land and Hello Kitty are so yummy and fruity! Grab one and you can enjoy either a peach, Japanese soda (ramune) or lemon flavored goodness. The individual packaging is adorable and the pack includes one collectible sticker out of 20 different ones! A must for all Hello Kitty fan!' £3.30. On the tiny packet, using a translation app, I can read 'gentle feel' and 'of colour and light'. The corporate philosophy of Senjakume Honpo, through Google Translate, 'When we come across delicious food, we feel happy and naturally smile. Since its founding, Senjakume Honpo has expanded the creation of delicious bonds through candy. Even now, in order to deliver delicious smiles to many people, we are not only safe and secure, but we are also basically creating products that reflect the voices of our customers. That is why we, Senjakume Honpo, constantly carry out marketing such as market research.' The Message from the President begins, 'A grain of peace that spreads a delicious smile to people as the outlook on life and values has changed dramatically with the times.' It ends, 'To that end, we will continue to think about what we can do through candy and what we can do as a one-of-a-kind company.' They sound just like me. Ingredients: Sugar, Corn Syrup, Concentrated Fruit Juices, Creamy Powder, Organic Acids, Baking Soda, Flavorings, Natural Colorings. Nutrition information. Per Bag (71g). Energy: 278 kcal, Protein 0g, Fat 0g, Carbohydrate 69.5g, Sodium 60mg. 278 kcal = 278000 Calories. A medium size banana contains 105 calories, on average. A medium carrot provides 25 calories. One packet of Hello Kitty Colorful Bunny Mixed Fruit Candy = 11,120 carrots. Really? I wonder how yummy this Senjaku Hello Kitty Colourful Bunny Mixed Fruit Candy tastes? (Leigh likes Haribo.)

Samstag 1 April – *Fool's Day*

The adorable individual packaging, research tells me, is a vertical form filled seal (VFFS) pillow bag with a zig-zag edge using Modified Atmosphere Packaging (MAP) and made either of Polyethylene terephthalate (PET) or Polyethylene (PE) film. (For a brief while, I thought it was an Airtight Horizontal Flow Wrap – which sounds wonderful – but I was told that this process isn't used for wrapping small, individual items, only for those that can whizz along a horizontal product infeed mechanism, or a conveyor belt.) 'The most widely used petroleum-based plastics such as PET and PE are not biodegradable.' PET is known as polyester, when in textiles. The PE around the Hello Kitty hard candy is likely a Very-low-density polyethylene (VLDPE). It is mainly obtained from petroleum or natural gas. In 2017, researchers reported that the caterpillar of Galleria mellonella eats plastic garbage such as polyethylene. In 1985, Cocteau Twins released the Echoes in a Shallow Bay e.p., containing the track 'Melonella' – mellonella being the specific name of the wax moth Galleria mellonella. There is a dead moth near my desk, lying on the shelf beside the Buddha – it is not a mellonella. I keep it there. I don't know why. Around 100 million tonnes of polyethylene resins are produced annually, accounting for 34% of the total plastics market. I found out. I could find out. From my computer, connected via wifi and router to the internet. Via Google. The Senjakume company website, under Environmental Initiatives, states, 'Regarding products, based on the Containers and Packaging Recycling Law, we fulfil the obligation to notify and re-commercialize by displaying the product package.' There is a recycling logo on the reverse of the pillow bag. I am not going to research the Japanese Containers and Packaging Recycling Law. Though I could. (The top three Plastic Manufacturing Companies are the Dow Chemical Company, LyondellBasell and ExxonMobil.) Perhaps I should.

Strangely, Mouse has caught a moth, and is having fun with it. I have to end that death-play. Moth didn't survive. It wasn't superspecial, just carpet brown.

Sonntag 2 April – *Funday*

I have always wondered if I could write a good verbal fugue. Why? Why have I always wondered if I could write a good verbal fugue? I have always wondered why. Have I always wondered? I have – I have. Why, if I was good? Why, if I could write? Why have I always wondered if I could write a verbal fugue? I have always wondered if I could write. Why have I always wondered? Could I have always wondered if I could write? I could. Could I write, 'I have always wondered'? Could I? If I could write a good verbal fugue, why, I could write… I could write if I could write a verbal fugue. A verbal fugue. A good verbal fugue. *With a countersubject that was clear and melancholy, unlike the first. With a countersubject* (if a verbal fugue) *that was* good *and clear,* if *melancholy.* If I could write. I have always wondered if I have always wondered. Why have *a countersubject?* Why have *melancholy?* If I could write I could write *clear melancholy and good melancholy. First* I wondered, could I write? Could I write *unlike?* If I could, could I write *counter melancholy?* Why was *melancholy good?* Could I write *counter clear?* Why was *clear good?* If I could write – if I could write, I could write *clear unlike clear.* I could write *melancholy unlike melancholy.* Why? Why write *counter?* Why write *unlike? Clear was* good, if I could write a verbal fugue. Good. *Melancholy was clear,* if I could write. Good. If I could write a verbal fugue. If I could write, I *was clear.* I *was clear* – I *was clear* I *was subject.* I *was clear* I *was counter.* I *was clear* I *was unlike.* I *was melancholy and melancholy and melancholy.* Why have a verbal fugue? Why? If I have a why, why have I a why? Why I? If I *was unlike* I I could write. If I was *counter* I I could write. I could – I could. If I could, could I always? *Was* I always good? I *was* always good. (*Was* I always *good?* I *was* always *melancholy.*) (Always *counter.*) (With a *counter melancholy.*) I have always wondered if I could write a good verbal fugue. Have I? (I wondered.) I have – I have. Could I? (I wondered.) I could – I could, I could. I have always wondered if I could write a good, *clear and melancholy* verbal fugue *with a countersubject that was unlike the first.* And have I? I have.

Montag 3 April

Not so much weather behind me this morning as birdsong. The day is neutral; the birds ecstatic. Just because something is well known doesn't mean it's known well.

' – for the candles are burnt down and I am using the wax taper – which has a long snuff on it – the fire is at its last click – I am sitting with my back to it with one foot rather askew upon the rug and the other with the heel a little elevated from the carpet – I am writing this on the Maid's tragedy which I have read since tea with Great pleasure – Besides this volume of Beaumont & Fletcher – there are on the tabl two volumes of chaucer and a new work of Tom Moores call'd "Tom Cribb's memorial to Congress" – nothing in it – These are trifles but I require nothing so much of you as that you will give me a like description of yourselves, however it may be when you are writing to me – Could I see the same thing done of any great Man long since dead it would be a great delight: as to know in what position Shakespeare sat when he began 'To be or not to be" – such thing[s] become interesting from a distance of time or place.'

John Keats, March 12 Friday 1819, letter to George and Georgiana Keats. (In the same letter he writes, 'Every body is in his own mess.')

(Note: Keats isn't interested in his brother and his brother's wife as they are whenever – breakfasting or playing cards; he wants to be able, mentally, to place their dollish bodies in repose 'when you are writing'; the only activity worth choreographing this way.)

Perhaps the reason we have so few similar accounts, pen sketches, is that Keats makes any attempt to relate to Shakespeare writing his most famous speech. (I knew the opening by Primary School, because wise-looking adults sometimes said to me, 'Toby or not Toby, that is the question.') To limn your limbs thus, is to figure yourself – even before your death – a 'great Man long since dead'. The 'Man' is problematic; the 'great' is even more so. I'll write about it, greatness.

Dienstag 4 April

Mouse had been playing with a conker, rattling it around the hall floor; it's on my desk now. This one is from last year, so has gone much darker than it began – claret not rioja. If the baby comes out okay, and grows without accident, I'll go conkering with him. We'll fill our pockets, put them in a breakfast bowl when we get back. It'll be like a collection of rare woods with extraordinary grains, and exceptional polish jobs. This is the only one left. When they go crispy, I use them as starters on the fire. (Three fires we have all winter.) This one isn't normal, though – it hasn't been left in a bowl to go dusty. It's travelled with me, into work, in my pocket. I've thumbed it whilst walking through Bloomsbury. That's why the rough grey circle on top, the lesion area, has got a sheen to it. That's why the whole thing still has a bit of juice. Central heating hasn't done its work, and neglect. This particular conker is shaped like a heart – a real anatomical heart, not an emoji. Underneath, it has a curve like an almost circular dog poo; into the centre of that, a flange, an epiglottis-shaped, sperm-shaped sticky-up-bit seems to insert itself. The overall effect is like that of part of a particular plant I can picture but that I'll have to look up – a chilli-red anthurium, or Painted Tongue, or Flamingo Lily, with its yellow stamen. A Lion-tailed macaque. Turn it the other way up and it's the world's proudest Afro. It is black, red, burgundy, orange, mahogany, purple. It is all the colours, apart from chestnut, of a chestnut mare. I wonder if the baby will like horses? Or be afraid of them.

Dad said he thought Mum was 'on good form' since our visit, and that news of the baby had 'given her a real fillip'.

Mittwoch 5 April

With shame disguising pride, I confess to my ambition. When I was fifteen or sixteen years old, being driven to Bedford by my Mum, in my Mum's red Citroën – I would think it lucky if I passed under one of the two railway bridges (just before Kempston Hardwick, just before Ampthill Road) at the same time a London–Bedford or Bedford–London train was passing over it. These were big, dusty blue British Rail locomotives, dragging rickety carriages of smoky commuters – not glamorous InterCity earthbound Concordes. As we coincided with their noise, brick walls echoing with steel wheels, I would say to myself, 'I wish for greatness.' I know – I *know* – I shouldn't even be writing this down; I can only blame Keats. I bought my Everyman copy of *The Poems of John Keats* at Pemberton's Booksellers in Bedford, and first read it on the top deck of the 142 bus, heading home to Ampthill (on the same road, beneath the same railway bridges). I didn't go for the greatest hits – just started on the first page of the book, as if it were a novel. (Well, the first poem, not the Introduction; I was there for the poems.) 'I stood tip-toe upon a little hill.' It would have been a Saturday, unless it was the school holidays (shops were closed on Sundays; I didn't have time to get to Pemberton's on a weekday afternoon). I became bothered by Keats, and Keats was bothered by greatness – the question of greatness – what it was and how to achieve it, quickly. Greatness, the attempt at greatness, was the only justification for the trivial pursuit of being. As love and fame sank to nothingness, for Keats, they rose to totality for Toby Martin Litt. Later, in the battle between the two totalities (it's impossible to have two totalities, but both love and fame are total for Keats), I would say to myself, 'Happiness or greatness?' The correct answer was greatness. I soon enough became great at being unhappy.

Donnerstag 6 April

Keats was a romantic. I understood this to mean giving people lots of flowers, and generally behaving like every day was Valentine's Day, and speaking in an unnatural way that sometimes rhymes. But Romanticism was discredited. T.S. Eliot, whom I knew at school, and W.H. Auden, whom I met at university, were programmatically anti-Romantic. Later on, Romanticism was seen as having something to do with the birth of Fascism, or a weakness for Nazism. (Even though anti-Romantic Ezra Pound was pro-Mussolini.) (This is the fast-forward version of history, where the goosestep looks even more comic.) Adorno said, after Auschwitz, no poetry. But there were still poems. 'I have asked myself so often why I should be a Poet more than other Men, – seeing how great a thing it is, – how great things are to be gained by it – what a thing to be in the Mouth of Fame – that at last the idea has grown so monstrously beyond my seeming Power of attainment that the other day I nearly consented with myself to drop into a Phaeton – yet 't is a disgrace to fail even in a huge attempt, and at this moment I drive the thought from me.' To Leigh Hunt, 10 May 1817. Keats writes of the fame monster, making it into one of the seductive ones – I was seduced. You can deny the validity of your myth, but if it was your origin it still remains your origin. Greatness can be critiqued and deconstructed, it can be guilt-ridden and wormholed, but it's still where I started. Wrong for years. 'I find that I cannot exist without poetry – without eternal poetry – half the day will not do – the whole of it – I begin with a little, but the habit has made me a Leviathan...' 18 April 1817 to J.H. Reynolds. Another monster, a monster habit.

Freitag 7 April

Of the poetical character itself, Keats wrote, 'It is not itself – it has no self – it is everything and nothing – It has no character – it enjoys light and shade; it lives in gusto, be it foul or fair, high or low, rich or poor, mean or elevated – It has as much delight in conceiving an Iago as an Imogen. Iago, who says, "I am not what I am."' But this isn't what I meant to write about. I did want to say something more about greatness, about the attempt to be great. Greatness in writing is the capacity to painfully fascinate the future, to agonize writers as Keats agonized me, to effect change even when the writing is itself made permanent, to continue to create the possibility of possibilities. Greatness makes dead words live. (This is how I first came to understand it, not necessarily how I understand it now.) To be great is to be unavoidable (as Shakespeare is unavoidable), but that doesn't mean to be unignorable (Shakespeare is often ignored). We often ignore what we're failing to avoid. Against it, I'll say the idea of greatness destroys – by exploding – those who keep it as an ambition, rather than turning it into an ethic. 'Great works take great work' not 'Great men do great things'. (All nonsense, male-wise.) Jane Austen, Emily Brontë, Charlotte Brontë, George Eliot, Virginia Woolf, Muriel Spark. You can create an up-to-the-moment canon, but what doesn't mean what is older ceases to exist. If your writing God is J.D. Salinger or Angela Carter, you're not going to find it difficult to feel you're approaching their presence. Or Sylvia Plath. Or Raymond Carver. Or Chris Kraus. But also in existence, way back, are Plato, Sappho, Virgil, Ovid, Horace, Cicero. Keats knew them all. Even Cicero. Which writer now is as preoccupied with the greatness of the classical world as Keats?

Samstag 8 April

I sneezed, three times — sometimes I think I've become so self-conscious that sneezing is the only undivided thing I do. When I'm in the choo part of at-choo, I can't think of anything else. It's as if my whole head is cleared. And even if I had toothache, I don't think I'd feel it for the duration of the sneeze. This isn't like anything else. I can be preoccupied in the middle of a coughing fit. Even at orgasm, I can be thinking about the fact I'm still thinking — that I'm not obliterated, as I should be. I want pure pleasure and find the wanting's the impurity. With sneezing, it's different; there's no style to it, and the totality is guaranteed. This means that I am always amazed when I survive sneezing whilst driving at 70 mph. Perhaps people do die because they jerk the steering wheel, or pump the accelerator, or kick the brakes — because their sneezes are more physically elaborate than mine. Just now was typical: I go rigid, and then headbang once. If sneezing were a longer or more intense spasm, we couldn't have motorways. Somehow, even if I sneeze four or five times, I'm able to drive in a straight line without changing speed. This isn't a boast, it's a wonder. I've also sneezed going round a roundabout. But am I aware I'm still driving? In the very middle of it, the ch-, I don't think so. I blip out and burst back. At the desk, I return with a sense of occasion. Now I might do something I wasn't quite capable of before. I am wary, however, always thinking that this one might have popped an aneurysm. I remember one particular sneeze from my life. I was at university, in a record shop, browsing. At the moment I sneezed, my mouth was still open — I don't know how. The upward force of the sneeze hit the inside of my skull as if my whole spine was giving me an uppercut. A dizziness of twinkles followed. I was surprised my body would still surprise me that way. I'd sneezed badly, I'd mis-sneezed.

Sonntag 9 April

Keats taught me – and continues to teach me (although I am over twice his age at death) – that in order to write at the highest level, you need to be ready to write at the highest level. (I don't want to turn this into sport psychology, although it may have something to do with the sport, sporting, sportiveness.) I want to look at two kinds of writing Keats did that we no longer do: verse letters and occasional poems (or verses). (T.S. Eliot still wrote verse letters to Ezra Pound; I expect John Ashbery found someone to address, perhaps Frank O'Hara. But later than them?) (I'm not going to get into letters vs. emails – but I don't think we're approaching emails with the intent Keats approached a letter. (Here, I could say something I haven't heard before.)) Why did Keats write verse letters? In doing so, wasn't he just showing off? – look, he says, I can perform (onto the page) as an act of will. Well, yes, he was. 'Shall I treat you with a little extempore.' To the George Keatses, 15th April 1819. Firstly, he was putting himself under some small, semi-private pressure. He could always destroy or keep and not send his words, if he felt they failed, or failed in the wrong way. Verse letters are not about the success of the poetry but about the attempt to dwell within poetry (eternal), and to house the recipients there as well (in the fane, the bower). Yet one of the factors in what a verse letter, or a letter containing poetry, meant was its simple material existence. Paper was not cheap; a letter was an investment of money as well as time. (How much did paper for a letter cost Keats? As much as a meal? As much as a pamphlet?) To save paper, Keats – like everyone else – wrote many of his letters twice on each page, crossways. 'I will cross the letter with some lines from Lamia.' To John Taylor, 5th September 1819. This meant that some of his generalizations – no, his aperçus about poetry, but also his day-to-day *I'm fine how are yous?* are viewed, read, through the latticework of a sonnet or an ode. Keats overlaid verse and the quotidian, the quotidian and (sometimes) poetry. Imagine an equivalent: I am writing this email to you but I am also opening the possibility of speaking to the gods, or having the gods speak through me.

Montag 10 April

There's more to say about verse letters, but I'll move on to occasional poems (because the two are interplexed). Too much at once – one thing at a time. Just had coffee. 11:40 – whee! I said somewhere else about not Live but open writing, vividly living writing (I believe this is what Keats meant by poetry: momentarily alive, everlastingly vivid); I've written an essay about this being alive (excited and capable of immediate change) at all three points: the writer, the written, the reader. In this diary, I've started with Keats' description of himself as an openly living writer (with one foot rather askew on the rug) and could find dozens of breath-moments, pulse-points, in his poetry. ('This living hand, now warm and capable...' 'Still, still to hear her tender-taken breath.') But here's an example of that within an occasional poem, a momentary composition. 'In my journal [he called this letter a journal] I intend to copy the poems I write the days they are written – there is just room I see in this page to copy a little thing I wrote off to some Music *as it was playing* – / 'I had a dove and the sweet dove died...' To the George Keatses, November 1818. (My emphasis.) The poem had to be written before the music ceased. Similarly: 'One of the pleasantest bouts we have had was our walk to Burns' Cottage, over the Doon and past Kirk Alloway – I had determined to write a sonnet in the Cottage. I did but lauk it was so wretched I destroyed it – however a few days afterwards I wrote some lines cousin-German to the circumstance which I will transcribe or rather cross scribe in front of this.' To Benjamin Bailey 18th, 22nd July 1818. (The sonnet wasn't destroyed.) As an instance of this, 'As an instance of this – observe – I sat down yesterday to read King Lear once again the thing appeared to demand the prologue of a sonnet. I wrote it & began to read – ' To George and Tom Keats, 23rd, 24th 1818. There are many of these reaction or anticipation poems. On Seeing the Elgin Marbles, Lines on Seeing a Lock of Milton's Hair, On first looking into Chapman's Homer, Written on the day that Mr. Leigh Hunt left Prison. But there's a recess to even these lines, as they are copied – the original manuscript, and its record of the open moment of composition, is another leaf of paper, and so –

Copied out: Mr. Bicester. Now. To the matter. This is the most ironic and amusing story that has happened to me. Mr. Bicester taught me Hamlet for one term. Then continued to teach me in 'Use of English' turning the Shakespeare duties over to Mrs. Wutherington who I much preferred. Mr. Bicester, being brash and very unsubtle in his interpretation. For a 'fun' end of term activity Mr. Bicester asked his Use of English set to write a 'mock' report on our teachers. I replied. Saving my report till last and getting the irrelevances out of the way he proceeded to start the argument/discussion I had been itching for: – 'English – a breath of fresh air after last term's turgid interpretation' (I forgot to mention, on announcing our texts, Mr. Bicester told us he was happy as he thought *Hamlet* the greatest literary work ever). This was a fact I had forgotten until after the ensuing duel. I picked my ground: Claudius not appearing, in his first speech, as anything other than a good king to a first-time audience. We debated in front of a bored class thinking how pretentious I was. We both scored some 'hits'. Then came what he hoped was his final, winning sally. Mr. B, 'Well, good luck in your [Oxford] interview, if you get one.' TML, 'Well, if I do I will have done as well as you did.' Class, Silence. Then raucous laughter and complete amazement at such an arrogant bastardish kick in the bollocks to a member of staff – Oxbridge obviously being Mr. Bicester's weak spot/ bollocks. *My* report returned. 'Satisfactory, until his arrogance gets the better of him.' (Perhaps the most carefully worded report I ever got – 'I hate him' in laymen's terms.) However, Mr. Bicester deserves much credit. Obviously watching my interview and ensuing wait for results with an uncommon interest. Before my results came he came up and said, 'If you get in I will shake you by the hand.' Come results I did and he did. This shows he is probably much fairer than I. This must have taken some doing to a snotty and probably understandably smirking T.M. Litt. (Please don't think I got too much pleasure from the one-up aspect. What I had blurted out sounded very different from how it was meant to sound.) Scene change. Oxford – Toby Litt fresher. I decided to go and see a play at the Oxford Playhouse, as I hoped it would be good and I wanted to avoid the Fresher disco. Who should

I see standing there having a stabling fag than Anthony Bicester. In Oxford, coming to see *Hamlet* at the Playhouse and meeting young undergrad. Litt, going also. I think he saw the ironic side. I – 'Come to see your favourite play, have you?' He – 'Yes, the one that's my favourite but of course I can't teach it for shit.'

Dienstag 11 April

'I have a great mind to make a prophecy and they say prophecies
work out their own fulfilment.
'Tis the witching time of night/ Orbèd is the moon and bright
/And the stars they glisten, glisten/ Seeming with bright eyes
to listen/ For what listen they?'

To the George Keatses, 14th–31st October 18??. Here an occasional
poem turns a letter into a verse letter. Keats makes the posted page
the live page by including in it the drafting of incomplete poems.
21st April 1819 finds 'La belle dame sans merci' change from having
'death's lilly on thy brow' to 'a lilly,' and she is met not in the 'Wilds'
but in the 'Meads,' and she feeds the knight at arms not 'honey dew'
but 'manna dew,' and he says of himself that he will 'sojourn' here,
not 'wither'. All of this, live for the reader – admitted, exhibited.
Yet Keats goes even further – how? – by wishing that his occasional
poems could respond, openly, vividly, to the momentary mood of
his reader. 'Ha! my dear Sister George, I wish I knew what humour
you were in that I might accommodate myself to any one of your
Amiabilities – Shall it be a Sonnet or a Pun or an Acrostic, a Riddle
or a Ballad – perhaps it may turn out a Song and perhaps turn out a
Sermon. I'll write you on my word the first and most likely the last
I ever shall do, because it has struck me – what shall it be about?

Give me your patience Sister while I frame/ Enitials verse-wise
of your golden name...

An acrostic on Georgiana Augusta Keats follows. A line for each letter.
We have no equivalent to this today. There isn't a similar mischievous
exercise of powers. It's both too pretentious and too unpretentious.

In his verse letters and occasional poems, Keats not only rehearses for performance, he performs a dress rehearsal. He draws attention to how he is drawing attention to himself, and concludes by dispatching the unfinished as final but still ready (upon opening) to speak, laugh, clasp hands, improvise. Other poets have live improvisations. The Renga poets of Japan (1050–1800) would sit around disjunctively linking their syllabic verses, 5–7–5 or 7–7 syllables (that became haiku). Rappers in 1980s freestyle battles spat their bars (still do) – just as Charlie Parker, Lester Young, Ben Webster took part in cutting contests in the thirties and forties and fifties. It's not enough to play well, you have to play well in the context of, you have to play off of, you have to outplay. The correct response to poetry is poetry. If you can't respond to 'King Lear' by writing a poem, ephebe, what motive will you find in the unmitigated world? Scottish flyting, I'm told, and Inuit boasting-roasting contests (that is no exact translation) – Inuit is the wrong word – these, too, were centuries' tradition of form and response. Keats wrote poems as comebacks. 'Answer to a Sonnet', 'On receiving a laurel crown from Leigh Hunt'. In a sense, his longest poems, 'Endymion' and 'Hyperion', were what he said back to Wordsworth, Milton, Shakespeare, and Homer. But I think he wanted to outlive if not to outlast them.

Change – metamorphosis of and in the reader. I haven't said enough on this. It is harder to demonstrate, though in all of this I'm saying my middle names are Exhibit A. My life changed on the 142 bus, even as I felt myself to be the stuckest of the stuck. The first effect of Keats' that I remember being impressed by, and enticed by, was – it's not just an effect; it's a disposition toward nature. The first time I felt Keats move, and moved to follow him, was when he pressed forward through foliage and flowers (as we progress through the leaves of a book):

> And when a tale is beautifully staid,/ We feel the safety of a hawthorn glade;/ When it is moving on luxurious wings,/ The soul is lost in pleasant smotherings:/ Fair dewy roses brush against our faces,/ And flowering laurels spring from diamond

Donnerstag 13 April

Vases;/ O'erhead we see the jasmine and sweet briar,/ And
bloomy grapes, laughing from green attire;/ While at our feet,
the voice of crystal bubbles/Charms us at once away from all
our troubles…'

(Yeats, too, rhymed bubbles with troubles; I don't think Heaney did.)
This movement is repeated but also negated in 'Ode to a Nightingale' –
which was the poem (along with the other Odes) that did for me
completely. Keats says he will fly after the nightingale, on wings of
Poesy, but in the next stanza has sudden feet. He urges flight, but
reaches blind stasis – and, for me, pure poetry.

But here there is no light,/ Save what form heaven is with
the breezes blown/ Through verduous glooms and winding
mossy ways./

I cannot see what flowers are at my feet,/ Nor what soft incense
hangs upon the boughs,/ But, in embalmèd darkness, guess each
sweet/ Wherewith the seasonable month endows/ The grass,
the thicket, and the fruit-tree wild;/ White hawthorn, and the
pastoral eglantine;/ Fast fading violets cover'd up in leaves;/
And mid-May's eldest child,/ The coming musk-rose, full of
dewy wine,/ The murmurous haunt of flies on summer eves.

We had read 'A Midsummer Night's Dream' at school, with Mrs.
Wutherington casting me as Cobweb then recasting me as Oberon.
I had heard 'There is a bank where the wild thyme grows.' Perhaps
I connected the two, and learned something about responsive poetry.
Also, I started to take in that one of Keats' recurring projects was the
curation of bowers (Coleridge, too, slummed it in the bowery). This
within the Ode to Psyche is for the minor Goddess being addressed –
but it's also for the reader. It is a place for them to reach and be at rest,
but only for a moment; the emphasis everywhere else is on alteration:

Freitag 14 April

> Yes, I will be they priest, and build a fane/ In some untrodden
> region of my mind/ Where branch'd thoughts, new grown with
> pleasant pain,/ Instead of pines shall murmur in the wind.../
> A very sanctuary will I dress...

Keats forces the reader to shift their disposition toward the world –
their metaphysical orientation. The best example of this I can give is
also the most famous:

> 'Beauty is truth, truth beauty,' – that is all/ Ye know on earth,
> and all ye need to know.

Although 'truth beauty' is there as rhetorical confirmation of 'Beauty
is truth,' I always feel it as a wrench. 'Beauty is truth' suggests that if
I seek out beautiful things, people, moods, then I will be rewarded
with the truth of the world. Fine – be a floaty aesthete, and Walter
Pater will be with you. But 'truth beauty' – to me, this transports
me to those unavoidable locations where the truth of illness, death,
birth, poverty is. Keats asserts that I will have to find beauty 'here
where men sit and hear each other groan/ Where palsy shakes a few,
sad, last grey hairs,/ Where youth grows pale, and spectre-thin, and
dies.' He then seems to speak as a God, addressing the reader as 'ye'.
(O ye of little faith.) He is philosophically declarative, epistemolog-
ically prescriptive, 'that is all/ Ye know on earth,' – meaning that all
ye know is two things that are not but feel contradictory. This is the
limit of human knowledge. That's a New Testament Moral. There's
lyricism to the mental frailty – as when Jesus tells the disciples to stop
asking him questions, they will get the answers hereafter (from his
father). The final phrase is Old Testament, 'and all ye need to know.'
The divine voice says, 'I could arrange it so your metaphysics were
different, but I choose not to. Like Job, you must suffer and accept
your suffering and accept your ignorance of the meaning of your
suffering.' Within two lines, Keats makes us completely change four
times. It is bewildering.

Samstag 15 April

Keats bewilders – he sets the reader within a safe wild. (Funny that my tutor at Oxford was a Shakespeare scholar called Wilders.) He ends his poems in a state of bewilderment. 'Do I wake or sleep?' And this is surely where an old-fashioned Russian Formalist reading of Keats' reading of Shakespeare comes in. The bewildering that occurs in 'A Midsummer Night's Dream,' 'As You Like It' and 'The Taming of the Shrew' – it's carnival time, and it's all to amend the bewildered. Mouse did a poo that came out of his litter tray shaped like a perfect fleur-de-lys; I felt bad flushing it just now. Why am I going on about Keats? It's not like anyone's going to go back to him for a start point. I've already started – I'm probably over halfway, however slowly I've been going (I mean hastily, for the most part). Didn't a similar vitalism end badly for the Beats? Spontaneous Bop Prosody. First thought, best thought. I respect them – deep bow – they survive better than most literary literature. I won't patronize them; they were complete, they were lucky, they were extremely brave. They were in exactly the wrong right country. What am I saying, now-wise? We mislead ourselves as to what life is. Thought and heartbeat, whoops and grace – we have our priorities all wrong (because we have priorities). Pay attention. Look closely. Take apart. This is nothing to do with Mindfulness. Mindfulness is Capitalism selling back to me the calm it stole from me. You don't crack the egg with Mindfulness. It's dry goods. You're not breaking open the head. You need to break open the head. Listen to flamenco, hear flamenco. You lack even lack. I'm too far gone, but you can save yourself. My back aches. I'm done for today. (Defend what you're doing.) Wrong life cannot be lived – or written – rightly.

I am buying myself stripey socks to cheer myself up; I am middle-aged.

• •

I once saw a bright grey car – it was parked on the long, the wearyingly straight and long Warwick Avenue, and I was walking from Culver House (where I was at boarding school) towards Bedford town centre (I can't remember why). The car, I think a Ford Cortina Mk3 or something British and sporty, was not painted but primed to be painted – and the primer was a grey that seemed to be brighter than a colour. Fluorescent clothes in yellow and pink were soon to become fashionable, if they weren't already. This car had a grey fluorescence, but it seemed more than natural or even artificial. I wondered that I was the only person stopping to look at it. Had it arrived from space? I remember pausing – perhaps it was radioactive. If you could see the waves coming off uranium, it would be something like this grey. It made you feel as if your eyes were melting in your skull. There must be some cost to seeing such a sight. The vision of the grey car – one of the strongest memories from that time.

• •

Sonntag 16 April

There is a long distance away from me, in every single direction — not infinite, but unimaginable. Up isn't really up; it might as well be down. Possibly, at this instant, it's diagonally off my left shoulder that the universe goes on for the greatest number of light years. I'm in a tumble dryer running on a planet orbiting a sun orbiting a galaxy moving away from the centre of all galaxies, and I feel a little dizzy. Sometimes, during zazen, the mini-vastation comes. To lose all sense of scale is one of the most useful perceptions. It's similar to when I read Heidegger saying that animals don't have a here. Maybe he's wrong — they don't have a left and right. They have a now, but it's a different now to ours. When you realize there's no point between electrons and superstrings up to everything that exists everywhere at which you can stop and say, 'This is neither big nor small…' It sounds so banal when you write it down. And so hippy. I'm sure it is an acid insight: this orange is as big and old as the universe. Maybe better not even to write this down. Did any good prose come out of LSD? I'm not freaked out by it, because I know scale will reassert itself shortly after I bow and stand up. If I felt I might never get back to it, that would be a bad trip. Zazen has nothing to do with aiming for insights like this. It's about sitting. But when you go back to Zen Master Dōgen's writings, you find he seems to be referring to an objective, non-human view of the universe. Not one, not two. Is that any less brain-mashing than the Holy Trinity? Perhaps religions need to establish impossibilities, in order to lock their believers in. I don't believe I'm a believer. Buddha wasn't a god, just a local realization — within a running tumble dryer. Womb.

Mid-April, the ground in the park already showing cracks.

Montag 17 April

Antithesis is too easy – and I'm sure the human desire to form either/
or sentences, or construct binary logics, has distorted the perceived
world beyond measure. (Not one, not two.) It may be the *male* desire,
rather than the much more widely human desires. (What if writing
has never progressed beyond Linear B's counting sheep?) By mentioning both sides of a likelihood, we feel we've covered all angles
of possibility – but there are more dimensions than three, and more
symmetries than ourselves and ourselves in our mirrors. (Instagram.)
What we're seeing is the gratification of someone else's vanity, and
because we're equally vain, and have chosen to focus on them, we're
totally – or almost totally – satisfied. (The winner of the beauty
contest, or the 100 Metres Olympic Final, is simply the person the
camera stays on the longest.) The slight loss of satisfaction is simply
the weakening of the light as it is reflected and reflected. Even with
digital reproduction, where the copy is the original, there is a small
and incalculable diminution. (A writer of fiction ends up believing that
if it's even sayable, it can't be true.) Whatever is repeatedly received
as the second half of the equation is progressively corrosive of the
validity of the statement. In finite logical structures, antithesis equals
equivalence. Is is is not. You are not yourself. You are neither/nor
yourself. You are incalculable. But that sounds too reassuring – you
are an abyss of unrealized possibilities, many horrific. By submitting
yourself to your own self-understanding, within language, you have
built a stone circle on an open plain. Unmistakably, you are here.
I'm not saying it's an evil thing, even if it's a bad thing. But a result is
not a truth, and an outcome doesn't stop time. There is simultaneity
and multiplicity, everywhere, always, and we do not not not not not
understand them.

'So all of this – are you great? Have you achieved the greatness you wished for?' I think my last book, blessed *Patience*, is the best thing I've done, and may be the best thing I'm able to do (do, not just write). 'That's evasive. Do you think your last book is great?' I don't know. 'You think it might be.' I think it contains elements of greatness – it's for readers to decide if they come together. 'You, as a reader of it.' For me, it does come together – I think it's better than I am. 'Is it a great novel?' Not if it's unread. Not if it's not read by those it can change. 'You think it's capable of changing people?' That, yes, I do. 'How?' It can – I hope – make them more alive, more compassionate. 'Don't generalize.' Specifically, it can change what they believe is a worthwhile, productive life – or change how they are disposed towards the worth and productivity of their own lives. If it succeeds, it should make them better people – better at being people. 'How?' The exercise of patience. 'You mean you've written a boring book, and people are virtuous if they get to the end of it?' I've written a book about the glories of frustration. 'Now you're just being paradoxical.' A life of best bits has no best bits. Mouse is on the page, off the page. 'Don't change the subject.' Mouse has white socks on all but two of his toes – his front left and rear left toes are pepper piebald, like the rest of him. It looks as if his slippers are only half on. 'Cats are kitsch.' I don't think so. 'Kittens in prose are cutesy.' Sometimes. 'Answer the original question.' I can't help thinking, if I were already great people would be paying more attention – more people, closer attention. 'That's a deliberately feeble argument. "Fruit Tree." You could give me a hundred examples of writers who were unsuccessful whilst alive. And you're not exactly ignored.' Mouse has gone. 'Has he taken his little feet with him?' Yes, he has. 'Ahhh.'

Mittwoch 19 April

Sometimes my pee smells like a baby's pee (even though we haven't (yet) got a baby, I still know what a baby's pee smells like – replete with, rippling with, vitamins). Mouse has black lines going out from the sides of his eyes, like he's gone too 1968 on the Cleopatra eyeliner. But there are other sideways stripes on his face, of the warpaint variety. There are black furrows on his forehead – these bleed into one another between his ears and re-form at the back of his sharp skull. What's the thing I've looked at most intensely? From square on, the black lines above Mouse's eyes make the shape of an 8-Bit stag's antlers. Was it early days, in love, wondering at Leigh? Eyelash frenzy of close-up presence of the end of loneliness? I have a magnifying glass that I use less often than I should. The last thing-creature I looked at was a dead moth. It was lion-hued, a sad going-brittle waste of best beauty. I still have it, on the Buddha shelf beside the Buddha. Offering. The majority of lifeforms that come onto the desk are insectoid. In summer, but also at other random times of the year – like last week – ladybirds arrive to ting the bell of the Anglepoise. They seem far more bumbling than bees. (They are beetlebums.) Moths rise up from the cater-cornered carpet – I have to kill them. My jumpers plead for them to be dust-to-dusted. Musca domestica don't tend to land – they just draw airborne oblongs beneath the ceiling light behind me. A silverfish would only be on the golden hardboard by invitation (carried through from the bathroom). Spiders, I'm surprised – and disappointed – there aren't more. I love spiders. A bird once flew in one window and out the other, a sparrow question mark. The life here is usually me and my bacteria. Dust mites beneath the printer. Will the baby have nits? I promise I will never get bored of combing his fine hair for nits.

Donnerstag 20 April

I am very aware that I can only afford to sit here as I do because I could once afford to buy expensive clothes, do drugs, fly to Ibiza, but instead I was boring and saved up the deposit on a flat – which I still own, and which most years brings in more money than my writing does. To the Tax Office, I am equally writer and landlord. This is one of the invisible things – contributing factors – to the fact of the desk, and my time at it; and I'm reluctant even to put it on paper, in case anyone ever reads it and thinks I'm a hypocrite. If I had spent all my advances on the fun of immediate living, vivid life, I would now have to work full-time. 'You did the sensible thing.' I did – I set aside some surplus income and turned it into capital and invested it in bricks and mortar. I bought a flat that was two bus changes from the centre of town, just before they built a tube line to take you there in fourteen minutes. 'It's no worse than anything else you might have done.' It's no better – I could have given all my money to Crisis or Shelter or the Green Party. 'And you would now have to work full-time.' I could have moved to live in Japan – like Steve Finbow and David Mitchell did. I could have more half-memories of nightclub toilets. I could have dated an actress. 'And you wouldn't have written as much as you have, or have as much time to write more.' People – readers – like those who misbehave and spaff it all away. I'd be more fondly thought of if I'd been a bad boy. 'You're incapable of being a bad boy – your mum made sure of that.' When I tried to write good commercial ideas, they never came out that way. Even the comic. My mainstream is other people's niche, and my niche is their what? 'You got what you wanted.' Did I? 'Accept who and what you are.' That's the last thing someone like me is going to do.

Freitag 21 April

Keats is not unproblematic. Why do I write sentences like that? It must be because, donnish as that phrasing sounds, I don't mean 'Keats is a problem'. Aside: Leigh told me her dream of last night. We were in a big old house – 'ramshackle but not unpleasant' – and we were getting ready to eat. The phone rang, and I answered. It was Herod. He wanted to come round to dinner. I tried to say no but he insisted. We didn't have much time to panic because the phone rang again. It was the Emperor. He insisted on coming round for dinner, too. I put the phone down, having failed to dissuade him. 'Well,' said Leigh, 'at least they'll have something to talk about.' Keats' model of artistic discovery is Imperial, extractivist, sometimes scientific. In 'On First Looking into Chapman's Homer' he paints himself as 'stout Cortez' 'Silent, upon a peak in Darien'. (I have never looked up exactly where Darien is.) Keats is Cortez because he's a finding new territory to explore. Having read Jared Diamond's *Guns, Germs and Steel*, I know this was anything but a good thing. Nothing was being humanly discovered, instead this was the moment before genocide and conquest – based on technology, Christianity, mendacity and viral immunity. The ancient world is 'the realms of gold' which Keats first figures himself having seen (and by implication 'done') as a tourist (a Grand Tourist). Context tells us he has done this not in a carriage or on horseback, but in a library on weekday mornings. He has gone 'west' yet never has he gone as far west as Chapman takes him. Again, it's implied that what Darien and Homer will give him, the reader, is greater realms and more gold (gold is neither better nor worse, it's a matter of grams). Gold is dug out of the ground, panned for, and not by bards, and not by the rulers of 'goodly states and of kingdoms'. However –

However, Keats – as an aside – has a secondary model of artistic discovery, presented only to be dismissed (like a Roman ante-feast). (But we're not going to give you *that* one, oh no...)

> Then felt I like some watcher of the skies/ When a new planet swims into his ken;...

Here, Keats is an astronomer – a Galileo, a Copernicus. He invests in the equipment he needs to sky-watch, perhaps within the court of a science-minded king; he develops his observational powers as a poet, and then he passively waits, within his technological and perceptual prosthesis. He doesn't voyage to make his discovery (except through time), it appears spontaneously within his vision (though within a liquid medium, as was the ocean Cortez and all his men crossed). (A muscle in my right arm, near the pulse point of the crook, is twitching. I wonder why.) The scientist gains knowledge of a new heavenly existence but gets no gold from the new planet itself. (Darien is a province in Eastern Panama.) Cortez, as Keats shows him, is also keen-sighted, but without technological assistance. He has 'eagle eyes' – he is the apex predator, observing from a chosen height. Keats glides above the page, ready to swoop on and kill whatever fits his appetite. This is the moment before. Afterwards is likely to be the insanity of *Aguirre: Wrath of God*. Human sacrifice interrupted by human sacrifice. Death and death and death and death. Followed by death.

The baby kicked. Leigh has decided he's a dolphin, and that Flipper is the perfect name for him.

Sonntag 23 April – *'Shakespeare's Birthday'*

If we don't ourselves want to recapitulate, recapitalize, Imperial conquest, we can't figure artistic discovery this way. Chapman was a literary translator; he imported one literary text of value into another literary culture. Keats does not for a moment suggest that being a tourist is facile, and that he should take up extended residence in the Western Isles; nor does he do the poet's equivalent and say, Chapman's English gives me a distant sense of how great Homer's Ancient Greek must be – I will learn the language. (As poets want to learn Spanish after reading translated Lorca.) (As I would like to know Russian, so as to read Osip and Nadezhda Mandelštam.) Keats is content to remain alienated, secondary. He is the bard of alienated, secondary, belated Gods – Hyperion and Endymion, not Chronos or Zeus; Fancy and Psyche, not Phoebe or Vesper. 'O latest born and loveliest vision far/ Of all Olympus' faded hierarchy!' How could he, honestly, be anything but a latecomer? How – after Homer and Dante but also Shakespeare and Milton (and Wordsworth) – could he see himself as anything but a tourist? At least Keats is honest about buying souvenirs from the gift shop rather than excavating treasures from the warrior's tomb or taking trophies during the battle. (Homer, too, came late – didn't sail with Helen.) But I want to say something more about what first attracted me to Keats (tertiary as I am (buying second-hand souvenirs from the charity shop)) – and about this business of bower-building. That's what Keats wants to do for the Goddess Psyche – even though he's a 'priest' – he wants to construct her a quasi-natural demi-architectural (trellis) 'sanctuary', in which Cupid can freely visit her for 'soft delight'. Butterfly kisses on the clitoris.

Montag 24 April

I agree with what I read and disagree with what I write. Or if not disagree, then feel I haven't really said the thing that needs to be said. For example, I think there's a falseness to the oversimple balance of this first sentence of the day. (Good start.) It was a statement that immediately needed qualifying; and I want to add another caveat to the opening. 'Or if not agree with, then try experimentally going along with.' (Experimentally or experientially?) Even when I know D.H. Lawrence or Emerson is wrong, oversimplified, unqualified, I enter their meaning and the meaning of their meaning; the world would be this way if the world were seen this way. It's not my world even though for the verbal moment it is. And I anticipate readers going along with seeing along with me. And so when I wrote that first sentence down, which I'm starting to wish I hadn't, I wanted it to sing with clear conviction, not mumble and hesitate with the confusion of the off-key. It was better, as my black pen tapdanced out the aphoristic letters, that I felt I was in the right area than that I – that I was pedantic, and so hateful. Here's a question: If I do agree with what I read, as I'm reading it, and disagree with what I write, as I'm writing it, then what happens when I'm reading what I'm writing as I'm writing it? Am I still the same disagreeable writer, or do I become – even for myself – a sympathetic author? (A figure of written authority, auctoritie.) Because at the same time as I am writing a sentence, I am reading what it might mean if I were to leave it in its present form. My eyes are going back over the opening word and phrase even as I'm here and then here and then considering whether a third here adds anything, which I think it probably doesn't. This self-criticism, literally, is what stops some writers writing: writers who might have been or might turn into good writers, but who become too early their own readers. They are caught between agreement and disagreement with themselves. They try to re-read what they haven't yet written – the finished version, not the momentarily sayable. (I disagree with what I re-read.)

Dienstag 25 April

I wanted to be embower'd – strange as that sounds. Escaped from boarding school, away from the bullies, I of course wanted a safe, beautiful place where there was soft delight, not hard dismay. I'd had enough of being hit; I wanted to be caressed. I also, quite soon, wanted to be a poet. Did I at first want to be Psyche or the priest? Was I keener on passively waiting for the temple to be built, and the nights of Love to begin? Or did I myself want to build, garden, interior decorate and stage-manage everything? Was I goddess or pander? I can't remember – all I can honestly say is that I wanted to be in this place, not another. And throughout the poem Keats maintains a doubleness: it's not a real, physical temple, though Psyche (soul) can enter and reside there; it exists only 'In some untrodden region of my mind…' I wanted to be safe from bullies within the mind of a poet who died in 1821. 'There is a region vast and unconfin'd/ Set out athwart the poet's patterned mind/ Wherein lie bowers, vales, rivers and rills,/ Colossal mountains, low, caressive hills,/ Expansive verdure where the safe flocks roam/ And in a tiny nooklet there, a home.' I wrote this when I was about a year and a half older than Keats was when he died. (Safe in heaven dead.) I stopped writing the poem after the obvious parody of 'nooklet'. (A place of greater safety.) In doing so, I missed the key components of a bower – which seem to me now based on a heavenly Persian garden (the insistence on flowing water as necessary for sensual repose).

Summer term started yesterday. I'll be seeing students for tutorials. End of term is 7 Juli.

Mittwoch 26 April

I would have to do a PhD – a PhD that's probably already been done – to find out the origins of the Romantic and so the Late Romantic bower. Dorothy and William had a place near Grasmere they went to, with Coleridge, that they called a bower. Coleridge wrote 'This Lime-Tree Bower My Prison'. I remember more bower-building in Coleridge than in William Wordsworth. (Dorothy saw her vocation as building a psychic bower for her brother.) Laudanum is a bower-seeking drug. It shouldn't be discounted, or sneered at, that sanctuary may be opioid-induced. 'My heart aches, and a drowsy numbness pains/ My sense, as though of hemlock I had drunk,/ Or emptied some dull opiate to the drains/ One minute past, and Lethe-wards had sunk…' (I have never done heroin.) For Keats, Poetry (let's start capitalizing it again) was a bower. 'A thing of beauty is a joy for ever:/ Its loveliness increases; it will never/ Pass into nothingness; but still will keep/ A bower quiet for us…' Bowers themselves are: 'Places of nestling green for Poets made…'

Tutorials today. I won't write that every time they happen – it's too bitty. But I think I may put all this thinking about Keats into my Summer lecture. Try to write something useful about what students can learn from a poet dead for two hundred years: How to write livingly. Four weeks to write it.

Donnerstag 27 April

I find myself writing so often about 'embarrassment' when what I mean is 'shame'. Writers are rarely subject to embarrassment, because they are not present for their worst humiliation, but they are shamed almost constantly – by themselves. If Keats were to have another model of creativity (that phrase suggests the utopian-utilitarian bits and bobs of the 1970s – polytechnics and arts labs), not Imperial (expansion of territory, bringing home the stolen bullion), what might it be? Keats shifts. In the letter to Shelley, it's 'load every rift with ore' – which is a beautifully strange image, but has gone further into Chapman's Homer's Darien. Rather than the reader (Cortez), the poet must be the creator of what the reader will extract from the text (gold). And so, Keats figures Shelley as himself less like conquistadors and more like Slartibartfast from The Hitchhiker's Guide to the Galaxy. Slartibartfast was one of the subcontracted creators of Earth, and was particularly proud of his work on the fjords. Rift-loading would have been on his workflow (along with volcano-priming, fossil-burying and other treasure-hiding). If not a God during Genesis, the poet (Keats implies) must be an angel during the Fall – they must enrich the nuances of creation. (The rifts are already there to be loaded with ore, like machine guns are loaded with bullet belts.) (Like Led Zeppelin, not coincidentally a heavy metal band, load every riff with awe.) The obvious shaming gesture here is for a contemporary writer, avoiding Keats, to go further still and ask how the poet comes by the gold? If they didn't extract it, they must have transmuted it from base matter. Here is poet as Full Metal Alchemist.

Freitag 28 April

Alchemy isn't magic – magic is the creation of something out of nothing. Alchemy expands the laws of chemistry; magic breaks the rules of physics. Is writing – great writing – writing when it's what I'd like to call 'great' – magic or alchemy? What is made out of what? Words are transmuted into great writing. There is nothing golden about the verb 'to be', and yet Hamlet's soliloquy makes the most basic form of it theatrical, memorable, unique, definitive. 'Toby, or not Toby.' He does it again with Iago and the first person singular present tense of the verb: 'I am not that I am'. And, with negation, with the opposite of this verb (to be here now) he goes even further with King Lear (not to be not anywhere never): 'Never never never never never.' A commonplace base metal has been made golden. Never has not come out of nowhere. Neither has King Lear himself, who was based on King Lir – and Shakespeare had seen an earlier play, and seen earlier stories about him. And those stories were based, ultimately, on a real person. What comes out of nothing is the energy needed to transmute lead into gold. Because we know that matter – the atoms – could be reconstituted, if we had a star on hand, inside a Dyson sphere. Yet the alchemist is quixotic – he does not see that a windmill is still a windmill. He's engaged in gilding his gelding. 'My mistress' eyes are...' Shakespeare is a bad example. We shouldn't use Shakespeare as an example any more.

Samstag 29 April

The air in the alchemist's workshop is no ordinary air — it tastes as though you could feed upon it (capon-cramm'd). Gulp in a few mouthfuls and that'll put some mercury in your evening, some magnesium in your proverbs, some lead in your pencil (if you have a pencil, perhaps you have a flowing fountain pen), some iron in your soul, silver in your quick, copper in your kettle (Popocatépetl), barium in your meal, Einsteinium in your cranium. Every surface is loaded with naso-visual delight. There are shelves jostling with jars, pipettes, retorts and glassware of every imaginable shape. Drawers labelled with arcane symbols rise to the low, blackened ceiling (for we are in a cellar — the event of explosions, we must be subterranean). Here is a human skull, and here the skull of another creature altogether. And books! — such thick books of vellum covered in ivory-hued skins! And manuscripts — entire cliffs of toppling, close-written observations and equations.

I don't think this diary entry is going to work. The effect I'm going for above is that of the beautiful, claustrophobic painting on my copy of *The Sword in the Stone*. It's by Alan Lee, and shows Merlin schooling the young Wart. Above him, a crocodile or a caiman hangs from the ceiling above them. It's full of wonderful, magical stuff. There's a retort, a celestial globe and a sundial.

Let me do some cramming, here, in hopes of my own Magic squares and rhebuses, narwhal's tusks and Rubik's Cubes. Moon rocks and bowler hats, the Millennium Falcon in Lego and something that fooled the experts on the Antiques Roadshow. I don't think we'll be able to re-adopt physical alchemy, but of course it was always only ever soul-transformation that was the real deal. And that can sometimes look like a girl on the top deck of a bus looking out at the high street through a gray rainbow wiped in the condensation. Even Robert Graves didn't believe in your actual alchemy; moon-magick for him.

Sonntag 30 April

And if I *had* to write it all in verse
what would I think to say, worth spending time upon –
years probably – that did not not just rehearse
the things I know already? I have gone
too fast before; that has been becoming clear,
and I need restrictions of some kind
to slow the flow, or else I disappear
into a blur of manner and of mind.
Somehow I doubt that *rhyming* is the halt
I lack – although it may be something like;
more probably it is the gradual freeze
of senses midway through the somersault,
chill waters tumbling down onto a lake –
fake lake. Facility is my disease.

However, in the past, when I have quit
the conscious mind, and written from the bliss,
I have done better than that 'Toby Litt'
could have achieved, if present as he is:
an anxious, willing, friendly, middle-class,
cisnormal, white, well-meaning but naïve
conglomeration of luck and disaster, self-disgust and shameful self-belief.
Perhaps self-absence is the only way –
the only *dao* – to make some progress now –
for otherwise all tortuous and bleak
is the world he wants his fiction to bespeak,
and that's no fun. No, he must not allow
the project to obliterate the play

Montag 1 Mai – *Worker's Holiday*

I have written stories of alchemy, of metamorphosis – sometimes it seemed my subjects had already started turning into a third thing before they were completely a second (which is surely better than some discrete genus of Darwinism). From outside, I can hear the football rattle of magpies in the ash trees./ It's hard to know how seriously I've thought about suicide. Ideation, yes; planning, not to the extent of investing money in accumulating useful medicines. I have felt I didn't have even the energy to give up. That's the phrase that comes, before the imagining of not being around, of permanent and blissfully blissless not-being: I give up. Often, I think about posting it where a few people will read it. I give up – I do, I give up. (When I read what's written there by others, I often switch from feeling okay to quit mode.) But it's the thirst for non-existence itself that's most powerful – immediate non-existence – 'to cease upon the midnight with no pain' – I don't care about displaying this, and the thought of others' comments is one of the things that stops me. I hold action in reserve. Curiosity also keeps me going. Has this changed since Flipper? I have a much greater responsibility to my own curiosity. I must continue to write barefoot; I owe that duty to my curiosity. I owe a much greater duty to my curiosity than to my duty. Why did I feel the need to lay aside the pen and scratch my scalp with all fingernails after writing that? Eyes scrunched, as if I'd stubbed my big toe on the corner of the future. Existentially pained, as if I'd said something I'll never understand: one of those recursive sentences, involutions. (I want not to want what I want.) Stop swanking: I must stay alive to buy things Flipper needs. Although I'm probably worth more biodegradable nappies as life insurance claim than freelance writer and university lecturer. No, I should be a second pair of hands, for when Leigh wants to share the weight. Here he comes, chunky legs kicking the air. Later on, I'll need to give Flipper the right advice to ignore, and only to credit after I'm dead. He'll need my counterexample if he's going to be his own man, assuming he's going to be a man. I'll be one of the pricks he kicks against; it'll hurt. Jesus, it'll hurt. God, it'll hurt. The party of the third part. Let's just get there first. I want to hold him. Let me hold him.

Dienstag 2 Mai

To whom – there's no reader now, outside the Halls of Pedantry, who'd count themselves whom-worthy, or assert themselves whom-requiring. But it's not 'To who…', so you have to rephrase. Who does a diary address? What assumption is there of knowledge and intimacy? Answer 1 is that it's written to and written for the person it is written by. (Firstly, the person inside the person writing, reading the words that person is writing for them to read.) And quick Answer 2 is that it's also, or sometimes explicitly, to itself, to 'Dear Diary'. (I've only ever written that as a joke.) The difference between 1 and 2 is that 1 nods along the whole time and doesn't need any help or explanation at the moment of writing. They know all they know of all the situations they are in. (No need to be reminded of an infrequent friend's surname.) But 2 stands back a little, and sometimes helps the diarist be a little clearer by crossing their arms and frowning. 'You haven't really told me what's going on.' This need for a little whispered context, a little footsie with the footnotes, brings in 3. This timely arrival is the diarist's future self – who is imagined rereading each day but without the immediate knowledge of what caused this annoyance or delight. (Who's this 'Keith'?) This 3 is where alienation makes its contribution. I'm sure some diaries begin as a contextless 'I feel' or 'I hope'. But they very soon need, 'So-and-so makes me feel' or 'I am still hoping for'. 3, who doesn't just cross their arms but sometimes shrugs or looks plainly bewildered, invites along their doppelganger, 4. 4 is the self not as future self (forgetful) but as other (ignorant). If I weren't me, what would I have felt about this? If I came fresh to the situation, what would I have hoped for? 4 looks neutrally, very likely to be bored or cynical, given the chance. 4 wants quirk history. But 4 is reflected, darkly, as 5 – the future as future, not the other's other but the completely alien. 5 is more mirror than person, and so it shows back vanities and delusions, spots and lines. Sometimes 5 is the past, too; it's the surviving ghosts of forebears. 'We are the form,' they say, 'don't disappoint.' Well, they don't speak, they just yearningly imply.

Mittwoch 3 Mai

The world does not need another word, not from any of us in particular, but if there were no words, there would be no world. Not as such. There would be an earth. But matter wouldn't matter.

Nothing depends on you. No-one gains by your gifts. Your heart attends you, but apart from that you are friendless. These concerns of yours, desk and pencils, Leigh and Flipper and Mum (and Dad), the point of them is to give a sense of scale to what would otherwise be a grain or a rock or a boulder or a mountain or a plain or a moon.

Walter sent me a postcard from Vietnam. He says he's getting married. Again.

Lots of tutorials. I'm not seeing Felix, which is a slight relief. Lola – who I saw yesterday – is writing a rom com, with murders. She said Samira has got an agent. They saw a memoir that got placed in a competition. Michael is thinking of going into a monastery. A Catholic monastery. Not much news of the others.

Donnerstag 4 Mai

'Bestial creature of no compunction or remorse, quite without shame and lacking all mercy – how are you this morning, Mouse?'

Mouse expresses himself artistically through the medium of cat-litter. Leigh is bigger and bigger, but remains elegant. When the windows in my room are open, I can hear the delighted screaming from the Primary School and the equally delighted screaming from the School for Looked-After Children. If I had grown up in a summery country, and been comfortable in bright sunlight, would I be doing what I'm doing? It was rainy day boredom turned boyish me to colouring pens and paper. It was wanting to be away from this dull planet, this Tatooine-with-sleet, made me start imagining desert-worlds, jungle-worlds. If the cricket pitch, and my friends, had always been available, all the year round – what kind of semi-wordlessness would have been mine? (Words but not *words*.) It must be climatological discontent, and that alone, made me. England made me. The place's fault. Of course, I don't believe this. But I don't credit a Chongqing or Budapest version of myself. He doesn't exist. If I enter a parallel maybe-world, I don't just wear different clothes – my inessential essence is the same/different. Teleport me anywhere and you strip out my *baráka*, strip off my particuliar patina. I'm localized, contingent; limited, constrained. I am far from inevitable. (Flipper.) Yet it's hard to imagine that what is now defining was once a whim, an affectation, a wish to impress a crush – at most a curiosity. How to bring up Flipper? Introduce him to as many varieties of variety as possible, then guide him towards becoming Chief Conductor of the Berlin Philharmonic? Trust he'll find something, if he's had the right combination of nutrients and never been beaten. Offer yourself, as you can't help but do, as an example. Choose anything, my son, but don't choose this. Be anyone, but don't be your old Dad.

Freitag 5 Mai

Is it worth writing? That's what writers ask — if I'm a typical writer, it's what I ask. It's a two-headed question, it bisects hideously, headiously. 'Is it worth writing what I'm writing?' that's the left head, the smaller with the sharper teeth and the sharper eyes. (The teeth, of course, in my case, are perfectly sharpened 6H pencils.) The right head is bigger, and it manifests and mouths this question: 'Is any writing worth writing?' Or maybe that, too, is a twin question — a two-mouthed twin head: 'Is any writing worth anything?' The monster is a time-traveller, because its questions are time-questions. Worth is time. 'Is it worth (spending or investing my time) writing what I'm writing?' and 'Is any writing really worth anyone's time?' Horrible. Take the financialization out of it. (Time isn't money.) 'Is it worth dying as much as I'm dying in order to write what I'm trying to write.' As I write it, I feel myself dying — in the stretches and reaches of doubt, when I don't feel myself vividly living (in words, for others). A straight line. Direct across the fens came Grendel. The airboat buzzes forwards through the Florida Everglades. The child and grandmother walk over the desert of human teeth. The Millennium Falcon makes the jump to lightspeed. Writers (like others, but in a more recorded way) are good at doubt — they doubt their worth and they doubt their doubting of their doubts. They do not doubt their death. 'When I have fears that I may cease to be/ Before my pen has…' Writing is — this sounds like a meme — Writing is doubt. I don't write *despite* doubt. I don't write *in the faces of the two-headed monster with three mouths for the price of two*. Writing is a dubious and questionable enterprise. 'Our doubt is our passion, and our passion is our task.' If you can keep both of your heads, when those around you are losing theirs. Writers are their own monsters. Vorpally and verbally armed, we seek and face our faces, hoping to outface them. Alice-alike. Why bother? I don't know what I should do. What should I do? I don't know what I should do.

Samstag 6 Mai

Such a limited life, this desk-life, but so many unaccustomed freedoms within its constraints. So many *theres* here since I saw there's no there there, no there anywhere. And I have at least attempted to become so many more people than myself. Even if it's only been fancy dress and drag rather than metamorphosis, we've had a rare old carnivalesque. Because all those other people, old chum, are turning into other other people. (Not crowdsurfing, decentred being.) (Argos in the Hall of Mirrors.) I think I've written a few things that I shouldn't really have written, not if I had been I as I wrote them. Deskbound. It may even be possible I've failed to do – failed to achieve – the impossible. But if I'd been merely the measly I with which I started, I'd just have stayed fascinated by my interests and repelled by my disgusts. 'I see, and sing, by my own eyes inspired...' I'd have pre-ordered and bulk-bought the bespoke. I'd have seen beauty in The Beautiful, and where the invisible stood, I'd have seen – and sensed – nowt but nothing. Instead, through language, and paying attention to language, where it says and fails to say, by sitting at my desk doing what I do, I've gone further than the first first person. Where? That's not for me to say. Most of the time, I'll have collapsed back into insensibility – how could I not? How could anyone not? Ideally, writing's not imperialism but cosmopolitanism; you haven't taken experiences, you have been taken by them. There should be no Elgin Marbles to be returned. But though I don't see myself as I am at the desk, that doesn't mean I don't have a certain visibility. This is my profile. IC1. 'Not everyone has the luck of departure/ or the privilege of absence.'

Smash from the kitchen, and Mouse (in beast mode) has broken the Buffy the Vampire Slayer glass – the one that was so faded. It had two pink-knobbly flowers in it.

Sonntag 7 Mai

The foetus – I don't like to write of it like that; or 'the embryo': the proto-baby, the ur-child. No. The thing inside Leigh is now the shape and size of whatever it is – week by week it flickers back and forth from fruit to vegetable. He's been a baby tomato and a gherkin, a satsuma and a – I don't think he's ever been a raspberry – or a loganberry – or a banana. He's not yet a marrow. Yesterday, Leigh thought she felt him move. Kick. What do I wear at my desk – at my desk in the morning? I wear comfortable clothes. Old underwear, but clean, not sharp-edged; many-times-washed T-shirts, frayed at the baggy neck – faded olive green, this one, two tours in 'Nam or Guam. My favourite trousers (even including black leggings) are made of a very strange, soft, cool, granular material – sand-coloured – a bit like wearing a desert at twilight. They were designed by Nicole Farhi, and I bought them when my books made me enough money to afford clothes not from Uniqlo or M&S. Like me, the sand-trousers have a big bum. (A literary agent once said writers' bums were like those of long-distance truck drivers – they better bloody well be comfortable. You don't want to do a fantasy epic balancing on your fin-tail coccyx.) The legs of them are slightly jodphurish in tapered-shape, and I've recently repaired them because the pockets were frayed out, the seams were re-splitting. I wish I knew what the fabric was – artificial moleskin? I also have a fat-years black knitted skull-cap-type bonce-hat from Nicole Farhi. Sometimes I see men with woollen hats that really suit them, as much as their beards do. I hope I have grown to suit this one. A warm head sometimes helps the sentences. In summer, I wish I could wear a skirt (a kilt would be too ridgy). I suppose (I hope) I look like a potter or a woodworker – someone who has a fixed place and takes the necessary time to make things there. Socks, sometimes; soft felt slippers, gone at the toes – but I take these off: write barefoot. (Posture tomorrow.) Most of all, along with the sand-trousers, my cardigan. Give it a separate day, why don't you?

Montag 8 Mai

I was in a mood, but I couldn't tell what it was – I knew it ran a long line out through me, horizontal to the ground. Then I recognized it as despair. The English way. (Outriding fences.) (Desesperado.) Despair, capitalized, as if by accident, because I put it at the sentence's start. All my writing is totally shit. What is the point of asking what is the point? (The grain of the hardboard is distractingly planetary.) Thomas Hardy has poemed most of it: 'in darkening dankness/ the yawning blankness.' Keats, 'In drear nighted December.' Shakespeare, 'When, in disgrace with fortune and men's eyes.' I feel, whatever my efforts, they will be lacking. They will suffer from, and make others suffer from, the lacks in me. And these are not even interesting lacks – I lack even the right lacks. (My lacklustre lacks.) Alack a day, etc. Wrong life cannot be lived rightly. The Question Concerning Technology. The Black Forest Gâteau. A word to come in the heart. Then I recognized I was merely being European, and I felt better. Tort. I could wear a chapeau on my a, if the mood took me. Flipper may make an appearance. Leigh is great and lovely. Our house is not being flooded or bombed. Good people read my books. Someone may publish my book, and it may – one day – be translated into German, Portuguese. And I started writing my Summer lecture a couple of days ago. Summer lecture, sounds a nice thing, doesn't it? I hear sirens, not coming for me. They're gone – and afterwards you're always in that state of not knowing if they were ambulance or police. It's very unlikely they were fire. What have you heard? Have you heard the sign of criminal life or legitimate death? Could be both. The state, rushing. Sometimes a flock of sirens passes along Croxted Road, and I think 'Major Terrorist Incident' – especially so if there is a helicopter above it all. I never thought of that: helicopters don't need sirens. Here's another whatever wheee-oow wheee-oow.

Dienstag 9 Mai

I only have one kind of foodstuff on the desk, almonds. Most of them come from California, where there are numbered and lettered groves, but I once brought back a wooden bowlful picked from the ground beneath the trees around the holiday house on a hilltop up a treacherous road in the desert in the National Park in Andalucia in summer. The spaceship-shaped nuts were holed like the woodworm had e'en been at 'em. (That was a lovely period for joy at the desk. I can't remember what I was writing; I was reading the Paradiso.) I wouldn't dare tell anyone how to eat an almond, but there's a particular way I like to do it – around eleven o'clock, to keep working, make sure lunch is delayed as long as it can be. First, I hold the almond lengthways across my incisors (also trying, if possible, to keep it dry). It's not flat, like the Millennium Falcon, but upright, like the Millennium Falcon going through a narrow canyon. It's not flat, like a flounder, but upright, like a cod. It's not flat like a lilo but upright like a cow. I bring my chipped teeth down through the seam of it – cracking the two now even more almond-shaped halves apart. They separate, and I take a moment to look inside them. On both, there are usually indentations – as if they've been nibbled at – and fingernail-like darkenings, where the oil has been compressed within the flesh. At this point, they look like two small boats that have been nibbled by two giant mice. All they need is a mast, a sail, some rigging, a rudder, a tiller, a weighted keel – and they'd be ready for a tiny sailor in a tiny life-jacket. Or maybe for a tiny monk with a tiny oar, they could already do for a coracle. Sometimes, before I finish them off, I mark them with my thumbnail. Stripes. Eyes. Now, vertical, they look like African ritual masks – this is the pale face of the invader. Finally, I crunch them between my molars, trying to taste each one as if it were my last. They taste subtle; they taste – after all these incorporated years – of prose, of commas and full-stops.

Mittwoch 10 Mai

A sunny, sunny day, with birdsong aplenty. Last night I thought I heard an owl – quite a grating-nutmeg sound – but it might have been some form of fox nefariousness. (A diary just fell off the desk, as I was putting it onto a pile of notebooks – fell off and into the bin. But it didn't go the whole way in.) Before I start writing in a medium-sized black notebook, I realize that I press down the leaves in the trough – there's a word for it, the ginnel, the gutter (I mean the long, vertical gap where left and right pages darken and meet). The guttering? The gulch? With the hands of my left fingers – I wrote that: With the forefingers of my left hand, I push down the seagull wings of the two sides. Away and near a couple of times is how I go, and then, from the top, I bring my thumbnail down, fatherly flattener. The fingers press flat, but the nail puts a crease in the folded paper (because each page, somewhere, is both ways on both sides: is verso-recto on the left and verso-recto on the right). The void? The page-crack? I would like the page completely flat to write on, but it isn't. From left to right it is undulant like a calm sea; occasionally, I'll feel a grain beneath the smoothness, and have to hunt through by finger-feel to find the graphite-shrapnel or tiny cube of sugar that somehow went from kitchen to my head to page (this happens). The grinning gap? The centrefold. When I read paperbacks, moist ones, I like to see the creases increasing in their spines as I move through them. In my experience, early bending makes it less likely the glue will harden and (unworked, unneeded) crack in half in future. The notebooks, I hope, are sewn, and have no danger of this. Sometimes, after I've massaged the spine to render it supine, I brush my hand across the page – readying it – as I have seen African Muslims wipe their faces after supplications. Then I blow across it, just to be sure. Respire. Suspire. Expire.

Donnerstag 11 Mai

Sound of rain outside, sloppy. Yesterday I was inaccurate – having prepped this page, before trying to make an impression on it. Having observed that prepping. I don't separately rub with fingers then crease with thumb. I do both alternately, pushing away from me with fore-finger and middle finger, then dragging back towards my chest with levelled thumb. This may be minor but 'fundamental accuracy of statement' (and observation) 'is the ONE sole morality of writing'. Ezra Pound quoted by Raymond Carver in 'On Writing' in *Call If You Need Me*. Oh, Ezra – ONE (in capitals) sole. I know it's emphatic, but it's still pleonasm personified. One more word than the meaning needs. Pleonasm in the very place pleonasm shouldn't be (a *maximus* writing-life maxim). Shaking your superflux like a Polaroid picture. World enough and time – spacious and specious. Can a sole of anything be plural? Does this possibility need warding off? Doesn't sole, by definition, have a sole soul – flying solo, solus, in solitude? (Mamma mia, Padre Pio.) I am in high spirits. Ezra put it perfectly, for all souls are plural – each is every other. I imagined an afterlife, more equitable than hell-purgatory-heaven (forget limbo), in which every created being was reincarnated as every other created being, until all had been each and each had been all. Every pain you cause, you suffer; every gift you give, you also receive. Pity is entirely self-pity, but is entirely selfless, because there is no origin. (Selfless – not philanthropic but altruistic.) We know no home. Origin is perpetual, reincarnation is momently momentous. I am he as you are he (and the Walrus) (and the Egg Man) as you are s/he as s/he is me and we are altogether now (and Paul) (and Flipper). Chorus: We know no home. 'Every night I tell myself "I am the Cosmos".' It's for this reason that existence is suffering, and simply sitting still in the same comfortable position is nirvana. Know your place, you know-nothing. 'Had place that moment and altered all.' Ezra put it perfectly, for any fundamentally accurate Learner Writer sees that either *ONE* or *sole* can and should be cut – and they then enact the lesson Ezra intends. They rewrite.

Freitag 12 Mai

I have always felt/ thought/believed/preferred – I have always – this is a phrase writers bring out when they want to generalize about themselves (writers of a certain sort, class, or in a certain confident mood). This is how I am, and this is how I have always consistently been since my beginning. Which raises at least two questions: *When is the start of self-identity?* and *How much does self-identity depend on self-consistency?* (How much does identity depend on consistency of belief?) For example, at their most ludicrous, writers sometimes say things like, I have always felt Proust to be a greater writer than Joyce. Now this timestamps the assertion (of opinion but also identity). If I'm generous, though I'd prefer to be merciless, the earliest this conviction could be formed was when the writer had read some Proust and some Joyce. Factoring in extreme precocity, I'd say the earliest this is possible is around eleven years old. This leaves two implications: That before forming this literary acquaintance, the 'I' in the sentence was not yet 'I'. And that it was reading Proust and Joyce, and deciding one was greater than the other, that made 'I' into 'I'. Both these statements could be perfectly true. The trouble is, writers often progress through life making a series of such generalizations – which can't all be true because they can only have had one originary moment (or, generously, period) as the declarative 'I'. If they say, at another time, I have always felt profoundly drawn to the ocean, then we would backdate this. In all likelihood they (as 'I') went to the sea before they opened *Ulysses*. But this would mean the 'I' who formed a positive impression of the sea was essentially the same 'I' as began to love Proust. There's no contradiction here. But that's a different kind of 'I' – it didn't come into deep and essential being through comparative reading of Modernist writers; it was there and, magpie-like, accumulated trinket tastes. I'll add one more example: I have always liked green more than red. This is something that could be asserted of a baby – though I'll continue tomorrow. Mouse is purring.

Samstag 13 Mai

It's possible, I suppose, a baby could – in some way – feel better disposed toward green colour tones than red ones. Babies, I'm told, dislike and reject certain foods even though, on the basis of survival, they'd be better not to spit them out. (I mean when they get onto solids – six months, or whenever.) Maybe 'infant' is a better word than 'baby', though more callous. I want to suggest the little chunky thing can't sit up by itself, but can feel agitated when Mummy wears her red jumper and soothed when it's her green. (Leigh does not wear jumpers. And she doesn't wear red. I think she's got two green dresses. And one wool skirt.) What this writerly assertion would raise is the question whether I, now, can really remember the likes and dislikes of 'I' in the cradle, 'I' in the recliner. This is the hard version of 'always' – hard to defend (logically, autobiographically). We'd have to parse this sentence 'I' (for as long as I can remember) have always liked green more than red. And so different kinds of 'I' make these different statements. It's hyperbole, I know. Always is always hyperbolic; always is always questionable. I'll be generous, though – with my assertive self as much as with any other writer. I have always… means, at this moment, 'the version of myself that I am (for however long or short a time it has lasted) would like to emphasize the consistency of my opinion on this matter…' In other words, 'I'm trying to impress you, and what I'd really really like you to believe about me is…' (I'm wondering whether, from now on, I should make it a rule (an aspiration towards a rule) never to say: 'I have always' – and to try in general to avoid always. Could I do that for the rest of this year, if no longer?) One thing you can say definitely is that the person who says 'I have always…' is the kind of person who, at least sometimes, says 'I have always…' And that is a very particular kind of person. (It may not be the kind of person many people like, though they may admire their gall and respect them for being so fully out as a prick.)

Sonntag 14 Mai

Looking back over them today, something I sometimes do, I don't like the way the last two entries are written. Although I'm partly (kinda) parodying posh-speak, posh-write, I also can't find a way of saying (want to use the word 'asserting', because I don't mean speaking) certain things (want to use the word 'propositions', because it's what you assert) without using (don't want to use 'employing', because using is perfectly okay) certain words (don't want to use 'terms', because that suggests they are all technical, which only some of them are). Here I go again. I am thinking, directly-indirectly, about my mother. She wanted me to speak correctly – I think the correct way (her way) is correctly rather than properly. If I spoke lazily, or inaccurately, she picked me up on it. Or just winced, so I knew. (English is my mother-tongue.) The problem is that certain kinds of accuracy (i.e., those involving the word 'accuracy', and sentences that include bracketed clauses (sub-sentences in brackets) and even more, that bring in i.e.) – speaking correctly is speaking poshly; or comes across that way to lots of people. Because the idea of correct English makes out that lots of Englishes are incorrect. Mum is a scientist – her degree, Biology. I should represent her accurately, therefore. Even in her illness. She values accuracy above properness. Correction: She wants me not to speak inaccurately (but she does have a class basis and bias for the judgements she makes). 'I ain't' is no less accurate than 'I'm not' or 'I am not'; 'I ain't never done nothin' is problematic; and would make Mum wince. 'I ain't never been to no Eton' is fine and dandy. Mum hates 'ain't', and is likely to think the less of people who use it (and even less of those who say 'I fucking ain't'). This is how a lot of people in Ampthill and Bedfordshire more generally seem to speak. 'I ain't fucking doin' nothin' wrong.' They are, in her opinion, people who speak both inaccurately and incorrectly. (And ungraciously.) They *have* done something wrong. Oh dear, this has gone even further off track.

Montag 15 Mai

What I'm trying to get at is – the language I use may be dead. Or rather, a dead idiolect within a living language that has already moved on. The commonest phrases now are deliberately inaccurate. We have (via California) developed an addiction to approximation. 'So, I'm kinda like... y'know.' In my mother's terms – by my mother's standards – this speaker isn't saying what they mean as well as they might say it. I'd say, their lack of specificity is highly specific. 'And Sasha's like kind of totally like yeah, you know?' Most of the time, the listener will understand – through inflection and gesture – exactly what the speaker intends them to understand. But someone without the clues of presence would get a more accurate picture of Sasha's attitude from this sentence. 'He was extremely keen on the idea of us going out on Friday night – and said yes immediately.' But no-one speaks like that. (My mother speaks a bit like that.) And so, who can write like that? I don't want to write in a repulsive language. And I don't want to write in a dead language – dead bit off to one side of a living, changing, vaguing-voguing language. I don't want to write in my mother's voice, or for the imagined approval of my mother (she will never read this). My mother, right now, not my mum, my mom, my mamma, my ma. However (because I used 'but' a few lines above, although I know 'however' comes across as quite school essay prize), when I write, I am after 'fundamental accuracy of statement', and so I go for the version of verbal accuracy (cousin if not brother to correctness) that I was first taught. And I can see myself walking back from Russell Primary School with Mum, on a sunny afternoon, perhaps with her pushing my brother in a blue-striped pushchair – perhaps stopping off at Deller's for some sweet cigarettes or sherbet dib-dabs – and her telling me not to say it like that, but to say it like so. She speaks kindly but firmly, and always clearly. And I realize that 'fundamental accuracy' is not fundamentally accurate. See over.

Dienstag 16 Mai

'fundamental accuracy' – for a statement to be accurate (like a description of a greenfinch) it needs to approximate at all possible points to the original Whatever is being described: object, mood, argument, dream. There may be choices, within this. The greenfinch could be described as golden-green or green-golden or green-flecked with yellow or light green or iridescently golden-green, but there is an original bird from which the descriptive statement can deviate, to which the descriptive statement strives to be true. This, you could say, is the foundation of the statement (the nature of the greenness of the greenfinch). It is the fundamental that the greenfinch (we can all agree) is green and not red. (I am red-green colourblind, and I still see a greenfinch as green. Maybe not an average green. A greenfinch is one of the colours I see as green.) Now, this seems to me to render Pound's 'fundamental accuracy' as pleonastic as his 'ONE sole'. Accuracy of statement is itself fundamental, because there is only one thing about which to be accurate. One world, one heart. How could any statement be unfundamentally accurate? By 'fundamental accuracy,' Ezra is saying 'exactly exactly,' just as with 'ONE sole' he was saying 'singularly single'. (He's being phatic as much as emphatic.) His maxim could be more accurately phrased: 'accuracy of statement is the sole morality of writing' – and no-one would have remembered or quoted it. He would have sounded like a Victorian patriarch, rather than a cocky Modernist. Ezra had to hector. Is that what I'm getting at – that all his accuracy comes across as hectoring? Just like kind of let it go, bruv, you know what I mean? Dads – or even Dads-to-be (hopefully) – shouldn't imitate the youth. God, I'm old – I can't even refer to young people any more without putting on a suit and standing in front of a blackboard (not whiteboard, not SmartBoard). Chalk and talk and walk.

Mittwoch 17 Mai

Finished writing my lecture. Perhaps because I had thought about it so much, I didn't find it hard. Even used a couple of paragraphs from this diary. About gold and Cortez. It's very easy to make writing seem difficult. The discourse of writers can often seem to be one of constant complaint: Kafka, Pessoa, Woolf (maybe not as much as the men). Writing is extremely easy; it's writing anything that's anything that kills. You can be trogging along and then click into a sudden sentence, find that it has codified a moment's dull light or brought an offhand mood into sayability. But there are the dead paragraphs above, and the words you're now trying to gather – scrape, scrape – where you seem to be trying to make a skeleton out of baking powder. There's no change of a spine, only the negative of a shadow. You are, in fact, already, despite your labouring soul, lost between commas, doing the exact opposite of what you wanted to do. You are constructing collapse. I could say that finding a way to accept this, and use the downslope and deliquescent energy, is wholesome. Karate! But it's a degradation when the skeleton you're trying to make is your own, and you're left with whispers and sweepings. That's the worst of it. Desiccated coconut. Other times, you can direct or succumb. It's even possible to witness – bell hooks gave one of her books the title *remembered rapture*. At last, someone inclined to being honest about the ecstatic. There is nothing better than writing better than you should, because the language has force. You can surf the elegant line of a spine – no need to construct what you're already using. Be a dude of syntax. There are years of hours to be spent in the barrel, with the recursive acoustics of echo and roar and trickle and again echo. Kafka catching an absolute monster! Pessoa cutting back on his cutbacks! Woolf ripping it all the way in, smooth as smooth! Meanwhile, life is good. Pop the blister. Enjoy your joy, man.

Donnerstag 18 Mai

Today I woke up early and began bargaining. How many weeks premature might the baby be born, to give Mum more time to meet him and spend time with him? Time times time. Babies survive from twenty-two weeks, or even earlier. Leigh and her brother were tiny premmies, and they weren't brain-damaged or unhealthy in any way. How about if the baby were born at thirty weeks, or twenty-eight? He'd probably need to go into an incubator (they're not called that), but Mum is still well enough to visit. If he were here, outside, alive, at the end of the M1, she would make that trip. She could have a long rest afterwards, in our bed, or stay the whole night. And the baby might even be exceptional, although early; they – the doctors – might look over all his working parts and say he was fine to go home. They don't want healthy babies, even slightly tiny ones, clogging up Maternity. Mum could meet the baby – who'd probably have a human name by then – (we're trying out calling the baby Bumper) – in our sitting room – (Leigh bringing him down, pink cheeked and radiant (that's the both of them)), or we could show her timidly into his bedroom full of hard-won sleep. (I feel nervous even thinking about this, because him being at home may never happen. More likely, almost inevitable, Mum will not visit us here again.) 'How about twenty-six weeks?' I thought, in bed. That's not long. Could we cope with that, to make sure grandmother meets and holds grandson? They've sort of met, through the womb, the orb of Leigh's tummy. It wasn't contact but it was congress. I would like Mum to feel the baby's warmth, and to warm it with her own.

Freitag 19 Mai – *Typing*

My typing is – if it were a child's painting, you'd say it was expressive; meaning lots of it ended up on the floor. I can touch-type. I taught myself that when I started at subtitling. As I was going to spend nine and a half hours a day inputting TV dialogue, I thought I better do it efficiently (and learn to work without eyes on the keyboard). Before then, I had been two-finger typing for years; I'd done four and a half unpublished novels. (A play, hundreds of poems, some short stories, essays.) Nowadays, I constantly make typos. back at ITFC, I learned (along with touch typing) to use the shortcut function to autocorrect the most common mistypes. Adn so ebfore teh wrods apepear no scrnee they have already been altered from the first form my fingers find for them to the readable. I really should be better and faster than I am. My friend Tomaš Mika did 100 wpm on a manual – typing samizdat overnight for Ivan Klíma. At my best I was around 70 wpm. I'll do a couple of tests, when I switch on the desktop. It's probably 45 or 50 now. Most of the time I'm looking to my right, where a notebook sits on a small wooden easel I bought; shaped like a capital A with two cross-bars, one high (for structure), one low (as a shelf with a ruler-shaped piece of aluminium in a one-inch-wide trough, raised edges). I have a bespoke thing, in darker (stained) wood – The Bershaw Book Rest – Made in England. This is more like a music stand stolen from the brownest piano in the world. It's more suitable for what I want but (as is the way with dooberries) I use it less often than the one which falls over and spills my tea. Trying the Bershaw now, it is much more fit for purpose. I promise to use you more often in future, my bought-at-a-car-boot-sale and dustily-neglected-thingamajig. You even have brass flanges to hold the pages flat. How have I ignored you so long? You're a life-changer. (Between 55 wpm and 70 wpm.)

Samstag 20 Mai

Doodles happen, occasionally; I'm not aware of doing them – and they usually appear on the opposite page. I draw owls, or monsters covered in hair (like Captain Caveman). When I'm trying to get an ink pen going, I will do pointed scribbles on scrap paper. I know when I draw by accident, it tends to be better than when I set myself up to copy or cartoon; and so, I have a scrapbook (on the shelves to my right) in which I paste the best. Looking through it, if I did now, I'd see that my default doodle changes. Before automatic owls, I doodled Vikings, long-haired Japanese horror-girls, skeletons and/or skulls, Salvador Dalí's moustache, a cartoon version of myself, running hares, rain. Maybe they align with what I'm trying to write, I haven't checked. If I ever *use* drawing, it's when I sketch a character I'm writing. I do this so badly, it's so failed, that it sends me back to the sentences knowing they're the only place it'll happen. My outlines are okay, but as soon as I try to cross-hatch, add 3-D, it goes to shit. Maybe this is also true of my characters. They seem believably contradictory to me, with fingernails and shoes that don't always rhyme with their humour. They veer in surprisingly logical or satisfyingly illogical ways. But though not my children, they're my offspring – and I can't judge their shallowness. Maybe I am indeed a cartoonist, with a cartoon soul. Mouse scampers off downstairs, chasing the ghost of a cat who lived here in the 1960s. I know I can completely misjudge. I'm a shithead, like everyone else.

Walter had a scan yesterday; blood in his stool; he'll get the results on Monday – an operation by the end of next week, perhaps. His fifth wife left him. Not sure if the two things are connected.

Sonntag 21 Mai

How do you know if you're any good? You don't. You don't, and you never will – not now, not ever. How do you know if this version of this sentence is better than that version of this sentence? You don't, but you feel you might know if it was worse. How do you know you'll ever reach a decent level? You don't. How do you increase your daily wordcount? You don't – that's not a good idea, not in and of itself. How do you know your first reader didn't skip? You don't. How do you know the voice of doubt isn't bang on? You don't. How do you know you shouldn't have become a painter or an accountant? You don't. How do you know what's best for you and your writing isn't seven years in solitary? You don't, and unfortunately, you'll never find out. How do you know if your closest friends from childhood no longer really believe it'll happen for you? You don't. How do you know what to change about yourself in order to become halfway bearable? You don't. How do you know, even if you get published, that what you've written isn't ultimately forgettable trash? You don't. How do you know your editor isn't about to drop you? You don't. How do you know your agent doesn't make bleugh faces to their assistant when you're on the phone? You don't. How do you know whether anyone will read what you've written in 2 years' time, let alone 200? You don't, you ludicrous numpty. Of course you don't. How do you know you haven't written on year after year when your best effort was a love poem you scribbled as a parody when you were sixteen and a half? You don't. (And you chucked it away.) How do you find your way back to your true original inspiration which was what made you want to write (not be a writer) in the first place? You don't – or maybe you do, but it's changed because you've become corrupted by despair and disgusted by your own innocence. How do you know whether it isn't finally time, after all these decades of misplaced effort, to abandon this hopeless quest for beauty, and give yourself a chance to just relax and do some fucking normal living? How do – You don't. How – You just don't, alright? You don't. Don't don't don't-y don't. So, do you stop all this nonsense right now? Do you quit? You don't.

Montag 22 Mai

This Tagebuch is open as flat as it can go, after pressing. The opposite page lies opposite the page on which I'm writing these words. Today it's the left-hand page, through which I can see the verlan of the day before yesterday's words, SLEDOOD, and more blackly on which is yesterday's entry. When I write in my diary, every page is used – usually the day after it is dated. But when I work in my notebook, the opposite page (always the left) is only used for additions to, notes about and different versions of the writing on the page opposite the opposite page. There is literally room for improvement. In some ways, where the writing takes place is more the opposite opposite page than the page (or The Page) – because even with the first word, the bounce back and forth is implicit. Sometimes no word lands on the opposite page, to rebound into the sentence, the paragraph. The opposite page seems wasted. On other days, it's fuller than the first draft page. This may be because one sentence has taken fourteen goes, or because five sentences have each needed three or four. An opening, top right of them both, may be entirely crossed out, with an arrow pointing to a new try, in pencil, upper left. Other words that fly across the gutter are given marks ⋆ o & +, and if these aren't clear enough, lines with arrowheads are drawn. Very rarely, I can't ready my own handwriting, or understand my own intentions – because all of this stuff on the opposite page and the opposite opposite page is practical instructions to typist-me. I know I will want to know what I wanted me to do. By the time I get to typing, I may have gone back to both pages, one or two times – and each visit is with a different pencil or pen. Most often I return to my bouncing with a pencil. Where the page is greyest is where things have got gnarliest. When I cross out, it's one or two horizontal lines, just to make sure those words are permanently gone. Thank you but no thank you. When both pages are typed up, they get four diagonal slash lines in pencil – like the claw marks of a werewolf. Done.

Walter didn't get his test results today. Maybe tomorrow.

Dienstag 23 Mai

'Get it down!' This was my main bit of writing advice, for years – received, not given. I was the beneficiary. The giver was Vic Sage, husband of Lorna Sage, academic, short story writer, bon viveur, and to end the sentence I need a word that doesn't exist in English. What it would mean was that anyone who met him could see that Vic saw very clearly – saw them very clearly but also everything else he chose to see, or couldn't help himself seeing. 'Percipient' would be close but also completely off. It's too passive, because Vic had critical intelligence, too. He wasn't just the Hubble, he was the whole research programme and science institute behind it. If 'seer' weren't polluted with every wrong kind of gubbins, from Romantic to New Age to Day Trading, it would be a little nearer. The missing word also needs to contain the sense of memory: that once Vic read something, he could quote it; if he glanced your way, you were anatomized forever. I miss him. I need that – 'Get it down!' was his encouragement, and also – by implication – his warning of the bleak consequences of not getting it down. He looked like an aged but not dissatisfied satyr. I spoke to him one time, at a party in his house, and he was the drunkest person I've ever encountered who was still conscious; next time I saw him, he remembered every detail of what I'd said, and resumed the discussion. (I've forgotten what it was.) Next time, I think, happened to be two years later in the British Library cafeteria. And Vic's is good advice, basic and bracing. But 'Get it down!' doesn't address where I am – after years of getting it down, or trying to get it down – looking back at what I've done and sensing that it isn't down at all. It. Here, in this diary, repeatedly, I've gone at Keats and vivid life and the open and the possibility of possibilities. It is still wild. It is loping through inhuman forests, squatting among chimpanzees, giving just cause to murderers. It is the why of cities, their angles and trash, that I stand no chance of describing – because I don't know they exist. It is submerged, nascent, fucking, solar. It is ungetdownable, because it is the up.

Gave my lecture. Seemed to go okay. College bar afterwards. Felix saying he found Keats self-indulgent.

Mittwoch 24 Mai

The hairs of the Mouse find their way onto the page, even when the bestial creature hasn't come into my room for days. Like this hair. And this. I know they are his because – unlike mine or Leigh's – they stick themselves down, as if the paper were a party balloon that had been rubbed against a jumper. Even the drag of my little finger across them, to move them enough to show they're not a line left by closing the diary on a pencil – even scraping and then blowing can fail to shift the clingiest. They are moist (my least favourite word). The thin, slightly zigzaggy hairs are moist with oil that keeps Mouse dry and keeps me flicking and scratching to get them into the bin. (And here Mouse is, licking his haunches with a sound like squelching, then padding off.) Although I can write around ink spills and coffee blips, I have to get rid of hairs. Occasionally, Mouse isn't the guilty one, and it's one of my own eyelashes. These are easily told apart from eyebrow- or head-hairs, by their clear curve and elegant taper. Eyelashes have an endpoint where other hairs just have a cut-off. They are like the quills of a porcupine – I know, because in my pencil pot I have a porcupine quill, and I've pricked my palm on it many times, reaching for something to do some corrections with. The sharp end is now broken, like a spear after defeat in battle; pieces of it got stuck in me. (Dangerous business, writing.) It has the profile of a javelin and, within that Olympic outline, irregular stripes of chocolate brown and ivory white. The ends are white. To write about it, I've picked it out and put it on the opposite page. It's not quite the height of the diary. The page edges frame The Porcupine's Quill, rather than allowing it to assert the third of its numerous dimensions (although the Anglepoise helps it to cast a shadow). It's as long as my hand from tallest fingertip to first wrist fold. I wish I could write with it. And I wish I could remember how I got it. A childless trip to the zoo, perhaps; to draw animals. I know I didn't buy it – it feels retrieved, not bought. I'd be more ashamed of it, if I'd paid for it. Where did the prickly creature live? Did it bustle about a cage in Regent's Park? Do porcupines have eyelashes? How long are they?

Donnerstag 25 Mai

It's a question – what do I see when I write, and what do readers see when they read what I've written? (Latter, I'll never know.) I don't mean these sentences now. Perhaps for 'reader', they would see themselves reading (either as they are at that moment, or an idealized or younger self-version), or perhaps they'd have an image of a reader – a girl in a library, a large man on the tube. What I mean is, what do I see and they see in the purely visual? If, for example, I try to describe an exact kind of (not shade of) red. What happens when I write red, or they read red? At the moment I'm doing the doing, I'm not aware of a headful of exact redness. It's as though I've clocked it, made my mind up about it, then opened an invisible floating thesaurus. (I see it more clearly with hands over eyes.) Partly, I'm seeing the sound of the word I want; I'm aware of the vowels and diphthongs dominant around it. I also see the shape – row on narrow row of low letters, or tall ascenders and jaggy descenders. This word isn't for a label, in neat calligraphy, on a piece of white card; it is in a particular place, at a particular moment, after these words and before these, on this wave of sense, within this sea of discourse. Red, crimson, blood-red, vermilion, dark orange, pillar box, scarlet, pinkish, ochre, fleshy, strawberry – there aren't that many possibilities. (I haven't visited Dr. Roget's Emporium.) (I will.) And it would be a very special occasion, and a very rich narrator, for me to pick vermilion. (Hopkins' silion, gash gold-vermilion.) The ambient thesaurus in my head contains a few words of French, Czech, German and Mandarin. (Moulin Rouge, RUDÉ PRÁVO, Rote Armee Fraktion, and I don't know the Mandarin.) Most of the time, I'm in a linguistic rather than colouristic space. Damask. But when I say I, of course I don't mean I. Maroon. When writing, I split into lots of different awarenesses. Carmine. I'm me reading, and a reader, and a distant future reader, and the narrator, and the consistency of the narrative voice, and the critic, and the hater, and the writer who decided to spend time on this, and the mischief-maker, and the scientist, and the drummer, and as much as I can be I'm the English language, and English Literature, and the physical world. Rose.

Freitag 26 Mai

Yesterday was artificial, because I realized something about writing colours about a year ago: you can push really hard to convey one colour by itself, 'She wore a dufflecoat the colour of strawberries in their first hour of mould.' And I sense the prose there is pushy and the colour is effortful. But when you put one colour beside another, even in their most basic primary form, the inner eye starts to see and feel them very brightly. 'She wore green tights even with her red dufflecoat.' That pops, doesn't it? (This is especially true of colours opposite one another on the wheel.) You can, once you've got the crisp edge between them making both more intensely what they are (redder red, greener green) – you can add a slight push, to specify. 'She wore lime green tights even with her dusty red dufflecoat.' Or, to try it a different way: 'She wore pale orange tights beneath her dusty violet dufflecoat.' (This is a different she, isn't it?) Or: 'She wore navy blue tights beneath her dark blue dufflecoat – I never got to see her skirt, but I was convinced it was black.' (This is another different she, and a different narrator.) (This is Mum in 1959, and her anonymous admirer.) If you add one more colour to the edgy ones, the effect can be dizzying. 'She wore pink tights beneath her green dufflecoat even though her bobble hat was brown.' I think this trick is what makes the colours so seeable in Tolstoy, Chekhov, Robert Byron, Virginia Woolf. (The word I've been avoiding is juxtapose.) 'Halfway between the path and the grey mountains was a squat white house with yellow curtains.' To make the edge between colours crisp, just place them closely on the page. 'His hair looked very red above his grey herringbone jacket.' From this, the lesson I learnt is, Don't describe one colour, name two or three – but name them accurately.

Walter's test results were okay. He had an abscess, apparently, but it was 'self-draining' – and the surgeon doesn't want to operate. Phew. He said he thought he was immortal. I did, too. History teachers should never die. It's wrong.

Samstag 27 Mai

I didn't answer the question as to what the reader sees, when they're reading my red sentence or my dufflecoat sentences. And as I'm not in any head but mine, I can only speculate or speak about my private experience. There are some books that I read as if I were watching a film – I forget the words and I follow the action. These books are rare and, as I became more self-conscious as a writer, I became worse as an enraptured reader. Just as violinists don't tend to listen to other violinists for pleasure, because they can't avoid anxiety and pickiness, jealousy and annoyance, so I am not an amateur reader. I put pencil notes in the margin. Other books or stories – and I'm thinking of non-fiction – I'd say I'm a similar reader to writer. I don't read as a unitary I; I split, painlessly, into different readers taking different, part-shared pleasures. One reader, for example, follows the sound of the words, but they're not unaware of the literal sense. The literal sense reader, who was trained by Mum and English teachers, is front and centre, sometimes commenting aloud, and demanding their comments be written in the margin. Leaving aside the professional readers, who are looking to steal what they can (jewel thief looking for sparkly individual words; industrial spy photographing the architectural plans) – the readers looking over the literal reader's shoulders take their pleasure from, say, memories of my own that are prompted by the current scene; or they squint and do their best to see the distances between the objects depicted, the arrangement of the characters' bodies, the exact colours and shapes; or they try to hear the acoustics of the room, the stress and accent of the dialogue. One waits for the opportunity to weep. One prays for violence. One sits cross-legged on the mat, and enjoys the story as it's told to them. Another, the librarian, sits next to the memoirist and runs off to look up quotes and allusions. There are several judges who consult with the other readers about whether what they're reading is guilty of extreme originality, and – if so – is that enough to undermine our delight in witnessing confusion, comeuppance, collapse, catharsis. All these readers blink in and out of existence, change size and density, absorb one another or attempt murder.

Sonntag 28 Mai

Home to see Mum. Photo albums out (I got them). In an early one, a small square black-and-white photograph of my mother-to-be in her dufflecoat – dark blue, though; not any other colour. She is fourteen or fifteen years old, and a girl absolutely of her time. Helen Mary Grindley of Hereford is hopeful but she knows there are nuclear bombs. Hiroshima and Nagasaki were obliterated 129 and 126 days before she was born. Those who protested for CND often wore dufflecoats. It was a look that would now be called iconic. Helen's brother James went on one of the Aldermaston Marches. (I don't know what colours he was wearing.) Over forty years later, an American man attended James's memorial service because he'd seen it announced in the Hereford paper – he had chatted to James whilst marching to London, and had remembered him clearly all those decades. My mother-to-be was a scientist but a biologist, a zoologist, not a nuclear physicist. The 1950s were a cold time in the Cold War. Dufflecoats and sturdy shoes, thick woollen socks and Aran jumpers that smelled of sheep when damp – these are the clothes of a survivalist culture. They're not just for the present walk home from choir practice, but for the nuclear winter in the offing. A bleached world of diminished pleasures. The clothes my mother-to-be wore lasted a long time; the shoes could be re-soled, the jumper darned. (Even in the Eighties, Helen held fast to Make Do and Mend.) Similar classes of English girls today never wear clothes so lumpen, so weighty. Their winters are never as cold. They don't have to wait for hours by the phone box on the corner. (Some of them do.) They don't have to wash their clothes by hand, and put them through the mangle. (No, not that.) Their homes are double glazed, central heated – and someone else pays the bills. Clothes are cheap and disposable. I think my mother brought me up not to trust this pre-nuclear winter world. I don't own a dufflecoat; I own a thick grey greatcoat. Even in summer, I wear sensible shoes.

• •

My mother's – Mum's new wig looks extraordinarily like a better, neater version of Mum's hair. I think, in a cruel way, this is just how Mum's hairdresser (in Bedford, same for fifteen years), if not Mum herself, has always wanted her hair to look. Less of a side-parting, more of a bob. She showed it to us on a wig-stand, because she knows she's going to lose her hair in the next six to eight weeks. (Ovarian cancer is now elsewhere cancer – she doesn't want to say exactly where. I haven't pressed her. Dad hasn't blabbed. The next round of chemotherapy is going to be 'more aggressive'.) We were formally introduced. 'Here it is. You better get used to it now.' Then, a little later, to Leigh rather than to me, 'What do you think?' It is a more regular, less streaky gray than Mum's actual hair – and probably a little finer – but it's a beautiful and comforting and appalling thing. I don't want parts of my Mum to be replaced by New and Improved. She was never superhappy with her hair, but it always sent a message to me (as did Dad's baldness) that there were more important things than hair, and that you shouldn't expect always to be getting everything right. I don't think I understood this until today – some children must never get the message, 'You are more important to me than my appearance, dear little ones' or 'It's both the things you keep and the ones you lose that make you what you are, my chickens'. Some children must be orphaned by a dress, a sports car, a shade of lipstick, a fishing rod. Some children must expect to always come second or third. Mum never made me feel like that, except once or twice when they went out to the theatre in London and I was afraid the IRA would bomb them.

I feel guilty for sitting here thinking of Mum in the past tense. If I wanted, I could commit to hope, *this* next round of chemotherapy might work – but I don't have enough hope to commit to hope.

• •

Montag 29 Mai

I don't know where sentences come from – particularly the second half of sentences. When I start to write the words, beginning with a capital letter (which, if I know nothing else, I tend to make an A) – at that point, what happens after the comma, or even after the first phrase, isn't known to me-holding-the-pen. The underwriter may know; they may have planned a whole paragraph, with varied structures and something to look at. But I am left finding it out, word by uncapitalized word, torch in midst of misty fog in haunted house of cobwebs and dust. I am sure some writers write surely. Each statement foreknown before engaged upon. This is what it sounds like and this is what it means and these are the rules of composition (cut the first 'and' and insert a comma) to which it is obedient. I can do that. I can switch to that – aware a second 'but' is about to happen, too close to the last one. But I feel untruthful as I write what I know, and also write implying that I know what I know. Isn't what I'm always saying, in every wing of every haunted house I describe, that I don't know what might be there, beyond the torchbeam, tables and chairs and paintings and subclauses? Yes, but what I'm after is a form of being that's a *maybe* rather than an *is*. Into view it comes, Tarkovsky or *Silent Hill*, as if it were myself as a ten-year-old happily playing the jamjar drumkit, or as if it might-might be a crimson-black wall-stain of bitter nostalgia for lost rhythms, or as if it might even have been thought of as being a slight sense in my mother that something might have pulsed less vaguely between us if there hadn't been so much shame. I began that last sentence without consciously wishing to humiliate my own coded ghost. Boom-tssk. It's not free or automatic writing, or spontaneous bop prosody, or even Henry James dictating to Theodora Bosanquet into the late afternoon whilst leaning against the mantel. Of course of course, I don't yet know what it wants me to want of it. All anyone can say is the sayable, but if all you hope to make is the makeable then you'll end up with a house, not a haunting. (Houses are built and hauntings happen.)

Dienstag 30 Mai

'What if there's nothing to say?' The thought of it gives me an opening, and through the opening flows ink. Like many writers (I first wrote *most*, then realized I'm not even close to being all of them), I have fantasies of being charismatic in my own absence – Thomas Pynchon, Socrates, The Pearl Poet, Donna Tartt. Outside, it is a beautiful morning about which there seems little to say but it's a beautiful morning – blue sky, clouds high and white, small breeze. Emily Dickinson. A fountain pen only works because of the emptiness which runs, a controlled viscus, from cartridge to nib. Gerard Manley Hopkins. Only one of mine, the Parker, was ever advertised as having a heart. All wordprocessed words hit the page, which is a screen, as dry goods – never any liquidity, no slow fading shine. The dot of the i, just gone by, was like the highlight in a painted pupil (Rembrandt with a two-bristled brush). Or like the single glint all primary school cartoonists learn to give kittens and puppies and long-nosed men looking over brick walls. Didn't you used to be Kilroy? I woz ere. Sometimes there are windowpanes in the glint, but there is also imposed soul. The ink is no longer dead-eyed. Ere woz I. The glistening is a form of listening – listening to life as it is when it is alive rather than when it's archived, digitized. Or like the sun rebounding off the Indian Ocean, witnessed by the no-one currently stationed on the moon. Woz I ere? It's a trick, you could say, an artist's low transcendence – a shortcut to the sublime. There's nothing in it. All you're doing is being falsely correct, dotting the i's. The life is in the characters in the scenes in the words in the eyes in the imaginations of the readers. These characters came fully formed through typewriter ribbons, hardly moist, and they continue to impersonate themselves behind shiny screens. There's more glare there than in your reflectivity. I fink I woz. Maybe so. I am only speaking for myself, not expecting tika-taka texters to regress to wetter lettering. This is a matter of choice. Or like the three beaming water droplets, each distinctly radiant, on a smooth-loping leaf in a flower painting of 1715.

Mittwoch 31 Mai

If I said I felt ordinary today, that would imply that on most days or at least on some other days I felt if not extraordinary then non-ordinary; and while ordinary (at the top of this day) comes across as meaning sub-par or flat, the implication is that I have descended rather than ascended to a level of ordinariness. Which is probably the case but, I suppose, paradoxically, it's only on days when I feel down to ordinary that I'm aware most of the time I consider myself at least above average. I know average is not ordinary, and that – for golfers, for most golfers – par is a distant dream, viewed from their handicapped start point. Where they play and live is always sub-par, if not per hole, then per round, per life. The earlier sentence is wrong and unlovely: I consider myself average in most things (height, charisma, endowment) but above in the things I value most (writing and writing). It is true that I have more money than average, if we sold everything (much of it is access to debt). And my education went to a much higher than average level, because there aren't so many PhDs around. I am below average in sexual attractiveness – which for most people is the most important thing. (Could I say, it's what someone ordinary wants beyond all things: to be irresistibly handsome or gorgeous. After which, the money will come.) I must have given up on that when I realized it was never going to be possible. All my aspiration transferred across to becoming capable of putting together a little verbal gorgeousness – handsomeness just sounds wrong. The level of compensation is pitiful. Midway through this day, I had to (why am I writing about myself like this?) – I had to get up from the desk and wash the pen clean. I wanted freer, faster flow. It worked for the pen, and not for the prose; that remained, and remains, ordinary.

I see the equivalent of gray and grey. My vision is filled with a flowing mist of frail metallic practicality, above a bottom two-thirds of gruff dry silty sand.

Donnerstag 1 Juni

It's hard to believe the light on the desk comes either directly or indirectly from the sun. Even though I know it is caused, travels, is refracted, bounces, arrives, bounces into my eye – even though I've seen diagrams, studied physics, it's easier to think that every object has colours which they beam out into any receiver. There seems such waste with solar light particles. Think of all of them, in my room, and then think how tiny a proportion go into my pupils. Two small black portals – a fraction of the area of surfaces being hit and invisibly lit. If Mouse is in here, that's two more black portals – unless he's sleeping. If I look at it, I can see the room, and the distances between wall and window, carpet and ceiling light. The particles are ricocheting from one to another, hardboard to printer to pencil to woodface, like perpetual pachinko without gravity but with energy. So much detail, so many possible pieces of information, so unimaginable to be omniscient – seeing everything all the time from every different angle, even from inside, and never forgetting a moment. To be present in the grenade as it explodes, the arm as it falls to the flank, the child in the fifth-storey apartment as it tries to make itself smaller, the nail behind the family photograph showing great-grandparents, the gilding in the edge of the frame of the family photograph, the headscarf of the mother five and a half miles away at her sister's, the gloss of her sister's hair-dye in the glass bottle in her sister's bathroom cabinet, the two street cats licking spilt yoghurt halfway back, the dust that was there even before the dust about to be created by the collapse of the compound wall, the phone in the thrower's pocket, the lettering in the books he read six months ago, the grey spittle at the edge of his father's mouth as he talked of football and prophecy on his last morning, the handles on his mother's coffin five feet below the dry rocks of the cemetery, the injured remains of his mother within the coffin. To be equally, neutrally present as a witness; or to care exactly the same about everything you see.

Freitag 2 Juni

Gah! – tea sideways onto this page, the desk, my fingers and my trousers. I dab it up with white and black napkins kept from cafes (for just this, and for pen-filling). Cuntybumfuck. Spilling things and dropping things – I do get unnecessarily angry; because, given the amount of picking up and moving, and my lack of focus, I always have moments of not just clumsiness but incoherence. For example, I will try to place the mug on top of a resting pencil. Reaching for a rubber, I will instead hit the glass of water with stiff fingers. Even when gazing at the ink being sucked into the cartridge, I will shudder and move too far to the right – gifting a spatter to the surface of the coffee, now cold. (I'll still drink it.) Someone once said, in a positive-thinking way, 'Don't say, "I'm so stupid" or "I'm so clumsy" say "I'm so human."' ('We're human,' said the monks at Eiheiji.) But I am stupidly humanly clumsy. My humanity is clumsy. My humanness is stupid. If I had never spilled or dropped, I would be some form of linear equation – giving an identical result every time. But I am more clumsy than I should be – what with all the fucking zazen and the bloody fucking attempts at cunting patience. If I spill, I swear; if I splash, I enter self-hatred – a cathedral of for fuck's sake. Why? Why now? Why can't I just get on with what I need to get on with: wet ink on dry paper with wet drinks in externally dry containers? A place for everything. Leave off. Accident can help a Frank Auerbach or a Francis Bacon, but I've never had a wordchoice helped by bleed or smudge. And I've lost notes and specificities. Just can't make it out. If I were less angry, I would be less stupid.

Samstag 3 Juni

Small triumphs of the day – carrying an overfilled cup of coffee up the stairs without spilling it on the carpet; subsequently, not becoming mired in anxiety.

Where I am, I am safe – and I feel that, although I don't always think of it. There are no hand-grenades ripping up Norwood Road, and no sniper fire snapping across the forecourt of the petrol station. I am safe and I am also alone. (Mouse is in bed with Leigh, sitting on her face and telling her that he loves her.) Because of what life was like at boarding school, I associate being safe with being alone. If someone is present, there's a chance they'll be a bully. At boarding school, it was a high chance; since, it has lowered. But I think that when I was forming an idea of what I could be, what I should do, I knew I wanted it to be as isolated as possible. I needed to be as independent of other people, and as completely responsible for my own way, as a round-the-world sailor – as Bernard Moitessier on his beautiful sailboat *Joshua* in 1968 and 1969. Bernard was out of radio contact, and I don't ask for guidance and advice from agent and publisher. Whether I've had a good day or a bad day, I don't speak about it to Leigh. Maybe if Flipper toddles in and asks what Daddy write, I will tell him. I will tell him the title. What I most prefer, however, is to be left alone with the words – and through the words come everything else: the reach of the sentence and the run of the character. Writing as sailing: you could take the analogy a long way, you could circumnavigate an infinite horizon of waviness and cloudiness. I am not going to drown on dry hardboard, but I can hit the doldrums, lose my bearings, get pitch-poled in the worst of a gale. My main-mast can shatter. I have my own albatrosses, which I am careful not to shoot, and my own dolphins, who seem to like speed best of all. (Leigh just came in to ask if I wanted coffee.) At night, I sight submerged glows that I can't identify; in the morning, their mystery is an embarrassment. Behind me I leave a long line. I dream of harbour as a new place from which to depart. Sun and clouds and waves and stars and wind and all of these are words, the most important of which is 'and'.

Sonntag 4 Juni – *Obit*

What would I have people say of me? He helped. He wasn't evil. Consumed relatively little. He did his best, even if sometimes we couldn't quite understand why he thought it important to do exactly what he was doing. He was the best writer of his generation, and also by far the most interesting on an intellectual level – but emotional too; alive! Oh god, I always really fancied him, but I just never – you know – got up the nerve to tell him. Very well read. I like his songs – there's one he wrote with Emily Hall that's just gorgeous, about twilight, and gets me every time; I mean, he only wrote the words, and it's really the melody... He remembered me very clearly, although we only met twice and that was twenty years apart. Through his social engagement, he wasn't completely out of touch with the proletariat, although a clearer example of alienation you could not find. He was a friend to the Armenian people. A surprisingly good listener. The only straight man who ever told me to be more melodramatic. An astringent critic, but not vindictive. It is one of the great regrets of my life that I never got to meet him, and to tell him how much his works had meant to me and my wife. He was no slouch in bed. The awards committee made a grave mistake in not calling in his novel that year. A good bloke. A good mate. Always interesting company. He was actually quite a decent swimmer. Could have been a breaststroke champion if he'd only put the effort in, early on. You'd want him on your team at the pub quiz. As a travelling companion, I found him very easy company – if you wanted to be quiet, he would sense that and let you have your space. He was a generous teacher, and he never took himself too seriously. Funny, the guy was seriously funny. Absolute legend. Twitter is a poorer, less giving place for his passing. Kind – very kind. I never really loved anyone else – not in quite the same way. Some people just have that natural charisma thing, don't they? I mean, like Bob Dylan or Barbra Streisand – walk into a room and everyone knows you're there. Really, the best orgasms of my life. Nice clothes. He just liked to sit and look at the sea. Could have been one of our most important philosophers, but chose another path. Who? Oh, I thought you meant someone else. I should do what people will actually say of me. Later.

Montag 5 Juni

By now I'm used to my days being German days, when I write them down. I have even started to think of Wednesdays as Mittwochs, and to wonder whether Flipper will be born on a Montag or a Samstag. (Fingers crossed.) Perhaps I can make a thing of it, and next year have an Irish Gaelic diary, or Pidgin, or Finnish. If we're lucky, I will be writing about James or John or Dylan or Freddie or Lucas or George or Henry or David or Aelfred (or Django or Johannes or Minty or Flipper) – whatever we decide to call him once we see him. I suppose we can choose two or three names. If the scan had shown a girl, we were thinking of May or Muriel or Anna or Hannah – there aren't so many because we didn't have as long to think and didn't talk about it as much. Even when he's born and we've gone to the Registry Office (fingers double crossed), James will still be a little bit Dylan, a little bit Muriel. My Dad always told me he wanted my name to be Hector. I've never met a Hector. (I've met Tobys, usually my age.) It's a loser's name, Hector, but he was thinking of a children's television programme called *Hector's House*. I must still be a little bit Hector. Thinking of this, and writing it, makes me horribly anxious. If Flipper isn't born, these will all become names we can't use – cursed names, though Leigh wouldn't say that – associated names that, if there's a next time, a next endless nine months, we couldn't choose from. We would be on to other choices, most of them second (otherwise we'd be considering them now). But there might just about be another pregnancy even with Child 1 safely alive. And then these names would all be possible again. You have to think of yourself shouting whatever it is down the aisle of a supermarket, or telling a taxi driver that's what your child is called. Hence not Aelfred, though I quite like Alfie.

Dienstag 6 Juni

Mouse, bestial creature, just brought in a very tiny head of a very small bird. He dropped it on the carpet behind me. It was possibly a sparrow; I hope it wasn't a robin. The perfect thing looked like it had been stolen from a zoological museum.

I buried the head three inches down under a piece of slate, so Mouse couldn't dig it up again.

Later: I am working very hard, but not very successfully, on not taking this death as an omen. Everything's an omen right now: milk-spills, what happens to characters in novels, student emails.

Writing about the sparrow-robin was meant to release me of the image of it, not install it in my head as the base of a miniature totem pole.

Mittwoch 7 Juni

The Bugaboo is delivered. At last, we can stop thinking buggies-buggies-buggies. I assemble it, reassured by the chunkiness of its design – reassured by its designedness. This gives me something to do, the practicality of Dadness: I must build. We've assembled a lot of what we need, now. Everyone tells us winter babies are a good thing, for schooling. Keep them warm rather than cool. Old for their (school) years. If Leigh goes into labour after stopping the blood-thinning injections, it could be just over a month.

Phone: Asking Mum what she'd like to be referred to, in relation to Flipper. (And so, what we'll call her, after her death.) What would you like? – Granny, Gran, Grandma? Not Nan or Nana. She would like Grandma.

Evening, we watch 'Birth – Eight Women's Stories'. None of them are catastrophic – a baby needing an operation at Great Ormond Street was the worst. One came out looking grey and floppy, as if made of clay – it vived quickly. None of the women needed to be cut. I suppose we should have expected the doc to be sunny side up. One woman, at 45, who reminded me of Brenda, hadn't known she was pregnant until five months, delivered in an hour, sat up in bed, ate a salad and looked at the baby to convince herself it was real.

Donnerstag 8 Juni

A boy is a bomb – and I can't say what a girl, or any other alternative, is like. But a boy is devastating, especially to a mother, because maleness like his is what's responsible for so much violence. There's no guarantee he will participate and not oppose. But when he's announced as male, the mother knows she's in a war *against* – a war against violence, against what maleness is seen to bring and cause and want. (Perhaps when they say, 'It's a girl,' the mother knows she's in a war *with*.) Because all her female friends have had girls, or if they had a boy, he came second – because of this fluke, Leigh expected Flipper to be a girl. It wasn't a rational expectation, that we'd have the same as them, but we'd already been promised about ten years' free baby clothes (not all pink, but very little blue). I think if Flipper had been a girl (had been designated a girl, whatever s/he turns out to be later), I would be more relieved and more anxious. 'Thank God I'm not dealing with the possibility of an exact repeat of myself' and 'Oh God I'm up against something that could be completely different to me'. With the scan, and the pointing to his pear-shaped balls and penis, a whole universe of Saturdays collapsed into non-existence – no ballet, no horse-riding, no boy bands. (These things are still possible: Flipper may love horses above all things.) No, it was a whole timeline of assumptions that went. It was very unlikely I'd have to spend hours learning a huge amount about teenage lipstick brands. When waiting for him to come home, when he was late from a party, I wouldn't so often think rape. Instead, I would likely wonder what trouble he has been getting into. I would ask, 'What's he capable of doing?' not – and I know how this sounds – not 'What's going to be done to her?' These aren't voluntary thoughts; I'm not having them because I hope to make the world safer. Along with blue and pink, in Mothercare and everywhere else, comes 'Will he be a murderer?' and 'Will she be murdered?' (Actually, when we did go to Mothercare, I was quite preoccupied with death – my own. It's not a shop that makes me want to stick around and finance this binary.) Babygro either/or: Daddy's Little Princess or Mummy's Little Terror.

Freitag 9 Juni

Cold War spies used to conceal microdots in the dots of the i's and j's of their letters. I've noticed that I don't always dot my i's – or not as I'm going along – only within some words, and only at a certain pace of writing. The faster, the fewer. And when I'm rereading, or reconsidering, or just going a bit drifty, I'll look back up the page and dot dot dot – add add add – just as I'll bring around the hook of a y or complete the curve of a c. I'll join the hole at the top of an o, so it doesn't get mistaken for a u; and sometimes, if a word isn't clear enough, I'll cross the fudged version out and write a better above it. I don't want there to be any doubt. I'm sure if you analyzed a few pages closely, you'd find the rules. After an f, he doesn't dot, unless the next letter is a t or a z. (What's my algorithm?) The same goes for joining letters. My hand knows which ones it hangs around on the page for, and which it leaves to fend for themselves. That last one – *th* in *themselves* – is my most unsatisfactory join. Because the bar of the t goes straight down as the upright of the h, which means the h is only tall enough to be an n. No-one will misread it; no-one will read it. (Words with *tn* in? Witness, Britney, Satnav.) I sometimes imagine a future scholar, closely concerned with textual history – drafts, inks, breakthroughs, dubious readings. But I fear no such humans will exist. Who will visit the basement archives when the roof's on fire? Everyone will be watching the roof burn, reposting it – just as they are doing now. More likely, Flipper will read my diaries. Hello, Flipper. Did we tell you you were once called Flipper? Am I still alive? I must be dead, or you wouldn't be reading this. Are you grieving? Don't. I crossed my final t. (The Crossing of the Bar.) I dotted my last i. (Doesn't work – my little I is dotless.) Finality.

Samstag 10 Juni

I have a healthy hang, after drinking vodka and wine at last night's dinner party. I feel purified, emptied – but this leaves me with little to say. It is a rare feeling, not to be so pent up. Instead, to be released from the imminence and immanence of importance – of trying to do, to write, something important. Each letter of each toppling word. Literature is a consistent gesturing towards Literature. Literature is always in spasm. And, really, there's no such thing. For almost everyone, that supplementary concern has been disposed of. All their time is a happy hang, voided of futurity, undependent on angry ancestors. If you can matter to your contemporaries, that's enough. Grab a few million likes. So few of them out there read books, though, that it's hard to imagine a future where a book remakes an epoch. Being important is no longer important. And *I* don't really want to be important, I want to – I want to write something that's better than I have any right to write, because it's something I shouldn't have written. (Me being me.) To do this, I have to open myself to the newly writeable, whatever that might be. All the time, in every time, there are fresh obstructions, and different ways of bumping up against being. Some of them are naff, and overfamiliar even as they are being unearthed, like another field of pyramids (not sphinxes, those are cool). But others are others, and Cézanne seeing the seeing of apples.

Sonntag 11 Juni

Blackbird. It has rained thickly all night, and has just started to rain once more, after stopping at dawn. In the damp of the trees beside the railway track a blackbird is singing. Though the moment I note it, it stops. One of the ways to expose the limits of language – ah, there it is – is to ask it to describe birdsong. There are monotonous calls: cheep-cheep cheep-cheep all day. Words can accommodate that. And there are other fitter languages – the music of, most precisely, Olivier Messiaen. The imitation and analogy of Charlie Parker and John Coltrane is also around as a breathtaking alternative; Evan Parker, too. But as soon as I say of this birdsong, it's a free but controlled whistling, changing note to trill and run to paradiddle, it's like I've poured battery acid on a cactus. The bird's aria, coloratura, is one octave up from human speech – though not from comfortable operatic voice. When it flies, and it flies fleeter and flittier than a blackbird flies, it's jeu d'esprit and jouissance, but when it lands it folds itself up into aperçu. There are pure contradictions about it: excessive efficiency, devout mischief, indirect directness. When I hear it, I feel intricately sheltered, and when it ends, the entire world is two steps further away. It is average virtuosity, an outflowing of inwardness, beneficent genetics. It is liquid and crystal and display. There are phrases I'd like to have rendered as carved wood, so that I could run my thumb around their smooth cusps and ridges and thorns. Nothing about its texture is sandpapery; it's all pocket-conker, long kept. And there's always one startling note that is sounded far inside the heart, not outsome. I am not sung to, I am sung from, I am sung by. (This is the best I can do.)

Montag 12 Juni

I went wrong last month with the girl in the dufflecoat. Anyone reading that (no-one is going to read this) would think I was making a point about eccentrics, kooks wearing bright colours — or if they didn't make that assumption whilst reading, they'd have that impression afterwards (when they remembered what they'd read). It's what has stayed with me. I should have stuck with, 'She wore navy blue tights beneath her dark blue dufflecoat.' The edge between navy and dark blue is crisp enough, even though it doesn't pop. (Dig it.) I was describing my mother-to-be, not Sally Bowles or Edie Sedgwick or Isabella Blow. I meant to mean Reading University in the early 1960s, not Weimar Germany, Warhol's Factory or London Fashion Week backstage at Alexander McQueen. Of course, pale orange and dusty violet are more characterful (for the reader) than blue and blue. But with Sally and Edie and Isabella, it's the blue beneath the orange and the ultraviolet within the violet that cuts through eventually. We know the Manic Pixie Dream Girl working behind the counter in the Multi-Coloured Swap Shop doesn't exist, although for a long time I wanted to get on board the Magic Bus and go there and meet her. I am not alone in that although I am alone in this. No one is going to read these words, except me; I'm not correcting anything except myself. No one has formed a mental image of the dufflecoat. What am I up to? I am trying to footnote an echo. But as I am my only reader, my sense memories count for something. I am the only data I have. The single extant print of the art-film (*Dufflecoat*) can only ever play in one cinema. When writing novels, I do this all the time — judge a description by my misjudgement of it, when remembering or rereading. It's a very windy day, outside and in.

Tutorials. Two from the workshop group. Andy, who seemed to be glad to see me. He's been working as a delivery driver. Grace, who said she should have done an MA in Psychosocial Studies but didn't regret learning to write short stories. She's writing a Young Adult novel about skullduggery in a nunnery, under a pseudonym — Faith.

Dienstag 13 Juni

Disaster! – the red bobble from the end of the clip on the black cap of the black retro pen is gone! I have searched my pockets, the floor beneath the desk, the fluffy bottom of the steel cup – without result. The pen looks more elegant now, but has lost its spot of 1920s sass. It's all brass and black. I don't lose many things; I am too cautiously deskbound. And so, suspicion falls on Mouse – though I can't remember him showing interest in the retro pen before. Not as he does with white earphones (chewy) or black pencil sharpener (spinny). Pulling off the bobble would be beyond his nouse, but playing footsie with it – if it was already free – that would spark his joy. Which means that by now it might have rolled beneath the floorboards of the living room, or pinged under the cellar door, or hustled into the corner of the kitchen where live the flip-flops and Wellington boots. (Mouse isn't malicious, but sometimes he's a right little git.) Should I get another retro, even though this one writes (physically, if not psychically) as well as ever? Over the next few days, I'll see whether the pen becomes a thing of ridiculous grief – a permanent missing in action – or whether loss turns out to be lightening – another excrescence gone. Yet again, I teach myself I can live without something I thought I needed. Quite probably, my mother taught me the word bobble, as she taught me the words red, no, marmalade (mispronounced marlamade) and bang (my first word). Bang! I, Bobo, drive into the glare of the ring in my stripey charabanc, with Rolo and Holo. The jalopy backfires twice more, and smoke comes out of the exaggerated exhaust. We three tumble out onto sawdust, feeling the fear of the younger children and the loathing of their mothers. No-one but the fathers – fellow clowns – wants us interrupting the palominos and wire-walkers. As I check the engine, Rolo kicks my bum and Holo kicks his. But the audience is turning vicious; we have failed to master them. I hear jeers, whistles. When I've been upended beneath the bonnet and crawled out through the boot, to no applause, I find myself facing an angry red-headed boy, pointing up at me, pointing at my eyes, the spotlight on him – 'That's not a real clown – he's got no nose!'

My beard has stopped tickling – instead, it aches. Leigh, big.

Mittwoch 14 Juni

For a while I'd been looking forward to writing about i-dotting –
I thought it would be an interesting minor thing, a significant detail,
and fun, light, or if not fun then cocooning. The writer who can
think about such tiny habits is not in a warzone or being persecuted
(although they may, now I think, be in prison, in solitary). I tell my
students about the differences between breathless, time-pressured prose
and expansive, leisured prose – that it's parodic to have a character
being chased by an axe-murderer notice the flowers in a vase on the
table, unless they're going to use the vase as a weapon of self-defence.
But if they're in the waiting room at the dentists', a very accurate
description of the flowers, and the vase, and the transit of its shadow,
could tell you a lot. (Maybe they're not at leisure – maybe it's their
anxiety forces them to notice. When we are trying to avoid thinking
about something, consciously or unconsciously, we always focus on
another thing.) When I noticed the i's, and decided I could make a
little of it, I felt now was the right, the sweet point in time. But, as
sometimes happens, more often than seems decent, the writing wasn't
all that – I didn't manage to write The Authorized Version. I can't
explain why, and if I could I'd spend time correcting or avoiding the
same-again-slide-away from the funk of the matter. It's like dreaming
an architecture, seeing a room, building a house to contain that room,
decorating and furnishing that room – then entering that room, to find
it has the atmosphere of, that it feels like the room next door to the
room you wanted. The cube of air itself, cut out of treetop space, is
off-kilter – unpopulated by ghosts, or populated by the wrong ghosts.
You flubbed the entire poetics, and will probably be the only person
who ever cares or knows.

If the red bobble dropped off the clip over the desk, which is most likely, then it would have landed on something hard – it would have made a double or treble tink! – plasticky and light, but audible. Why didn't I hear it? Like the fall of a small bauble. Alternatively, if it came away when I was pulling the pen out of a pocket where it was clipped, then it might not have made much sound when it hit my shoe or a carpet, but why didn't I notice the bobble was gone when I went to replace the used pen? Both mysteries. Just now, I looked again – observed by Mouse – beneath the desk, and before that under the printer. I don't think I'm going to get it back again. Mouse saw me on all fours. When I try to think of objects I've lost, and still regret, still mourn, there aren't a host waiting to manifest – spirits at a séance. We come at your call. Your sweet summons is all we ever required. We have messages. And there they float – the absences – ready to spew curiously muslin-like ectoplasm or throw some poor spirit-medium across the front parlour. (Call her Maggie, or Meg for short.) Just when it was getting interesting. Meg was terrible shaken. Can you feel a cold hand? Did something brush your cheek while I was asking you to look the other way? We have urgent messages. Hearken! What you stand to lose, beloved ones, will not be lost. Now, I'm feeling a strong female presence. Does the letter H mean anything to anyone here? It's impossible! Why cannot we speak directly to our nearest and dearest? There they sit – trusting and waiting. Why do we have to deal with these abominable shams? There is protocol. But now one of those awful disruptive spirits – presences – has erupted among us; and the table is bucking and the candles flickering. Please, please, wait your turn! Many have been waiting patiently for years. We cannot hearken to everyone at once. It is a child – an angry boy – oh so angry. The table flips. All stand aghast. Ah, no – I see him now – there in front of the curtain. Can you not see him? It is a clown. Has anyone here lost a tiny clown? With a red bobble for a nose.

Donnerstag 15 Juni

A greyer than gray day. Writing is performed onto/on the page –
there's the live moment of getting it down, then further live moments
of rewriting. I don't like the word *Live*. It suggests Live Bed Show,
Live from Norwich. Vivid is better, but sounds self-aggrandizing. Too
much eyebrow pencil. Really, it's the could-go-either way moment.
Could-go-any-way. The open moment. Writing which is open to
being different, to being a different being, to different language, and
to whatever of the various-fissiparous world may choose to enter. Lots
of writing, of my own writing, is in no way like this. Hens in their
coop not hawks in their stoop. You can pre-vision the campaign of
your writing, give it certain metaphysical rations to be going on with.
But then you're selling yourself to yourself. Live is 1970s Liveness.
Dotting or not dotting the i's, because ongoingly wording the world,
is or seemed to be an image of vivid life; worth writing because itself
showing up the performance, rather than hiding behind the page – the
typical page where every i is every other i. Not even every hundredth
i, as with a letterpress with very limited type; digitally identical, as
information – Press Send. Vivid is day-glo D.H. Lawrence. Hens lay
eggs, hawks kill other birds. (Say hello to Vivian.) Do we want to read
about the routine of hatching or the indeterminacy of a vertical dive
towards death through cold air? (It's not either/or, but it is.) (Left the
vivid air signed.) I assert that there has to be the open possibility of
change at all three points: in the writing, in the writer, in the reader.
I assert that the possibility of change has to be opened at all three
points. Change as transformation. You must change your life. (You
must choose a new brand of Vivid.) Second thoughts, things got
wrong, ignorances, hares-pursued – this is our way in the world. We
are neither epitaphs nor slogans.

Freitag 16 Juni

Yawning and then more yawning, with a bit of rubbing my face in between. 7:31 am. Bad night. Mother-dreams and then thoughts. I put my left palm over my eyes, as if it were a poker player's eyeshade; then press closer in, eyemask. It's asymmetrical, because the left thumb rides up the ridge of my left temple, and my fingers fan out over my right cheek. The darkening isn't equal, either. With the pad of the left hand lodging itself in the socket of my left eye, that becomes twice as shaded as the other eye, which sees light through the pink jalousie of middle, ring and little. If I want to equalize, or try to, I shift the pad higher and cup the tensed fingers as if they were holding a small crab in seawater. The thumb still goes up, and as it touches and supports the temple, I feel the weight of my skull. When I'm like this, I'm usually not writing with ease – I need to close my eyes, and get rid of some light, in order to hear something of the next sentence, or make out the disharmony of an abandonment. *This will not do. This might go.* I'm not despairing, or mimicking despair, as this is a position that works. The pen is still in the right hand, nib hovering or trembling. *Shall I cross this out? Is another word not needed?* But if I rest the pen in the gutter, and put a hand on each eye, then it's a different kind of dive. It's also a better fit, darker, with the heel of the palm dug in below the cheekbones and the fingers cool on the brow, and, in between, the space above the eyelids occupied by snug flesh. Elbows brace, and I'm set for however long. I breathe down into a triangle but also slightly up my sleeves, if I have sleeves. *It's bad, yes, but it's not as bad as it was. It could be good. I think I need to stop thinking.* When my eyes again look at the page, they see the trace of not-seeing. And I find it clarifying: the words are completely the same, but I'm new.

Samstag 17 Juni

He's going to die – like the other ones did – and (like them) we're going to have to mourn him, even though he was never born, and maybe never stood a chance of being born; something chromosomal (it sounds like the alarm chime of an iPhone) – a chromosomal defect will cause the forming cells of him, the potential life-changing character of him, to be ejected. Into the toilet bowl, like number 3. (I think of number 3 as a girl; numbers 1 and 2 remain indeterminate.) I woke in fright, all the cold sweat and certainty of the worst coming to pass. I'd like to write something – something *something* – not this – this angst-splurge – but I can't think of anything beyond a grief that may never be. 'Most of all I can't forget/ the things that haven't happened yet.' I am shy of the pain. I'd like it to stay in another universe – one of the infinite number in which I'm already all-crying-broken. There's an equally infinite number where I'm like I am here, and infinity where Flipper really is born a dolphin. Mouse is lying on my desk, blissfully being chucked under the chin with my left hand. His forepaws are holding my wrist in place. What rules will I bend for Flipper? I wouldn't let any other cat up on my desk. How will I ever be able to tell Flipper *No*?– if he is born, he should have everything he wants. He'll be the absolute gift, unrefusable. How many days to go? Mouse's white whiskers shoot off like particle trajectories. More, he says, more.

Sonntag 18 Juni – *Father's Day*

Just about to go round to Holly and Nirpal's for dinner, the phone rings. Leigh answers. It is Dave. She says his name and is delighted to speak to him. She wanted to know whether... But then she stops, listens, is devastated by something, starts crying. From her questions, I can tell that Janice lost the baby, their third. Leigh is really shattered. It is only when she is off the phone that she tells me, and I start crying, too. Janice and Dave went for a scan at 35 weeks and found the baby had died. They were offered induction then or the next day. They decided to go home and Janice went into labour naturally. All this happened a month ago. They haven't felt able to tell anyone. I am horrified. All I can say to Leigh is, 'That's such a terrible thing.' The baby was a girl. They got to spend some time with her. There was a funeral but they didn't invite anyone. Leigh asks can we see them and Dave says they're not ready quite yet. I texted Nirpal to say we'll be late just after Leigh took the call. We can't decide whether to go or not. I am worrying about Leigh, about our baby. I am thinking of the plot of *Ghost Story* – about my characters Agatha and Paddy losing a baby so late on. Writing this while Leigh speaks to Janice, long conversation.

We decided to go and I called Nirpal to let him know what happened, before we got there. I'm glad we went. Leigh is going to write to Janice.

Montag 19 Juni – *True grit*

If I can feel grit beneath the cover of the diary, between it and the surface of the desk, it more than irks me. I have to find it and, if possible, flick it into the bin – so that it doesn't become annoying underfoot. The page, with a particle of stone or cat-litter or wood beneath, feels as if it's vibrating with a flaccid resonance. Twanging. How can the words be right if they are pivoting microscopically? What I see and what I saw, it needs to come out plainly – no sandcastle, no teeter, no crunch. I am beached enough as it is, and founded upon pulp and knitted fibre. If I'm on a page where the pen hits a tiny bump, I can usually tell beneath how many pages the princess-pea lies. Under just the first page, there's edges and a cubic sugar crystal might scape sideways. Two pages down, and the ride will be smoother over but the paper might still be left in an angular new peak. Between three and five, the thing is still a certainty – a hillock – but with different gradients and a decreasing chance of crumble. Still further down, I don't bother counting; it's there, it bloats a letter or kinks a line, I find it, it's moved on. Imagine the jam jar full of them, over the years – sand from the drabbest beach, unrefined sugar, shards of graphite. Often my eyes aren't good enough anymore to see individual grains. I find them by finger feel, rub them into a running ridge, and then make the money gesture over the bin.

Dienstag 20 Juni

Sweeping is the first thing I do – after getting out of bed, going down-stairs, putting the kettle on, emptying the top shelf of the dishwasher, scalding the teapot, putting four teaspoons of tea in, pouring on the hot water, pouring hot water into two mugs, emptying the bottom shelf of the dishwasher (with interruptions to stir the tea), emptying the mugs, pouring the milk, pouring out the tea, taking the mugs upstairs – hopefully without spilling – to Leigh and then to the desk. Sweep, sweep-sweep and, if necessary, SWEEP, all with the palm of my left hand because if I do it with the palm of my right it might pick up crumbs of rubber or shreds of pencil lead, which might then drop onto the page I'm about to start. Until I wrote this, I hadn't consciously known I did this. Sometimes, I now realize, if I know the hardboard is likely to be gritty, I get at it with a paper napkin kept from a café trip. Depending on how dirty this gets, it's either dropped in the wastepaper bin or returned to the scrunch pile in the postcard box. After which, all of which I can do semi-somnambulant, I will reach for a pen from the pen-pot and the diary from the notebook pile, find the next day, the next new page, and – not necessarily awake, nor always intent on conscious production – puzzled, ambitious, tactile, intent, ecstatic, nihilistic, truthful – dull, empty, stupid, pathetic, arrogant, impatient, regretful – hating my handwriting but accepting its legibility – already far far too late for the kind of thing to which I aspire, but perhaps also a little or a lot too early for whatever would replace that ambition, for someone like me – with an ache in my spine, blurry eyes and feathery breathing –

Mittwoch 21 Juni – *Summer Solstice*

I am disappointed with my use of the word *something*; I have noticed I use it much too much. Sometimes it appears two or three times, meaning two or three different things, within the same page or paragraph. Holding something, doing something, waiting for something, standing in for something that is so unknown it can only be referred to as something. There's something lazy about this habit, but it's also an attempt to get at an ineffability that's destroyed by abstraction if you give in to articulacy and call it *an ineffability*. A thing of nothing. This thing of darknesse I acknowledge. On some pages, I feel I ring through changes on something, anything, nothing – along with somewhere, anywhere, nowhere, and someone, anyone, no-one. I remember seeing a writer in a documentary; he had a card stuck to his computer with all the words he could no longer allow himself to use. *However* was there, and *therefore*, and obvious ones like *actually* and *really*. It is better to be specific, says the writing advice, but sometimes we don't know what we're being specific about. We have the calipers but not the insane or criminal head that went between them; the subject has escaped before we could observe it/them. Something in the way. Should it be I am disappointed *with* or I am disappointed *by*? He was a great disappointment to himself for something he had once failed to do for someone. Isn't that what opens the door on the abyss, fifty storeys down? Some somethings, the dust falls on them, and the cracks show up when they're lit from the side.

Leigh's just back from work. How is she? How was her day? My love.

Donnerstag 22 Juni

Dust is – The dust in the air (I hear Mouse crunching his dry food behind me – like the sound of being tackled really hard in rugby: gristle and crunch) – the dust in the air is in the air, and the air isn't empty. My cancers (working). Our house is on a quiet road but two doors away from a busy road, and thirty paces away from a petrol station, and within close sight of a railway line, and beneath the flight path to Heathrow. If I start to die of lung cancer, there will be various factors – blames – possibilities I'll think of. One of the main ones will be the location of our house. (I'm suddenly aware of the lymph nodes in my neck. they feel gristled, ready to go rogue.) I breathe particles and in between them I breathe, in the smaller, spacier spaces, I breath particulates. Very rarely, I can smell the petrol – it was one of my favourite smells, when I was a boy. Petrol meant drives with my father to service stations, antique shops, warehouses and houses way off in the country – where someone repaired wickerwork or fixed grandmother clocks. It meant the Peugeot 503 on long straight French roads between parallel rows of poplar trees, or on autoroutes, or mountain roads as twisty as the blood vessels of the human kidney – which are called? Petrol. Santa Pod Raceway. Cape Canaveral. We will need a car to take Flipper to the hospital, if there's an emergency, and to visit his grandparents, if he survives his emergencies. I sneezed, twice. Was it thinking about particulates, or writing about them, or would I have sneezed anyway even if I'd been on the subject of hermetically sealed chambers, vacuums, voids? And now I want to look up that bit of the body I want to mention – the Loops of Leprechaun? – the Hoops of Bayern Leverkuhsen? – but I know if I do, I will be drawn into screen-time, and I will write less. Later. As far as I know, I am not yet dying. Is there anything Mum would like me to do for her? Shall I write something for her? Does she want me to promise never to write anything about that? (Avoid that conversation.) The Loop of Henle – actually not as twisty as the distal convoluted tubule or the proximal convoluted tubule.

Freitag 23 Juni

Sometimes you have to start writing a page even when you have no sense what will go there – or if anything will appear but shame at your own emptiness, and wastefulness, and hopelessness. It is necessary to make a new beginning, today, another new beginning. If you don't open the door, no-one can enter. And here they suddenly are. Hello, friends. Not for some dead, arranged-months-ago get-together. Come in. How are you? What writers need are these out-of-the-blue visits and resurrections, as during a civil war. Friends and friends of friends bringing alcohol, a very little food, instruments and Eros – the Eros of good, hard talk. On the instant, the kitchen of your desk becomes a carnival, cha-cha-cha, a carnival of presence, a celebration of continued and entwined existence. There's a chair in the next room. And out of that, in the midst, while one cackles and another sings, she rolls a cigarette and he starts to weep, you hear brilliant news of an unexpected birth or a miraculous transformation. You find yourself in a story. Two people who were characterized as lighthouse keepers are now having the most beautiful, entertaining affair; the inert marriage of X and Y has exploded into fireworks of jealousy, and all because of a cockatoo; Z, who always believed themselves to be male, right from girlhood, has succeeded in becoming something far more extraordinary; A has died, but astonishingly not by their own hand – by that of B, a fascist who everyone knew for a fascist but didn't take seriously; and C has written an unprecedented work – and C is you. And does it matter the whole alphabet of acquaintances is comprised of ghosts? Who is to tell if there are many here, or only the one?

Samstag 24 Juni

Sometimes it is no kitchen-party, it is the Intensive Treatment Unit – and a decision has been made: to see if the patient (beloved) can sustain their own breathing. You sit beside them, and you wish there were something more original and caring you could do for them than hold their hand, but at this point, in this place, with this little opportunity for wit, originality is no longer a valued value, and care is all that counts. If you really care, you will care well; if you don't care to care, you will dismay and possibly distress and definitely dishonour a dying person. (I have switched from the metaphor I intended to write about Leigh's father's time in Frimley Park Hospital, his recovery, release, but then his second time. There he was, in his ITU bed, and there his family was, shuttling in and out (in pairs) from the Waiting Room. *Take a Break* magazine set aside.) Novels have Waiting Rooms, too; I'm not sure if there's an equivalent to holding their hand as they die. It's more like reaching inside their chest cavity and trying to restart their heart by mashing it in your fist. Come on, you fucker. The surrounds of a novel, or any ailing book, are not hospital-neutral. They are not pale blue, branded and wipeable. They're the velvet curtains of blood, the William Morris wallpaper of the lymph nodes, the cream brown cram of the guts. I have had enough of hospitals. I have stayed too long in Waiting Rooms. I want my two-year-old son on my shoulders on the highest point of the South Downs on the first sunny day of the year – even if that's in January – and I want him to be surveying what's around him with a wild and giddy amazement. Vision Creation Newsun. And I want a one-hundred-year warranty on his heart and other major organs, and that goes for all other dolphins, too – and a few thousand spare worlds for us to share. Up on the Downs.

Sonntag 25 Juni

When we encounter an abundance of charm, we should always expect a disposition toward its abuse. That which has the tendency to persuade and divert can hardly be less than cozening of its unfortunate possessor – unfortunate in that they have received the talents of a diplomat without the utility and appointment of their mission. I have known many men whose eloquence was unmatched – I mean, sir, that of all of them it was said their elegance was unmatched ; and in each case what was said had no lack of truth : every one of them had a moment of nonpareil in a lifetime of comparison. Yet what has been earned without toil will surely be spent without check ; for it is the pain and effort with which we invest our endeavors as we pursue them that makes us sensible of their worth. We may highly value a gift, however small, because we esteem the donor; but when we have seemed to receive our benison from such an inexhaustible distributor as Nature herself, our respect for her judgement and taste will be corrupted by our fore-knowledge of her future munificence. The diadem upon our brow is but a reflection of that greater diamond even this moment falling into the darken'd miner's open palm; and so, we are diminished by the mere possibility of increase. If we feel more is to come, we will think the less of what is present. I value personal qualities, sir, as far inferior to adherence to impersonal values. Sometimes it is a relief to contemn what we have long strained to condone, out of a wish towards Christian generosity and forbearance: yet what is wrong is wrong, and our Saviour's penultimate act will be to pass judgement. His final act will be to accept his Father's invitation to sit at His right hand. Amity must outdo division. (It's fun being Samuel Johnson, but a bit exhausting.)

Montag 26 Juni

Dust is of course constantly falling onto the desk – and I am quite fond of dust. When I can't think of anything to write, or it's made everything I can see obtrusively opaque, I wipe it away with spit and tissues (as I used to clean everything, when I was a boy – spit and hanky). The dust particularly likes the shiny silver base of the Anglepóise – that's where I notice it most. Some particles are just dots but others are shaped as half-moons, fingernails, ferns or spores. I suppose in summer a decent part of it *is* spores. On the nut beneath the bigger central spring, flanked by two sidekick springs, there is Quay dust. I love the films of the Quay Brothers, Stephen and Timothy, twins – their Mitteleuropean-besotted stop-motion puppet animation that is often at its best when deepest in dust. They must (like Quentin Crisp) curate their dust. It's not set-dressing dust, sprinkled from a shaker by a runner. Where it is, it has grown, matured, darkened, become oily and characterful. The QQuays – Pittsburgh-born, Borough-based – sometimes animate (full etymology) their dust. Turning-turning screws twizzling out of their lodgings and waltzing away through a grey carpeting. Their dust is the dust of Bruno Schulz, Robert Walser. *The Street of Crocodiles. Institute Benjamenta.* (Franz Kafka was hardly dusty at all – maybe a bit, in *The Trial*.) It is grey-brown, like a mouse, like parts of Mouse, and it is soft-sift, it is silky when it isn't tacky-sticky. If you blow on it, it doesn't flee, it wrinkles. There it lies, along the tops of my guiltiest unread books. I am old enough now that the pages of my teenage paperbacks are yellow or golden, and brittle and flaked. Brush the dust off *The Dictionary of Latin Tags and Phrases*. Off Burton's *Anatomy of Melancholy*. Off *The Reader's Encyclopedia*. On your finger, it forms an eyebrow. Doldrums – Leigh feeling super-heavy, she says.

Dienstag 27 Juni

Quick trip to Mum, just for a couple of hours around teatime. Even though I know this is how she wants it, I feel guilty for not staying. She is performing being better than she is, and can manage being bright and inquisitive for an hour and a half. She wants to know all about Leigh, about our latest hospital visit or meeting with the midwife team. When I ask her about her hospital visits and meetings with care teams, she says there isn't much to say. 'It's all the same, really,' she says – when everyone in the room knows it's anything but. I don't think she's ever asked for a prognosis, timescale. With babies you get a due date – what do you get for death? An undue date? An undo? A late, a pass, a – if it's like trains, it's a termination date. Arrivals and Departures. 'This train will terminate and stop at Terminal One.' Mum did mention she's stopped playing bridge, which is sadder than I can say. For her birthday, I once bought her bridge-themed pens and score cards – jacks, clubs, diamond and spades. She loved those, used them for the Wednesday night school. This was before she stopped having Dad as her partner – because, like competitive sailing, it disturbed the peace of their marriage. I said goodbye at four forty-five. How many more times will I think, 'This might be the last'? I was thinking that thought even when I went off to university. Leigh was fine when I got home; I'd already texted, when I had just left Mum and Dad's, sitting in our car under the apple tree that leans out over their garden wall. Mum wants her ashes sprinkled in the garden. Leigh wanted to know all about Mum, but, of course, I'd spent most of my time with Mum talking about her and the baby. Dad seemed okay – melancholy, unsure what to do. He makes Mum seem even smaller now.

Mittwoch 28 Juni

There's more to be said about dust – I wanted to make it the character in a book once. Sort of. The book was to take place in a world gradually being subsumed under QQuay-type dust. Not an original idea, I'm sure; one of the reasons I didn't write it was that I knew someone else would have done it better. 'There are seven types of dust.' That was a possible opening sentence that I knew wouldn't make it to the final draft; it's too novelly-discursive. I don't know how many types of dust there are. On the desk, the majority of it must be me-dust – off the top of my head, emerging from my scratched beard; then there's whatever floats in from the garden, or through the front door (alternatively, carried on our feet, drying out on the shoe rack, taking flight); then there's the pencil shavings. One of the crafty almost nothing things I love about being a writer is the sharpening of pencils. For years I've used a Palomino Blackwing sharpener, shaped a bit like one of the earliest tanks (without the slope of the tracks). It gently reduces the tip of the pencil to a longer than usual taper. (The fine point of his soul.) It does this by virtue of two holes, the first (on the left) to get the wood roughly in shape, the second to fine hone the graphite. After I sharpen a pencil, I always sniff it. That's the smell of my work – wood and lead, graphite and cedar. Sometimes I think that I'll end up killing myself this way, get brain cancer – what particulates are going up my nose? Afterwards, there's a ready point to be written with; and this makes me more willing to write. My handwriting won't be a shameful slur; it'll have something of the morning's acuity. (This is in pen. Diary in pen.) Pencil is usually for revision – for a second draft on top of the first, to save paper. Recently I bought two pencils from a beautiful new shop in town, one is Prussian Blue (imagine that) and the other is Dark phthalocyanine green. But usually I used Mono 100 HB pencils from the Japanese company Tombow. They are lacquer black with a gold band half an inch from the non-writing end, and a white line bissecting the bit some people would chew. (I'm not a chewer.) Made in Vietnam. For hi-precision DRAFTING (we hope). *Highest quality* (we wish). HOMO-GRAPH (we are).

Donnerstag 29 Juni

Today will be an in-between day, I can tell – but it's those that make a book. Days on which all you do is spellcheck, or search for words you know you have repeated too often (particularly, almost, thing, Nietzsche). Earlier on, you may change a character's name, and again, then change it back to what it was the first time you changed it. Later, I re-read until a sentence is bad enough to stop me. Perhaps there's an unwanted rhyme with the sentence above or perhaps, seeing it again, I realize it says the opposite of what it needs to say. Sometimes, at any stage, a paragraph is dead – you overdescribed, did too much research, or tried to reduce it to its most efficient form, and ended up sounding faux naïf. The worst comes when I begin to realize I wasn't writing what I thought I was writing. Read in an obvious way, with today's head on, it seems an appalling misjudgement, this whole book – a misjudgement that would appal anyone not themselves appalling. And yet, when you were writing it, during all those months, you thought people would be delighted. I seem to be doing this more and more often: three finished manuscripts to one published. But I need to write in orbit around the far side of the moon, in radio silence, info-shadow. If it's written with permission, it's trash – even before it's written, it's already trash. I tell my students there are no wasted hours, because that's what all writers need to hear. There are no wasted hours, but there are wasted years. And then, in a sentence or another book, something comes to exist that would never have been sayable without that waste – and it almost feels like it, the shitness, has been redeemed. (I feel like I'm going to be sick.)

People are now starting to congratulate me on my beard. 'Amazing.' It gives my face a sense of occasion it's always lacked (my too-thrusting nose, my underwhelming chin). I think I look like a sailor home from the sea, but already watching the tides and tasting the wind.

Freitag 30 Juni

Motes — what I see floating into the light of the Anglepoise aren't chunky enough to be described as motes. Most of them seem to be either specks or strands. They might be made of hair, but it isn't mine — mine is too heavy to rise in the air. I blame Mouse, and the carpet, and my clothes. If I haven't been moving around, about six or seven flyers per minute enter the spotlight. The smaller ones, more like single points when seen from my scale, descend from the unlit and are enthused by the warmer air. This can make it seem as if they are being pulled toward the lightbulb; not like moths, not at all like moths, because their flight paths are too unflappable. Heavier, the S- and C- and even Q-shapes rise but won't always be drawn into the brightness and warmth. (This bulb is easily touchable; only as hot as the final sip of tea before the tea gets too cold.) Now I'm noticing, I just saw an S-shape describe an S-shape, but of an S that has capsized. It already had sideways momentum, so entered the light descendingly leftwards — towards the black printer — then was smoothly swung around and lifted for a space but only until the midpoint, whereafter it smoothly crested and began to fall, still sideways-bound. And now I've been sitting here for a while, I see the frequency of the flights has diminished to two or one a minute. Of course it's me, entering the room, that pushes and swirls the air and everything in it. Unless the window is open, or Leigh has come in and gone away, I'm the only other energy source: the sun, the bulb and me. And the radiator. And my phone, if it's charging. And my laptop, if it's on. And my computer, if it too is on. And the pipes beneath the floorboards. And the printer, if it's on. And my watch, if it's wound. I could have written 'after which' but 'whereafter' perhaps because it's formal or archaic is a far more airborne word.

Leigh, big and fed up.

Samstag 1 Juli

To Mum and Dad's. Mum seemed very sleepy but perked up when talking to Leigh. Lunch of bought quiche and packet salad followed by mandarin slices in orange jelly. This is a joke from Mum, as she knows I don't like it, but she used to make it when I was little, and says I never said anything. Mum doesn't usually make jokes like this. Afterwards, when we were sitting around on the two sofas, I wasn't able to hear what Leigh and Mum were saying. This was partly because my brother had arrived and was talking to Dad. But also because, I think, Leigh and Mum were negotiating connections very fast – like dial-up modems used to do. When I asked Leigh later, during the trafficky drive home, what they were saying, she told me, 'Oh, it was just about the baby.' That's probably true, but it's also not true. At one point – I feel guilt about this, and didn't mention it in the car – my mother had asked permission (I heard her do this) and then had placed her left hand on Leigh's bump. It seems Flipper was asleep, because Mum didn't react to any movement – she just kept her hand there for a short while. And I felt guilty because I wanted to say, 'Get off.' Her hand looked pink, dry, boney, and most of all manky from the needles that have gone into the back of it. Her hand looked like a blood orange the day after you've grated off its zest. (She was wearing long sleeves, deliberately I'm sure, so we couldn't see the state of her arms.) Mum's hand didn't look the kind of thing I wanted touching the baby. I also thought it might be unlucky, this contact. So obvious: 'You're death, it's life – leave it a while before you interfere.' And also: 'Don't give the baby cancer – don't transfer your lurgy.' But Leigh was smiling, and I felt differently, I felt very ashamed when I looked at Mum's face. It was the hand I wanted away from Flipper. Mum's face, although the skull is coming through, was lovely and I wanted her to have everything in the world. If I could, have her inside the womb, too – so she could be safe and yet-to-become. Then I wouldn't be, wouldn't have been, and neither would Flipper. Why can't the treatment work? Why can't they save her, when they save so many awful, useless people? Famous fuckers. I feel guilty about even writing these thoughts.

Sonntag 2 Juli

'These subjects of yours are very meagre, and not worth the attention you give them. In fact, they're hardly subjects at all, they're more like objects. I mean, what's interesting or to be gained from dust? Dust is just dust. We have to live with it; we waste a lot of time trying to get rid of it – or we pay other people to spend their time dusting and vacuuming; and we do this so we don't need to spend our *own* time on such trivial matters. We have bigger fish to fry in bigger frying pans for bigger dinner parties for bigger numbers of guests. And it doesn't matter you're writing this (you *claim* to be writing this) in a diary no-one except one or two people will read. You're still wasting your own time – you're wasting your own literary talents spilling this much ink over the flagrantly trivial and excruciatingly uncommercial. Samuel Johnson, a writer I believe you admire, and have been known to imitate, said, "No man but a blockhead ever wrote, except for money." Are you a blockhead, sir? Are you deliberately impoverishing yourself? – and if you are, what benefit do you believe will thereby accrue, to you or anyone else? Do you think the dust will thank you, or remunerate you, for paying it all this attention? Why don't we make that inquiry? Why don't we ask the dust for the fruits of its experience? What has it learned by virtue of the illumination of your angle and your poise? How has it profited from its fame – from its little hour of flisking in the glib spotlight of your eye? Would it not tell you, sir, if it could speak as I can, that you are vainly frittering your fantastic vitality – for what has closely observed dust to do with the death of your beloved mother or the birth of your soon-to-be-beloved son? You, sir, are a fool – and only a fool pays mind to a fool.'

Montag 3 Juli

How can you say you're an atheist when the first thing you say when you see a bad car smash, multiple pile-up beside the motorway – your first words are, 'Oh God, oh God'? And how can you say you're not Christian if, when another car cuts you up and almost sends you into the central reservation, you shout, 'Jesus fuck!'? I know if it comes to Flipper living or Flipper dying, I'll be pleading with something – I'll be begging it (It) to let this version of the universe be the one in which Flipper lives, and doesn't suffer brain-damage, and can know who we are. It would probably be 'Oh God' rather than 'Oh Lord'. At moments of great stress, I've sometimes repeated The Lord's Prayer to myself. But it's a Primary School chant – it's in so deep, it's a connection with me when I was five and born and conscious and safe. 'Please, Whatever – ' that might be the way I start. Usually, I say to myself 'the Buddha the Buddha', but that's an approach to neutrality. An infant died two seconds ago, somewhere in this world, and I am not mourning it. It was another born, another died. If Flipper dies, he will be another another. (But I'm his father.) For others he'll be another distant another. (Or in the next delivery suite.) To be is to suffer. If he lives, he will suffer. Why am I thinking this? I'm thinking it because the spotting returned, a little heavier – and I don't want to ask any God or any Whatever for that not to happen. Again. If what you are when you are at your most desperate is a man on his knees beseeching invisible forces to spare him – that's you all the time. That's you, that is. God is what's left when nothing is left. Not 'God is what's left when nothing else is left', but 'God is what's left when nothing is left'. It's either God or

Dienstag 4 Juli

How do bubbles form in a glass of water? Do they form faster in a large or small glass? Does it matter whether the water is room temperature or chilled? Not scientific, but let me watch – I've fetched two Pyrex glasses, one fit for a small gin and tonic, the other for a double vodka. It is 10:15. Leigh at work. The water in the glasses doesn't have any bubbles in. It trembles slightly as a train goes past, north-south or vice-versa – I don't look back. When you pay attention, you can see flecks of dust already on the tense disc of the surfaces. (They're chatting in next door's garden.) Four drops of water splashed onto the buff cover of Keats' letters, when I set the glasses down. How long until a bubble forms? I'd guess twenty to twenty-five minutes. When you wake in the morning, the bedside glass – the midnight water – is stale and filled with equidistant pearls. The far edge of the bigger glass is now freckled with microbubbles – it's 10:55. Yes, they're definitely there, but I can't see any in the vodka glass. (Bubbles in a fresh gin and tonic are one of capitalism's loveliest phenomena.) Does a larger surface area mean bubbles form faster? Concluding unscientific. Always, for the writer. Who has time? The water in the smaller glass seems stiller – I would expect life to germinate first in the other one; where one of the microbubbles just detached and rose to the surface. And another, an escape pod hitting a silvery moon. The base of the bigger glass is populated with tiny mercury-like orbs, some of which overcome – get too big for their butts – and rise. Small glass is still unbubbled – perhaps the inner surfaces of it are smoother. (I've just noticed that, below their round rims, big glass is a septagon, small a nonagon.) (Sordid mornings when I didn't get up but drank bubble-blowsy water. Hungover, single.) I've meant to do this water-watching for a while – years – maybe since university. Glasses do this daily, as I work, but I've never done the Practical Observation. I saw patterns in the bubbles, diagonal lines, but they seem to have gone back to being apparently randomly distributed. 27 minutes since we began, the gin glass now looks as if it contains flat lemonade. The bubbles sway as they rise. A very few now where the vodka might be. I wish my eyes were better, more acute. Bubbles are beautiful. As in a glass sparkly. 11:15.

Mittwoch 5 Juli

There are things I say to myself, I don't know why. (Oh God.) For instance, I just stood up to go downstairs, have breakfast (muesli, it's 9:48, I've been writing since 7:59), and I said, 'I'm thinking about thinking about thinking about thinking.' These are the words I come out with when I'm trying to recall something that was just present but has run off. They have a clippety-clop galloping rhythm, or are like the trains behind me going south. If I go in the kitchen, I sometimes find myself saying, 'Wharf rats. Warfarin. Swarfega.' Wharf is a rare sound, in English, and I'm comforted by its oddity. (It's awful, it's waffle.) I said I don't know why I say them – that's not true. I know their function (mouth-rove, memory-sieve), but I don't know why these *particular* words. If I cough, I say Arsenal – because Eric Morecambe did. (Mr. Memory.) And because Leigh's Dad did, because Eric Morecambe did, because Mr. Memory did. It's a tribute cough. Most often, the words I say to myself are obvious and for themselves. 'Come on come on come on' (without commas) or 'What is it that…?' or 'And the thing is…' They're getting less special now, each one I write down, and I may be making that last one up. I'll have to listen to myself, while I'm watching myself. When I go back to work at the desk, after making coffee, I say, 'Boom-shaka-laka-boom-shaka-laka.' As far as I know, I don't say encouraging phrases. More often, I think, I am trying to tell myself not to be so stupid. I swear at the computers when they're doing what computers do, which is not doing what they're meant to do (unless what they're meant to do is enrage humans, so they're less productive).

Donnerstag 6 Juli

It's cruel to write those things, as I did a couple of days ago – about Mum's hand, and I suppose it was disgust. I have to admit it was disgust. Even if no-one's going to read it, it's a harsh thing to put down. Hate myself for it. But out of all that happened on that visit, the hand was the significant thing – it was a thing, although I'm uglily repeating the thing. It was a not-Mum thing as well as being entirely Mum. Shouldn't I be remembering her as she was when – as she's always been – when she was wonderful? Such an enthusiastic person, never glum, always Englishly geeing us along – me and my brother and my dad – through strops and spats, furies and feuds. Mum was of the dufflecoat generation: post-war, buttoned up but expert at cosiness, flirtation after choir, Ovaltine before bed, Cold War. She'd been brought up by those who kept smiling through, and knew she had no right to complain. Her parents were terrified of life – small, thin people who'd brought an aunt home to die of cancer. Mum was around that, as a girl of seven or eight. She only spoke of it to me once – on a drive to I can't remember where. A long enough drive for me to ask her about the Grindleys. She didn't say they were small, thin and terrified; I get that from the photographs of us together in the yard, behind the antique shop. They already look as old as I remember them from ten years later. Mum escaped that closure, that lid; she sang in the Three Choirs Festival, had her photograph taken for the local press, rocketed off to university, got a good zoology degree, got a good job with early computers (programming it using cards with holes), then she met Dad in St Albans, and he made her happy and she made him happy. They married much much too quickly and it was a disaster for anyone wanting to warn youngsters off marrying quickly. She brought up two healthy children, then went back to work – ending at the Citizens Advice Bureau. She's had to give that over, along with the bridge.

Freitag 7 Juli

Any writing about Mum's life misses her. She was positive – she was the one saying, 'Come on, one more push, grit your teeth you can do it.' But she also knew how to leave people alone. She taught me to stand out of the way on pavements; be aware of who's coming impatiently up behind you, with a huff and a puff of wolfish self-importance. Mum could be so polite that she made people nice who were not nice. They realized they were speaking to someone who wanted their best. Even with people in shops, she seemed to know them better than she should, but it wasn't an intrusive knowledge. It was supportive. Her manner would say, 'You're being impatient, but I can tell you don't really want to be impatient.' When I was a baby, she'd leave me in a big navy blue pram, outside the shops; when I could walk, she took me in with her and left my brother outside in the pram. She would count out the right change. She would say a heartfelt thank you, even if nothing else had really been said – apart from 'Could I have half a pound of dates, please?' In all this, she taught me my Ps and Qs as keystone letters of the alphabet. And all this rightness and properness and kindness, really – all this way of treating people better is now itself being treated, and dying despite that treatment. Like all relations, I want to say to the nurses and carers, 'This one's special.' But I think they can tell, because she's kind with nurses just as she was with shopkeepers. She spoke to shopkeepers as if they were customers about to make a very good choice: to buy, and never regret it. (Mum was a shopkeeper, too – for several years, in David Litt Antiques. Strange to think of.)

Final day of Summer term. Anxious about how to spend the coming weeks. What to read? And Autumn is Study Leave, and perhaps overlapping Parental Leave, and perhaps also Compassionate Leave.

Samstag 8 Juli

Listening to Bach's Suites for Unaccompanied Cello is a little bit like going for a gentle stroll with God Herself – around the rose garden, out through the paint-peeling back gate, and up to the eternal cliffs overlooking the infinite abyss. 'Roses are looking good this year,' says God, after taking a long deep breath of ozone, and you have no way of knowing what She means by 'good'. You doubt you even know whether by 'roses' She is referring to the roses you've just looked at, or something more like 'all roses everywhere' or 'the things I created and let be known as "roses"' or 'the creation you humans have bred into being roses' or, even, 'the prospects for humanity'. But this is wrong: the Suites are absolutely human. They know the routine of dusty attics and the glamour of a swim, they know grief for a birth and joy for a death, they know being ignored by enemies, and pivoting on love, and dancing backwards through curiosity, just as they know going for a gentle stroll with God. They know almost everything. They know they know, and they know how little knowledge there is in knowingness, and they know what it is to be known, and they know how much knowledge there is in unknowing. No, that last bit's too zen-smug. They know it's wiser to abandon yourself to clarity. Perceive the economics of the rose. The important thing is not who does the seeing but that the vision is had by someone. Like discoveries in pure maths. Yesterday, I found an exhausted bumble bee on the carpet under the reading chair. A heavy buzzer. I fetched a white saucer of sugared water for it, and watched as its hairy tongue – black fronds of a feather duster – squirted again and again out of its proboscis. Leigh looked at it, too. Its wings shivered as it revived; phew and pre-flight checks. The ends of its black legs were rubbery curves beneath the meniscus of the sugar water. We put it just as it was on the windowsill outside my room, to keep it away from Mouse, and half an hour later the saucer was empty –

Sonntag 9 Juli

Today and yesterday, I was trying to do some second draft corrections, but the sharpener (Blackwing, spinny) kept snapping the pencil lead – every time it got close to being good, I had to start again. Of course, this was distracting/frustrating, and I was frustrated I was getting so distracted. Something so minor, I should have been so much further into the forest, or at least the woods. There was no clearing for the alternative animals to enter. The words that would've been were replaced by cedar-smell of pencil shavings and the non-smell or ~~smell~~ of graphite. I was desk-bound, in a bad way. I shall have to do something, he said nobly – I shall be forced to buy my way out of this outsideness, this failure to operate. Meanwhile, I'll have to use the gold sharpener which makes squat not pointy ends. Interruption –

Drove home. Mum 'floppy,' so she was 'Lady Muck' and 'lazy' and stayed in bed most of the morning. 'I don't like you to see me like this.' She meant bald as much as floppy (although she was wearing the new wig, stylishly). I worry she'll suddenly get worse while we're in Suffolk.

Leigh, big and fed up of being big.

Montag 10 Juli

11:30 scan. King's. We waited over an hour and a half to be seen. I finished two magazines. All was 'normal' – measurements; the umbilical cord has three blood vessels; blood flow in the head took a while to find but was fine. I now have a photo above my desk. We saw Flip's lips, pouting; the rest of him was glimpses and strange angles. He is cephalic, hasn't moved, or has but has moved back. Raining still when we got outside.

Sometimes – today – this morning, what I start with seems to be grief. Someone else's grief. It's not prompted by anything, although I had difficult dreams: a man sat in my chair and refused to move, another man in another dream refused to sell me something. But as I was making tea, I started to think about Dave and Janice, and Marnie, then all the other children who have been born dead, and all the mothers who have had to deliver them. Just because some horror isn't happening to you, and has never happened to you, and in some cases may never happen to you (I will never have to take the bus home after a scan at the hospital, appearing to be a pregnant woman but knowing my unborn baby is dead inside me) – just because you are elsewhere doesn't mean that someone equally as important and attentive and hopeful and capable of suffering isn't right there, on the brink of it, or just tumbling into it.

Dienstag 11 Juli

I am looking forward to this holiday in a way I haven't looked forward to any holiday for years. We are going to be American, and it is not going to be a holiday but a vacation. It is very interesting that it isn't the other way round, with Americans going on holidays and Europeans taking vacations. They seem the more sanctified, while we seem more in need of ridding ourselves of ourselves. I know the meaning is departure from place – clear the cities, like the *Grand Départ* of Parisians in August, but I hear it more as the emptying out of soul-gubbins and self-stuff – the stuffiness of self. A vacation is an evacuation – as of bowel, as of troops, as of womb, as of civilians. Only these are the imagined workers, leaving through the little doors that open at the ends of the fingers and toes in this relaxation-visualization exercise. All those little women and others and men are leaving you now – can you feel them go? They are stepping back from the control-panels of your mind, and leaving behind the levers of your knees and elbows – but don't worry, your heart will still beat, your lungs will fill and empty and fill. Your heart and everything else doesn't need little people scurrying around. Perhaps, for you, they're not little people but little ants or robots. Howsoever you see them, feel them vacating your body, leaving it entirely relaxed – like an abandoned factory or a – no, just an abandoned factory. There's no more production-line, no more surplus labour. A peaceful revolution is happening, and the strikes have begun. Can you feel that? The last little workers are going out the little doors and onto the floor and strolling away from you – not scurrying, strolling – strolling with dignity. And you know that they'll come back if you need them – if there's a fire or a bomb goes off, or if your children need rescuing from a lion. The little workers can always appear magically back at their posts, but for now they are departing from you. If you listen closely, you can hear their little footsteps at the edges of the room – bye, bye, little workers. And they are closing little doors behind them. Now, I'd like you to count – in your head, not out loud – back from the number 10 all the way down to the number zero, and when you reach zero...

Mittwoch 12 Juli

I have been waiting for the new pencil sharpener I ordered to arrive in the post. I have only been waiting two days. Still waiting, though. But when I checked the website, I saw I hadn't ordered it, just put it on my watchlist. I was waiting to get paid before I spent that money. (It's not cheap.) Do I need a new pencil sharpener? Well, the current one has started to break leads. For about a month. They get almost to the right point of pointiness, then they snap – especially the Prussian Blue, which I've been using most. Also, it's not sharpening the wood as much as it used to do. This means that when I bring the pencil across the desk, grains of shavings drop there and on the page. I'll brush it off with a flick of the little finger, but then it's all on the hardboard. Disguising itself. Or, if I'm feeling punctilious, I'll sweep every bit directly into the bin. These are all tiny obstructions to work. For the nib of the pen, the sliver of wood is an upsticking root. For the palm, it's a lazy splinter that can't even be bothered to get stuck in. On the grand day the new sharpener arrives (Blackwing Long Point Pencil Sharpener – One Step), and assuming it works as well as the old one did, I'll just have half a dozen long-tapered pencils (including the Prussian Blue) ready to contribute, to do their thing, to accurately interpolate. It's not that I didn't try replacing the blade in the old sharpener. I did; and that sort of fixed it for a couple of days, but I think there's a bigger problem. The tip of the pencil comes out with a ridge halfway up it, as if one dunce's cap were wearing a second smaller one as a dunce's cap. Just now I tried to get rid of it, the ridge, by careful gentle pressured turning of the shaft – and snap. Inevitably, irksomely. But on the great day the new sharpener arrives, everything will be clarified. A bought technological product will redeem me. I have now definitely bought the new pencil sharpener. (Meanwhile, I could use a penknife, like charming craftspeople do in documentaries.) Am I writing about impotence and ageing? Flipper proves I'm in good working order, generally.

Donnerstag 13 Juli – *Bastille Day*

What are we doing? – what are we thinking we are doing? – increasing the population of this overpopulated planet by one; and not a frugal one, either. He won't be carried on Leigh's back in a soft piece of cloth. He will have a pram then a buggy then a pushchair then a scooter then a bike then a bigger bike. He won't be helped over a patch of grass to go pee-pee, he will have nappy after nappy. (We have researched, and found a service that collects, washes and returns reusable nappies. And if that doesn't work out, it'll have to be biodegradable middle-class nappies – without the plastic waistbands and absorbent crystals.) Even so, even if we mitigate as much as possible, it's still pure consumption from end to end. When I go in the chemists now, I notice all those little jam jars full of sweet and savory goo. When we go to the park, I see the amount of stuff a single Western baby has to travel with – what a caravanserai of coddling. Just in case. And all of this makes me think we shouldn't have – we should have been virtuous, and kept ourselves out of it. Good people still need to be born, but there's no guarantee Flipper won't end up running BP, or designing nuclear weapons, or driving an SUV the length of West Dulwich because they've run out of passata and the corner shop doesn't have the right brand. Not 'What are we doing?' but 'How guilty are we?' There's no doubting we are guilty. (Don't have any kids yourself.) But Flipper will only be a good if Flipper does good. We can try to be the guarantee of that. Well-meaning parents don't always bring up well-disposed children. I'm saying none of this to Leigh; I'm sure she's thinking it, too.

Freitag 14 Juli

I think about the baby dying more often than I do Leigh dying –
modern medicine, obstetrics, sonography. But there's a chance the
baby will die and Leigh will live, and then there's a smaller chance
that Leigh will die and I will be left alive with a new baby. I feel Leigh
dying is worse, because I know her and love her, and the baby's still an
abstraction, a maybe-baby. (Leigh would want herself to die and the
baby to live, I'm fairly sure.) (I'm not going to ask her.) Leigh might
still have another baby, after the death of this one, though it is difficult
to imagine us being brave enough to try for a while – and we haven't
got that many years left. It took time after the last miscarriage, but we
were being investigated. There was a future aim. Lying in bed, or at
my desk, I fast-forward through lives without Leigh but with Flipper.
Her mother comes to stay, to help me out. I don't want to, but I have
to bottle feed from the beginning. My mother reminds me I was bottle
fed. (In some of these lives, Mum is still impossibly here.) Among
all the other worries, it's the future conversations with my son that
get me most. How did it happen? Did I kill her? Would she be alive
without me? We'd share that guilt. I would really be the one who'd
killed her. In some fast-forwards, a female friend suddenly takes me
in hand – as Ballard describes in *The Kindness of Women*. There's grief-
sex, and trying to convince myself Leigh wouldn't have wanted me to
be alone. I see myself giving up my job, selling the house, moving to
somewhere small and cheap by the sea. I write the grief-book and do
interviews about it. I am suddenly old, and looking back on Flipper's
terrible, stymied life, or on his remarkable stability. All the times I've
told him what a great person his mother was, and how much she loved
him. And other times, I die, too – I kill myself and leave him in the
care of anyone; or I have cancer, and have to ask Tev and Simone if
they'd adopt. I go through all this, revise, wish against, fear.

Samstag 15 Juli

Drive to Suffolk.

Sonntag 16 Juli

Aldeburgh.

Montag 17 Juli

Dunwich.

Dienstag 18 Juli

Southwold.

Mittwoch 19 Juli

Walberswick.

Donnerstag 20 Juli

Westleton.

Freitag 21 Juli

Stayed in the cottage.

Samstag 22 Juli

Drove back to London. New pencil sharpener not here yet. It's coming from China.

Sonntag 23 Juli

And some days, like today, the air just feels friendly – even gravity seems to help. You have a difficult task, it's defeated you for weeks, and you watch as it completes itself, beneath your hands or within your mind. Sometimes the weather is on your side, and this weather may be hail rather than sunshine – perhaps the sting and drumroll of it is what you needed; the Unlikely falling from an unreal sky onto a sheltering city. It's not frogs or Lego, but it seems a slightly remixed physics – which allows the opening of possible possibilities. Or it might be the fright of the wind, stirring you like a heart-scan or word from a rival. Here is turbulence, the furl and unfurl of boughs of branches of leaves – undersides popping like Rodney Mullen's deck – seeming to be little more than energy being energetic. Surely there's spare for you. If even the humble H_2O plays kiss-chase with the moon-face moon, then your desire for the absolutely unreachable can cause you to swell and surge. Marble cliffs will collapse like sugar cubes; seawalls come tumbling down. Jerichoasts. And sometimes it's just the sun – the fact of the sun and the unlikelihood of our orbit; only thinking of that, seeing the smudge of its too-brightness behind smog and cumulonimbus and cirrus and satellites – thinking how difficult and different the real physics of it is, so that even Newton got it wrong by getting it right (he printed the timetable but misprinted the bus, the road) – cold and bouncy Space and its inhuman traverse, the weather of nebulae and the phut of black holes, the heaviosity of Higgs bosons and the wow of the fields of spooky-action-at-a-distance. When I stir my constellated coffee, I am not disconnected, though I'm hardly broadcasting. Look, I have motive force. Within a bubble of meaning, within an atmosphere of doubted doubts, I can refer to noumena, to unknown unknowns – and a start that has been pointed at is different to a star that hasn't been pointed at; I don't know how, or why, but it is. (It's been befriended.) Today I can say anything. Today you can say anything. You are forgiven and you can.

Montag 24 Juli

My mother said I never should – I should never sleep with anyone I didn't love. And this seems to me very similar advice to My-mother-said I-never-should *play*-with-the-gypsies-in-the-wood. The clapping-song-mother is saying, 'Don't become involved with people who don't love you enough to stay around.' My mother was saying, 'Don't become involved with people you don't feel enough towards to think there's a chance you'll remain with them.' My mother gave me this advice on the day I went off to university. 'And mama used to say, "Take your time young man."' Apparently Junior Giscombe's mother gave him the same advice. Had my mother heard his song on the radio? She came into my room especially – perhaps she'd said to my father, downstairs, that she was going to have a little talk with me; perhaps it was just between us. I don't think she spoke spontaneously, unable not to blurt out her main worry. This was what she chose to say, after thought – and now, this interests me. She didn't tell me, 'Don't do drugs,' and her main, her only message wasn't, 'Find some friends you can trust.' What she said, I see now, makes two assumptions: one, that I very much wanted to sleep with someone (and might do so even if I didn't love them); two, that without question someone I didn't love would be prepared to sleep with me. Now I'm writing this, I remember that she had just asked me – gently, in her clear, clarinet-like voice – 'I don't think you have already, have you?' Did my mother use the word *virgin*? I don't think so. 'Toby, I think you're still a virgin – aren't you?' With her standing in the middle of the room and me sitting on my virginal bed. Actually, that is a possibility; it's her kind of word. And yes I was embarrassed, and – I'm sure – didn't adequately return her love and concern. I might have said, 'Okay.' I think it unlikely I made a formal promise. 'No, Mum, I won't.' If I did, I broke it – but not in my first year, not until eighteen months later. Leigh and I haven't had full sex since the pregnancy test. We're too worried it will disturb things, cause a miscarriage. It isn't that I don't find her attractive – I like her increasingly. We're superstitious, perhaps. If we take a vow of celibacy, it will appease the Gods.

Dienstag 25 Juli

'It's not a good idea to sleep with someone you don't love.' That may have been how she phrased it. Five foot three tall, with – I think – a perm of undyed hair, and clothes that often contained dark pinks and rich greens but were never black or white or monotone. She liked nature patterns, still does, slightly abstracted; jungle leaves, not jungle print. 'My advice would be, don't sleep with anyone you don't love.' As I get older, I think it's wiser and wiser. But I still think it was the wrong advice. For me, for then. (Sorry, Mum.) It's not that I needed to be told, 'You should sleep with lots of people for practice.' Yet, in a way, that's exactly what I did need to do. What I felt, for years, was that I would essentially be married to whomever I first stuck with for more than a week – first fucked more than once. I didn't go out with people to see how it went. If they weren't perfect, I wasn't interested. Could I have been more Romantic? I don't think so. My lover will renovate my life (La Vita Nuova), and I don't want to end up with the wrong life; I want a castle, culture, creation. The advice an imaginary uncle would have given would have been better: 'Sleep with one person you quite like, to get the virginity thing out of the way – it's become too much of a thing. You need to see it isn't that much of a thing. Because once it's out the way, you'll be able to – you'll be a bit more of a fucking human being, not John fucking Keats mooning over Fanny fucking non-fucking Brawne.' (I don't know how my imaginary uncle knows about Keats, although I suppose my real uncle did. I have his edition of Shakespeare's plays.) Not that I would give this advice to my possible-son. Firstly, it might not be appropriate to him, to who and how he was; secondly, I think my mother's advice is good – generally – once you're not a virgin. But I am very glad I slept with women I didn't love, and I wish I had been more relaxed, more playful, more confident, and had slept with more of them.

Mittwoch 26 Juli

When I lay out my away-from-home writing kit, as I did in Suffolk, I realize it's a sequence of black objects: black notebook, black inkpen, black pencil, black pencil sharpener (until I had to settle for a blue one), black laptop (see earlier), black iPhone. I want non-brand, and as close to non-existence as possible. (Black is not not.) Maybe I should replace my desk with a black desk, although it would exhibit the dust. About that Sunday writing: Should I feel bad that sometimes I write with ease? – as though everything was in its right black form and right white place. This doesn't mean on darkling glowing days I write stuff worth keeping, just that it immediately go-go-goes. Writers aren't permitted 'easy' or 'fun' (like on my secret Sundays). We have to agonize – to be taken seriously, we have to agonize over how agonized we are required to be, to be taken seriously. (We must we must we must improve our must.) (If asked, represent angst.) But jeez there's enough suffering in the overall enterprise – allow us our biannual exaltation, grant us the occasional moment of grace. Plain sailing, surfing, aquaplaning. (What are words worth?) Some stories, some combinations of words, it's not that we produce them really quickly, it's that they have been waiting a long time to be said – and emerge under pressure.

Donnerstag 27 Juli

You can change your orientation, but not your origin. What's happened to you, and in you, has already happened – it may be redeemable, even rewritable, but it's not replayable. (All's past amend, unchangeable.) (Print is guilt.) The art that made me was the art that made me; the boy that books built. The European canon is here. The songs that saved your life. A train heading north comes skirling past.

Mouse is avoiding me this morning, since a brief recline. I can hear him, pushing a plastic bottletop around the hard floor of the hall.

We have bought things for Flipper – things we think he'll like. We've bought everything but I'm sure we've forgotten something. There have been conversations with the others in our NCT group – the ones who have already successfully birthed live children into the world of equipment and entertainment. 'More muslins than you think you'll ever need.' I'm convinced we already have this more, but Leigh buys more more. If I enter the room, there is the cot I assembled – not for nights, the Moses Basket for nights. It's hard to believe that: 3 am and you're in charge of a baby. Deep in the darknesse of everyone else's sleep, and you're responsible for a breathing thing – one you love to the point of paralysis. What should I do? I find it hard to go into the baby's room because it still might not yet become the baby's room. It might just be a childless couple horror. Could we keep all that shit, branded, efficient, if it was for nothing but hope for the next? I think we'd have to give it away – although I'd feel it was cursed, because we'd failed. To destroy a perfectly good cot would be immoral. Even one that terminated in a hyphen. Baby shoes. We actually have actual baby shoes. They're horrifically cute.

Freitag 28 Juli

Sitting at my desk, writing in my diary – writing about sitting at my desk, writing in my diary – writing about writing about sitting at my desk, writing in my diary about sitting at my desk etc. Behind me, outside, the wind is blowing the wind to bits. I only hear it because it hits the leaves on the trees, and the twigs from which they reach, and the branches from which they stretch, and the trunks from which they tend. Just like I only see the curlicues and spirals always present in the turbulent air around me when they are signified by crisp packets and leaf-litter and woodsmoke flying through the turbulence of the air in spirals and curlicues. I often sit here and try to think about what I've failed to think about, because I have never spotted it – never spotted that it could be thought about – and because of this, I see I am trying to spot my blindspots; but whoever succeeded in spotting their own blindspots? Philosophers, mainly, but mainly philosophers work by spotting the blindspots of other philosophers and then by philosophizing that those blindspots or something like those blindspots are also their own. How can you be a philosopher, a lover of the truth, when the main discovery of your philosophy is that you don't know what the truth is? What is it that you are a lover of? Are you capable of love at all – of love oh love oh careless love – if the object of your love is no object, is imperceptible, inconceivable? The first thing that philosophers demonstrate is that there are no such things as philosophers, there are only philophilosophers, lovers of the love of the truth. But the first thing that philophilosophers demonstrate is that there are no such things as philophilosophers, etc. Even though I am a writer, not a philosopher, I see that I can't see what I can't see – and yet if I see that I can't see something, that's surely a way of sensing the significance of its presence in the turbulence of its absence, isn't it? If I write. Therefore, I love the trees I cannot and will not ever see, but that – sitting at my desk, writing in my diary – the leafy wind infers for me. If I write and if I write about if.

If if writes

Samstag 29 Juli

Some days.

Like today.

I don't know why, but some days the air just feels friendly. Even gravity helps you.

You have a difficult task, it's defeated you for weeks – and you watch as it completes itself beneath your hands.

Sometimes the weather is on your side. It may be hail rather than sunshine – perhaps the sting and drumroll of that is what you need. The Unlikely, falling onto the city. It's not frogs or Lego, but it still seems like physics laughing.

Or it might be the fright of the wind, stirring you like a heart-scan or news of a rival. Here is turbulence, the furl and unfurl of boughs of branches of leaves – undersides popping like Rodney Mullen's deck – little more than energy being energetic. Surely there's spare for you?

And sometimes it's just sun – the fact of the sun and our orbit of it.

And a star that has been pointed at is different to a star that hasn't been pointed at.

I don't know how or why, but it is.

Today I can say everything.

And today you can say everything.

You are forgiven and you can.

Sonntag 30 Juli

I am sitting at a desk in a room different from the one you are in now. Unless, that is, which is very likely, you are me reading this back, sitting at the same desk in the same room. If that is the case, I leave it up to you to decide whether the changes to the room that have taken place, inadvertently or deliberately, between my now and your now, have altered it to the extent that it can no longer be thought of as the same room. Although I expect, whatever new paint there is on the walls or carpet on the floor, that we would agree the desk is the same, even if you and I are almost completely different people.

I am sitting at my desk in an inner room subtly different from the one you are in now. Unless, that is, which is fairly likely, you are me re-reading this book, sitting at this same desk in this same room. If this is the case, I'll leave it up to you to decide whether the changes in the inner room that have taken place, inadvertently and deliberately, between my now and your now, have altered it to an extent that it can no more be brought up as the same room. Although I expect that whatever new paint is on the walls or carpet on the floor, we could agree this desk is the same, even if we are completely different people.

I'm subtling at my desk inner room settling difference from throne urine wow. A nest, satis, witches veiling like Leigh, you army greed greed greed in his brook, subtling ass this aim desk hithers aim moon. Phthisis surcease, shy'll sleeve a stop stew tudor design sever exchanges environ vavoom shat hive shaken space, evidentially an deliver a sassy, atween minnow and uno, a vaulter hit twinset ent petite cannonball bee sawn-off ass this emerald. Also high aspect trot trot oven you panties nova Walsall Karl Pétain les fleurs, weaken angry fist test fizzer's aim, eye Venice weir gombeening tiff rent purple.

Yams sheetings shats nigh desc inna roo mescalin dish insurance shroom shine shearing ow. Annex, shat ish, wishes shaling lightly, yaw nigh creel creel creel inish shook, shuttlin ash hiss shame thesp shivers shame noo. Thesis saucisses, shill leaf

Montag 31 Juli

At the desk, I am in space – I know the earth doesn't go down forever, and that the exact point where I was a few moments ago is
hundreds or thousands of curving miles away, beyond the exosphere.
Yes, gravity; yes, the laws of nuclear reaction, of wave and particle,
that bring light to us – across invisible fields, through dust and non-
aether. And I am not only human, but I also (losing focus) go down
to a quantum level of interference and emergence. What occurs
there is full of bounce. Carbon, hydrogen, oxygen and a few trace
elements are writing this: calcium of the bones, water of the blood.
A choreography and beautiful riot of electrical activity flows around
my brain, which corresponds with but does not ape my mind. Even
so, the common sense of scale – reinforced by the measurements
of sport and the temporality of hospital waiting rooms – is where
I live. Sometimes I'll write about the melancholy of a robot or the
impersonality of gloop, but usually I am populated by small and tall
humans in rooms and beyond, in trouble and beyond. I'm the model
village in Legoland, seen by a Lego construction worker. I'm inside
the insides of my characters, looking out through their eyes, limited
by their limits.

Small humans.

Dienstag 1 August

The new new pencil sharpener has arrived. It works. Now I can forget it. Except it's blue, rather than black like everything else (retro pen, printer). An identical replacement to the original tank-shaped one is, as Dad would say, 'silly money'.

After his health scare, Walter has taken up skydiving.

Mittwoch 2 August

I think it's my – not my job, but I don't want to say vocation. Oh
God, it's my *task* to see things clearly, think them complexly, feel
them deeply, and then write them clearly. I was going to put *simply*;
that, however, suggests Hemingway-Carver. (Should I say think-feel/
feel-think (Hello, Mouse – settle down) to get rid of the dissoci-
ation of sensibility?) Despite Romanticism, and all the smeariness of
Wagner and the fragment-kultur afterwards, I think I'm still more
song structure. Electron microscope. Dowland, Gibbons – English
confines of moderated discord and ironic resolution. Pages dark with
print, like the oblong of a sonnet. Embarrassed – shamefaced beauty,
shyly adored. Oh dear. Blushing. He's so peachy. The postcards on
my big green baize noticeboard right now are Dürer: I should go to
the zoo, and look at the golden lion tamarins, the pangolin, the rats.
(Bye, Mouse – where you off to?) (I do appreciate you, kitten.) Or
up to the Horniman, to do some drawing. But I'm never going to get
anything other than basic animals (pigeon, crow, seagull, fox – yes,
rat) into my stories. Albrecht Dürer (1471–1528). I think he may be
my favourite artist, now – taking over from Hans Holbein. Maybe
I'm just going onto animals and off people (nobs) wearing bit of dead
animal; even if that is Christina of Denmark, Duchess of Milan. (I was
writing a whole book on her.) To see the bristles on a hog, and paint
them with a hog-bristle. Mouse has firework display of whiskers
curving-carving out from his split-V nose: tremor-touch of them as
he swifts my earhole. In his coat, stripes the colour of this off-white
paper alternate with stripes of ink-black, with desktop browns in
between – desk-in-sunlight browns. Dürer should be here. He'd see
better than I; but maybe he only drew from the dead sample. Never
read a biog of him. I expect he liked his chickens clucking, though
it's a bugger to get their shapes right. His horse of 1503! That's art.
Seeing and seeing and seeing, then lines.

Donnerstag 3 August

Time – I still have a bit of time, before the baby's born, or before whatever goes wrong goes wrong. (Fingerscross.) And Mum. If Dürer is my favourite artist then my favourite writer, if I've got my detail-head on, is Gerard Manley Hopkins (1844–1889). I don't think there's a word-combination I love more than 'dapple-dawn-drawn'. (It would've been too obvious for Elizabeth Fraser to give that as title to a Cocteau Twins song; instead, we have 'Pearly-dewdrops' Drops'. Same hymn.) You can sense Hopkins' bodily eagerness (beneath the cassock) to ram, ram, slam all he seefeels into fourteen lines. A magic square. No wonder of it. If I should die this very moment... He does colour, scale, motion. And *sound*, he doesn't want to miss a click. Ycleped: 'My heart in hiding/ Stirred for a bird, – ' Ridikka-lick-a-lick-alouse. Think of Keats (my ultimate), for like him Hopkins is compelled-compiled to load every rift with ore, ride every lift with awe, riff feathery odes galore, lift leathery toad with claw, if every either/or. He turns his back on turning his back on himself, with mischief aforethought. Gild every gift with gore. The richest rhymes, he can afford (though deliberately poor), and will pay 'sillion' if it gets him 'billion' and even more 'gold-vermilion'. All of Heaney, and most of me, comes from 'the achieve of, the mastery of the thing!' Like Rilke, he likes liking things. His ding-a-lings. As Celan (and Carroll), he buckles and hurls sense into translucence. What is the what. There's no chance for me to be so, to be so, so pliant, playful, plangent, plush. The rush and the push have been told to shh. Wilde killed vermilion, cerulean. What a gay day! Gaudy night. Whimsy petering out. It's queer fear here, and a crime to rhyme any time. Close your prose. Close it! Reading – a gaol. Thomas doubted Christ's cock, thrice. Bodied forth, the green carnation. G.M. foods: manly manna; generically mollified. Eat me! Soft-sift, all-alluvial, follow me follow, pukka-pukka-all-alukka hocus pocus do nimoka. If I could only, if only I could. Finnicky wank. I would if I could but I.

Freitag 4 August

Today is one of those annoying days where the day itself, the fact of its dayness, is annoying. Everything is interim; nothing gets to the thing of the thing. It's like one of those despicable jazz tracks that make people who might like saxophone, piano, bass and drums playing music together – makes almost everyone hate jazz. I mean, a track where every note is a passing note, every chord is midway between other chords, and so it makes the melody sound inconsequential. With no solid ground, there can be no foothold, and no stubbed toe. I know this is a fair existential comment on evanescent life, etc. But sometimes it's just fucking annoying that what's advertised and what's received is all just fannying around. That's how today makes me feel – jazzed and jizzed. Wankety wank. If I were a child in the 1970s, I would be described as *fractious*. On other days, everything feels like accomplishment; there are major chords on every half-breath. But even writing this is substandard to established reality. E minor diminished 7th. Stop the caffeine *ands*, with their consumerist question marks!?

Holly and Nirpal for dinner this evening. Our turn. We agreed we can talk about anything but teaching.

Samstag 5 August

I've spent too much time on this, instead of saleable fiction – I should write, instead, a gripping but moving story with a sympathetic central character readers can root for, with a bomb under the table, with dialogue. Somehow, if I'd tried, I doubt I would have written anything worth writing. I am both too preoccupied and not preoccupied enough (9 months of it) – when I'm in the middle of the shit, I can produce something; it's the peripheries give me lack (like fashion magazines or Pot Noodles). If/When Flipper is born, then I will have to earn more money. Perhaps I could write a crime series, featuring a detective completely not like any other detective, and completely not like me. It is hard to see my writing, rather than me teaching others to write, becoming profitable again. It is unlikely I will ever be a going concern. No, I don't *spend* time on this, I share time with it; and I'm not trying to create worth, add value added, discover gold. I am sitting with the potentially sayable. I am staying with the trouble. I am paying attention to the paying attention to the paying attention. And this *has* to be failure – it has to exist as *I don't know*. Does it? I don't know. Fuck it. It doesn't *have* to exist. I'm trying to find reasons for my unreasonableness. I blame Literature. All those fucking lovely writers who made me want to be a writer. Toby Literature. Not to become a writer, to *be* a writer. Donne. Keats. Beckett. Plath. Gorgeous cunts. They left me no choice. Modernists. Romantics. Metaphysicals. At a certain time, in my twenties, I heard footnotes echoing behind me – I was deluded enough to believe I would have a textual history. Mouse just puked on the landing. He brought up something green that wasn't grass. His timing couldn't have been more perfect – and how completely appropriate: animal nausea, kitten vom. I give up. I quit. See you tomorrow. Whatever was in the puke looked like chicken chow mein or entrails.

Sonntag 6 August

Sometimes, I write a comma and then immediately doubt the comma, and through that doubt, start to doubt myself as a writer on that day, and then myself as a writer at all, and then writing as an enterprise for anyone not dead. Is there really any need for that comma after that *Sometimes*? Isn't it just too English and finicky and teacher-pleasing and repulsive? Won't it stop people reading, because they'll think this is all written by a comma-y kind of person – and didn't they pick up this book to escape the particular punctuation of their lives? Is there really any need for this book anyway? Haven't enough books made and remade the moods of each moment? If I want the impossibility of writing, isn't there already Kafka, who writes the impossibility of writing better than anyone else ever could? Hasn't Kafka, in blessed fact, written page after incomparable page about the impossibility of writing anything at all? And if, on this day or that, Kafka isn't quite the right flavour combo of frustration, despair and collapse, then haven't – as a handy alternative – we already got Pessoa's boredom, melancholy and self-abandonment? Or Woolf's panic, self-disgust and despair? Or Plath's self-abandonment, pride and collapse? Shouldn't that opening sentence have read, 'Sometimes I write a comma and then immediately doubt the comma...'? Or rather, to avoid nonsense, 'Sometimes I omit a comma and then immediately doubt the omis-sion...'? Or better, 'Sometimes I omit a comma and then immediately doubt my use of the word "omit"...'? Or 'Sometimes I leave out a comma and then, after a moment, start to doubt my use of the word doubt – which grammatically started even before I used it...'? Did I not vow to leave *omit* behind me, along with *rather, therefore, hence* and *nor*? Have I acquired the writerly gravitas to ascend from *worry about* and *angst over* to *doubt*? Isn't it the most pretentious thing of all, for me (unKafka) to doubt my doubt? (Who has that time?) No, the most pretentious thing of all is for me to doubt my doubt about my use of the word *doubt*, in a sentence with a comma that hasn't been omitted.

According to Dad, Mum is much worse today.

Montag 7 August

'Why are there twigs under your loo?' Manny, Holly and Nirpal's youngest daughter, 8, asked this – after a visit upstairs while we were having tea, yesterday. They are not twigs, they are sticks of pine kindling. I bought them from the garage, but had to put some of them beneath the base of the toilet because it was starting to lurch to the side when we sat down. These improvised wedges have now been in place for about eighteen months. We will have to book a plumber to replace the rest of our broken bathroom, and it's not worth getting rid of the twigs before he comes. This year our house is one hundred and eleven years old. I can explore it whilst sitting here; all the small and big things that need to be fixed. When Leigh and I both take a shower on the same day, water drips down into the kitchen – just missing the sink, but hitting whatever's in the drying rack. Three of the ceiling lights in the kitchen haven't worked for six years. There's a back panel to the oven that didn't fit back in place when the old stove went fzzt and had to be replaced, so for two years we've had concrete and fat splashes. Where the floor of the kitchen meets the floor of the hall, a telephone extension wire is stuck down with black gaffer tape. The paint on the front windows is coming off in finger-size flakes. Moths have eaten holes into the stair carpet where horizontal meets vertical. Behind the books in my bookshelves, to my right, there is a damp breeze and a ragged diagonal rip in the wallpaper – which, I can tell from a pencil mark I made at its end a month ago, is growing. At the back of the kitchen, beside the square pillar making the edge of what used to be the pantry, there is a widening crack in the wall. I think we have subsidence. Why didn't I mention this before the black gaffer tape? And the twigs? The patterned glass panels in our green front door don't match, and neither do the opaque glass panes in the bathroom. I pray the cellar doesn't flood. Water leaks through the roof when it rains and blows northerly. (I don't know which wind direction for certain, but northerly sounds more decaying than southerly, or the other directions.) Another house on our road, similar to ours, sold for over a million pounds. I haven't bought new clothes since February.

Dienstag 8 August

I remember Walter telling me about one of his schoolfriends, Karl I think it was, who discovered the joys of end-hyphenating words that are – you realize as you approach or begin them – too long for a particular line. As soon as he started doing this, Karl felt grown-up, released, and wrote a whole exploratory story. Yes, he was an eight- or nine-year-old boy at the time, but he was still telling friends about it a decade later. Those mid-optional word hyphens ('eight- or nine-' not page-side) are the ones I find least satisfactory. They are like ragged edges of horizontals – guttering or broken ladders – that give you tetanus scrapes on your ankles as you walk past them. I mind them much more than the levitating em- and en-rules, arrows travelling too fast to need heads, or distant starships capable of near light-speed. Dashes won't blood-poison you, they'd just have left a perfect hole through you before you knew it – a self-healing hole, because they're supercool. Cosmic rays. Byron dashed through his prose, and Woolf, and Keats – used them instead of full-stops or commas – used them to show thought-breaths; with many dashes, the prose starts to skim over the page like ducks and drakes, interfuckingalactic ducks and drakes – across the smooth surface of the multiverse – flat yet curved – concave and simultaneously convex – we're inside it at the same moment we're escaping from it. w/r/t this & this & this. I wanted to invent my own punctuation mark – which would be a long dash with a small loop midway through it, on the top or the bottom: which would mean, 'this loosely follows, but paradoxically (in a good way)' for the up-loop, and 'this loosely follows, but paradoxically (in a way that will probably annoy you)' for the down-. w/r/t this & anti-this & anti-anti-this. (I'd also like a semi-semi- or, I suppose, quarter-colon, made of two commas; this would signal to the reader 'be prepared to be confused by the logic of this connection'.) My dash would be like a more specific, less neurotic colon – signalling that the sentence wasn't about to end, but might be about to jump to hyperspace – or squidge through a black hole –

Mittwoch 9 August

The twigs comment did it. Leigh forced me to find a plumber.
He's called Bill. Holly and Nirpal got him to do their kitchen and
everything else. He can come in October. Or maybe November.

Donnerstag 10 August

Not everyone knows what I'm talking about when I talk about a sentence. Very few people will carry their concern, even though they think they feel it, past the first five minutes. They will start to say to themselves, 'Is this really that important?' – meaning the presence or absence of a dash – and they will silently follow that up with, 'I wish we could move on to something else.' But we're not yet finished with the dash, which could be a gate or a slope or even a trip hazard (a tree-stump or a root) – one which turns a stroll into a stumbling run, if only for a couple of heartbeats. In any discipline – lute, ontology, skateboard, tango – it's those who are not only willing to bide a while but who are compelled to dwell, it's the obsessively present who begin to find the space within time.

That's a terrible way of expressing what manifests as filigree and fugue and fractal and funk. I sound like I'm saying nothing, and saying it in a corporate way. Time and Space and Space and Time. The dwellers acquire, no, they find themselves having grown entirely from within themselves, they sprout horns – qualities – balance, acuteness, reflex, expressivity – through caring about the world through caring (for now) about only one thing in it. They have also failed extravagantly at life-in-general.

And here I had to answer the front door to a pert middle-aged man, dressed up in a morning suit and smelling of affable-affordable aftershave. 'Natalie?' he asked. I said there wasn't a Natalie here. He looked surprised. 'Are you the father of the groom?' I asked. 'A funeral director,' he said. He had a hearse parked further down our road. I said I wasn't aware of anyone nearby who'd recently died. He said thank you, or indicated thank you, and went away. When I went upstairs and told Leigh she said Natalie was the name of the person we bought the house off. 'Strange,' she said. We know a Natalia, much further down the street.

Freitag 11 August

I would not say I've been *happiest*, it isn't that simple, but I have been most ecstatic – ecstatic to the furthest extent – and also most content, halfway through a sentence, midway down a page, sometime during a forgotten working morning. I have passed from one verbal inevitability to another, both illusions. In this close involvement, I – Local Writer Finds National Success With First Novel – have entirely ceased to matter. It feels as if I could not be interrupted, because what I am doing is important to more than just me. What needs saying needs saying not just for the sake of the work but for the sake of the world – and that is why the world is saying it, flowingly, through me. It means something that this feels like this means something. I have reached the condition of musicians who feel they are not *playing* but are *being played by* the music they are making. And this is the truth, even though I know that the inevitabilities are delusions, not illusions. They are subjectively mine, not out there for others, like the blueness of the sky. And I know Leigh sometimes comes in because she can't get a website to work, or she's heard someone's died – so interruptions are allowed. It would be too perfect if that was her now, coming down from the attic; it wasn't – it was sudden helicopter blades sounding for a second like footfalls. I realized yesterday that similes, which I've always found a bit suspect, because they are reversible, and the tiger can roar like a fire just as easily as the fire roars like a tiger, so who learns what? – maybe you're more familiar with fires than tigers, but they're both only ideas – then yesterday I clocked how similes are ecological, because they insist on connection. We are not separate from all the things to which we can be compared. A sentence glows with interdependence – each filament within it relating to, responding to, each other filament. It's all jungle music, from roots to dawn chorus.

Samstag 12 August

How much some people would hate it, hate me, if they read this, or even heard a rumour of its existence – that someone who could have been writing them an entertaining story of a man with a gun seeking justice was, instead, keeping a diary in which he noticed dust, his hands on his face, commas. Although it's safely private, I'm still defensive. I don't want to be hated. I still feel bullied out of certain attitudes. I want to be generally liked, and I think this is a terrible fault. It goes along with another pair of faults: the desire to please and the desire not to displease. I've written pages of self-justification, when I should be just like Haters gonna hate hate hate. That may be as wise as wisdom gets, on the issue of being hated. What would I put down here that I don't, out of fear of what people (who'll never read it or be told about it) might think? Positive things, I think. Statements that seem self-aggrandizing or conceited. Stuff about desire, sex, fantasies, yearnings. My own hatreds. I suppose, even to myself, I want to come across as better than I am. You're above that. And so I write from above and outside the figure bending over the desk. No, that's only occasionally – most of the time I'm fully down with my bad self, and the truth of what I'm trying to say is in the pads of my fingers, the smaller bones of my hand, the lifted weight of my wrist. Perhaps I should go back and cross out anything disembodied. No, I'm not all that self-censoring. I may start an entry with the feeling of being hated, but I usually manage to escape it, shake it off. Otherwise I wouldn't write the word *yearnings* or admit to their being a truth of what I'm trying to say. My back really hurts. Leigh has a painful stye – she just bathed it in salty water, and shouted ow! When I asked if she was okay (she's in the bathroom), she said she thought she'd put in too much salt. She's having a shower now. Wide splashes.

Sonntag 13 August

I see my desire made manifest, and ready to destroy me (as desires do, so my mother taught me). Once, I fantasized about girls who would be cruel to me; now I think of kindly women – I think of forgiveness: forgiveness for lapses of mind and collapses of body. I've been very reluctant to write about sex, in relation to me. No-one wants to hear about it, least of all myself. At a certain age, with me, it changed from desire for sex to desire for desire. I see my desire made manifest, and she is unwilling to destroy me – she can't be arsed; she has other, younger preoccupations. Desire feels anything but desire, in regard to me. This is a ridiculous but stereotypical situation. And then usually I realize I am attracted to Q because they remind me of B – of someone from much earlier in the alphabet. It can take me weeks to realize who B was, and it's usually dismaying. B was someone I liked but never desired. But with a younger appearance, and greater kindliness, and the possibility of possibilities, Q has become a week or a month's preoccupation. Nothing happens. I stick with Leigh. (Until I wrote her name, this was semi-fictionalized. Of course, I never consider any other woman, however kindly-looking.) I see my desire made manifest, and she is no longer – as she was for so many years – Louise Brooks. But the way I've been writing about her, she may still be Lulu. This neat little apocalypse, with dotted i's and dangling participles. Bearded as I am, and Father William-like, it is Picasso's *Le peintre et son modèle*. I don't have to look seventy years old; I could go back to looking forty-five (by shaving), and it would make no difference. Why sleep with someone who's merely desperate for writing tips? Your life remains monogamously faithful to your life, however many lives you fuck. He was a very changeable man. I think it must be worse for the promiscuous, when they look back at their erotic success: they've genuinely lost something rather than its illusion. As you get older, it becomes much easier to understand prostitution. (I don't mean sex work, I mean prostitution – as in self-prostitution.) The desire of some men to give an order and know it can't but be obeyed. The desire of some men to express a desire and know it will be fulfilled.

Montag 14 August

There are things so small-to-non-existent that I've never bothered writing them, but that now seems the very reason they should be written. I often begin with the imperceptible, in one form or another – and that's what I'm doing in this beginning, though more deliberately than usual. Because I am fairly sure that in these fifty-seven words so far, I haven't given the reader anything to see – except the ink on the paper. Seventy-six words, up until that full-stop. And full-stop – or period elsewhere – is visual, but less so than *paper* and *ink*. The narrow-lined off-white paper of this right-hand page of a black-covered diary. Black ink landing shiny from the inky nib of this black fountain pen between the narrow grey lines on the off-white. That's what I'm seeing, and yet other readers would see completely – or almost completely – other papers and inks, even in these clear sentences. Paper: some would see the tight ridges in laid paper whilst others would see the thinness of a reporter's notepad. Ink: some would see the clotted start of a page of blue biro, scratchings and spittings before there's a hollow flow; others would have no pen, they'd just see the round meniscus-ringed surface of the black ink in an inkpot. Other others would see ink-spills, ink-splashes, Scarfe and Steadman, and so many dry and wet variants that are beyond me – although I wrote the word *ink* in ink. But this is simple, carnival; we are all at the same party, the same Black and White Ball. It's those fifty-seven words above that really fascinate me. What are the other others seeing then, when I've given them nothing to see? When I write *small* do they force a child or something coming into focus under a microscope? Or going back to *things*, are monsters what they squeeze out? Or cartoon outlines of The Thing? Or models of Platonic solids in beige plastic? And when *imperceptible* comes along, is there an effort to picture that as a gap in plain view? I don't know, and I never will know. (See also 24 Mai.)

Dienstag 15 August

And what if I were to experience – to be present for – the total absence of absence. (I have felt something like this, fleetingly, while sitting, but a feeling isn't a presentation, an envelopment.) (I realize this opening sentence may be a meaningless statement, and yet it is less meaningless than *hearing silence* or *perceiving emptiness*.) Usually, we are not only separate from what's around us, but we're aware of everything out there in the worldy world being alienated from every other thing. Yes, sometimes we look at a sublime landscape and see creation or biome; we have a good sleep and feel we've woken to a refreshed vision of a renewed green. But in order to understand, we isolate. We do this as much to ourselves as to a Lego brick or a poem or a regional economy. And it's not that we maintain this, because even Descartes moves in five days and a few thousand words from I to totality – it's that we willingly put on the blinkers even for a moment. This creates the possibility of absence in a different way than of what's beyond our peripheral vision. (He's behind you!) I realize a diamond can't be valued from a satellite. Maybe, though, the problem is in this perpetual creation of value. 'What is being seen?' should replace 'What will this be worth for me when I exchange it with others?' or 'What can I use this for?' The problem is, we're hardwired for hardware – we treat the world as an ironmongery or an armoury. Yesterday, lying in bed around six am, I was stung by a wasp – or rather, my right hand reached for a hardness, moving, that my left elbow had felt. When the fingers tried to grab it, the crawler-thing, my thumb felt a stab and then a blossom of pain. This was very beautiful – as if a red and white chrysanthemum were expanding inside me. Of course, I swore, and tried to squeeze out the venom. I crushed the wasp against the wall with a bedside book. I took two paracetamol. But I wasn't ungrateful, and I can still feel the echo of the clarity of the sting.

Mittwoch 16 August

Tomorrow it will be one month until Leigh's due date. Her bump is very full and tight. She feels, she says, as you do on the afternoon of Christmas Day – after lunch, chocolates and cake. Her bellybutton hasn't popped. No brown line. The heartburn a bit better (she's eating fresh pineapple). Is uncomfortable in bed – with a mountain of pillows. I have to climb it to say hello.

Donnerstag 17 August

What's there when nothing is there? It's a good question generally, but I mean in the writing, when it seems I've said everything I have to say – written all the stories anyone wants from me, including myself, and made all the small observations. Because it seems I want no more of that do-able stuff; it's only the impossible interests me. And so, because I won't allow the faux-impossible, I've left myself with nothing. Not exactly 'I have nothing to say and I'm going to say it.' Because John Cage has a big fat 'I' as a start-point, and he also has the accoutrement of language. Because my nothing is as really nothing as I can make it, I'm removing myself, too – but for the moment leaving something articulate: a voice-activated voice that has yet to stop asking things of itself. It can't see but it can remember what it has seen. Not 'I have nothing to say…' but 'What kind of saying comes out of nothing?' And you, whoever you are, say, 'But that's impossible. Nothing produces nothing.' Not 'I have nothing…' but 'What is the subject of a subject without a subject?' And you, whoever you insist on being, say, 'I am not going to listen to more pretentious silence, or read more blank space – I did enough of that back in the twentieth century. I got nothing from it.' Not, 'I have not…' but 'Unnothing.' And you, whoever you were, go, depart in miffedness – taking your absence with you. Regard: A nothing after anger is exactly the same as a nothing after love. Although, because a nothing has no qualities, a nothing is not self-similar. It does not constantly change but it is never at any moment what it previously was. This, however, is an example of a nothing with time to be a nothing. This is a nothing waiting for a bus. And everybody knows nothing has no time to be what it isn't. If there is time, there is not nothing, if there is no time, there is no time.

Freitag 18 August

Yesterday, Leigh took her last aspirin and did her last Heparin injection. I'd prefer it if she were to keep going with something – even a placebo that we knew was a placebo. (It probably can't be a placebo, in that case.) No-one has mentioned any risk to the baby, at this stage, from blood-clotting. More likely is, she'll go into labour. She slept well last night for the first time in weeks. Also, had slippery elm in warm milk. Don't know if the two are connected.

Samstag 19 August

Lots of humans, I've observed, don't really like it outside the womb. When properly understood, their lives aren't about alcohol or overeating or power-grabbing or heroin, they are about the rigorous pursuit of a decades-long attempt to get back, get back to where they once belonged, before they belonged anywhere, because there was nowhere to belong. Captain Beefheart spoke dismissively of the kind of music he didn't make. He called this 'mamma heartbeat music' – by which I think he meant regular 4/4 beat (bahdoom bahdoom bahdoom bahdoom) surrounded by comforting chords that always eventually resolve themselves. Harmonies, optional. Some of us need this blood-boom blood-bloom blood-room blood-room. What's it like to be in the blood-room? What's life like for Flipper? Outside the womb, we're pulled down onto the surface of a sphere – one so vast it took most of human history to discover it was a sphere; inside the womb, we're afloat at a changing distance from the soft surface of a sphere – one that fits itself and our growth without us even realizing it. This unseen red cave is a place of sensation without comparison; it isn't warm or cold or perfect – the temperature is always temperate: blood-heat swishing through a swishing through of blood-heat. It is a non-place place of distance without separation, of location without travel; there's no measurement because everything is always found to be becoming at its origin. Time doesn't exist, proceed or lapse, as it does outside. There is emergence without event; things – and I really mean things (fingers, toes) don't happen, they come to be, they arise – and what they are is also where they are and when they are. Everything single feels self-caused, without even the vaguest structure of philosophy or physics or number. Of course, there is no I to experience this – and experience is exactly the wrong word. Experience depends on difference. The unborn baby is a hook hanging on itself. There is no upper case I, but there's the dot free-floating that seems as if j just as well as i might be whom it might join.

Sonntag 20 August – *My birthday*

If she doesn't love me anymore, perhaps there's someone else? If she doesn't love me, she doesn't love me – if she doesn't love someone else, she doesn't love someone else. Perhaps she doesn't love someone else. Perhaps, if she doesn't love someone else, she doesn't love. Perhaps she doesn't love any more. What I fear is the loss of love, and the loneliness that follows. What I fear is the loss of love, and the loneliness that follows the loss of love. I fear the loneliness if perhaps there's someone else. The loneliness that follows if she doesn't love me any more. The loneliness, the loss, the love, the loss. Perhaps she doesn't love any. And perhaps she doesn't any more fear the loss of someone else. Perhaps she doesn't love love. I fear she doesn't love me any more, and she doesn't fear the loss of me. Doesn't she? Perhaps she doesn't. Perhaps. Perhaps she doesn't love me any more. Perhaps she doesn't any more fear the loneliness of the loss of love. Doesn't she? Doesn't any? More follows – more and more love, more and more loss, more and more loneliness that she perhaps doesn't any more fear. I fear. I fear she is what someone else doesn't love any more. I fear the fear of loss of love of someone else. Perhaps and if, if and perhaps. The if of love – perhaps the if of more love. More follows. More of that. The more the love, the more the loneliness. That follows if that follows, and that doesn't if that doesn't. More and more. What if she doesn't fear loss of love? What if she doesn't any more love that someone, that someone that I fear? More more. I fear that she doesn't any more love that someone that is someone. I fear that she doesn't any more love that someone that is someone that is me. Is the loss the fear? Is the love the perhaps? Else the loneliness, and else the love. Perhaps what I fear is that she doesn't fear the loss of someone else and that she doesn't fear the loss of me. What is the loneliness that follows the loss of love if she doesn't love any any more? What is the loss? Someone is the loss. What is the if? Someone is the if. Perhaps I fear the loss of more loneliness. I love the loneliness and I love more the loss. The loneliness of loss that follows if I love someone that doesn't love me, that doesn't love someone else, that doesn't love. More of that. And the love. More of that. And the love.

Montag 21 August

I think of emotions as operatic, and I wonder if I'll feel them in the delivery room, or wherever my mother dies (if I'm there). (We're planning for a hospice near Dad.) Being English, v. English, as well as an imaginatively-adopted Mitteleuropean, I feel ashamed of my BIG emotions and embarrassed by the idea of **BIGGER** ones. This would not be the case were I a flamenco singer (though I am fairly sure some famous Italian tenors are psychopaths with unusually fluid tubes). I feel I have not felt all I should by way of love. Hasn't it mostly been recitative rather than aria? Has my brittle, upright heart performed anything like *Butterfly*, *Tosca*, or even *Peter Grimes*? (or even *The Magic Flute*?) Going so far into the emotion that you become the personification of that emotion – I am Jealousy, I am Rage, I am Love. Enthused, overtaken, possessed – ringing with it, singing with it. To the exclusion of everything else, everyone else. No *ahem* or *sorry*. I am comprised of grief. Cut me open and find remorse. But then I think, No, I bloody well *have*, especially when I felt I was losing it (Love). Melodramatic scenes in Big Sur. (Leigh was about to leave.) Opera composers (Bellini, Puccini, Wagner and Berg) distend the incandescent moment into a three- or thirty-minute glow. Humans are faster than arias. If they are English, by the time the soprano is reaching E above C, they are already putting the kettle on. But when they feel they fucking *feel* – only with irony aforethought, and an afterburn of abashedness. The bereaved will interrupt their sorrow, their weeping, to say, 'I'm sorry.' Do women from Iran apologize for crying over their dead children? Do the daughters of County Wicklow, or Kerala, or the Aka Pygmies, or the Roma of Romania – do they lose their flow mid-mourn? Do they ironize their aria with self-deprecation? 'Well, would you look at me now?' Maybe in Australia they do, or Canada, or even in fact India. (Big places, I know – but bits of bits of these places: Alice Springs, the suburbs to the south.) Places to which English abashment was exported, in return for gold, slaves, minerals, tea.

Dienstag 22 August

I can imagine that in Japan, grief could be expressed entirely through formal apology, the calibration of a bow, the crispness of its closure. In bits of bits of Kyoto. When my son is (maybe, I hope) safely born, will I sing over him wholeheartedly then shut up as I am silently applauded by the rest of the world who as they clap think, 'Ah, at last the English are becoming human.' (Princess Di.)

Sarabande. There is something ecstatic about breathing into a cat's mouth – especially when that cat is a skinny, happy kitten like Mouse. You look at them, and you have no idea what they see when they look at you. (Look at you, looking at them!) But when you're breathing together, nose to nose, and that's what you're thinking about, thinking your breathing and breathing your thinking, and the cat is undistracted, then it's like being groomed by a chimpanzee while grooming a chimpanzee. I was once stared out in an aquarium, by a tilapia, or some other overlordly fish with scales like scars and lips like a porn star's. It held my gaze, the fish, and defied me to look away. 'You know this is an atrocity,' it didn't say but conveyed. 'You know and I know. And I have an I to know it, and that is why it is an atrocity. If I were just an object, this would be no worse than keeping jewellery in a jewel box. But this is different – this is torture.' When I look at kitteny Mouse looking at me, I see the New Testament, not the Old. He seems to be suggesting there's some glee we could achieve together, some mischief to be co-constructed, but I'm too humanly stupid to be taught. (It must be killing, with a little prelude of torture.) He doesn't despair, though – only very old cats despair – and they despair *of*, they don't abandon hope in their own capacities. Mouse is fragrant, if slightly fishy; his breath is whiskery and his whiskers are breathlike. The inside of his mouth, seen when he yawns but always there, is like a short story – those pink ridges, those sudden teeth. (Novel equals big cat – even sabre tooth tiger.) After he has yawned, he looks satisfied, as if he has been assured he will never be poor. Life is a boat of white bone on a river of red blood.

Mittwoch 23 August

Leigh gave a cry in the middle of the night. I thought, *Here we go*. But she had just shifted awkwardly. In the morning, a couple of stretchmarks had appeared. 'Slippery elm is not a wonder-cure,' she said. Bad-ish night. She was upset, after getting dressed. She said she wanted things to go back to normal. She's worried she won't get enough academic work done before… Also, the wear of carrying the weight. We put pictures up in Flipper's room (the tortoises in blue, Quentin Blake, big Občanské fórum comet). Leigh sorted through the three bags of clothes my brother gave us.

I stared at the calendar for a few moments this morning – on which of these days will Flipper be born? It's possible he'll be so overdue he'll go into October. That would be difficult. Leigh is still sleeping badly, still kept awake by heartburn and backache. Horrible heartburn. I am building up to the day by working. I wrote a story this morning. Whilst I can do these, I am staying away from the novel. I should be reading more but I can't even find time to watch the research books I have lying around, late at the library.

The new pencil sharpener has arrived. It creates an inward curve towards the point – like an elastic membrane being drawn to a single atom. But I'm not sure the end is as exact as I'd like it to be. Yes, it's usable, but it's not what I wanted –

I just spent half an hour changing blades on the sharpeners, to see if I could bring the old two-step back to life. No joy. The new one will have to do.

No, who am I trying to kid? It won't do. Maybe it'll be okay for the shopping list pencils in the kitchen, sad old things. I'll have to order another like the old one, but a different shape (rhomboid) or colour (blue). I like the new sharpener's curve, but the point is annoyingly approximate. At least it works, and doesn't break the leads. I suppose that's something to be grateful for. Quel drame!

Teatime NCT reunion. Farha and Ted bring their baby.

Donnerstag 24 August – *Sartre*

On the desk is a Penguin paperback of Jean-Paul Sartre's *Words*, his autobiography (an astonishing book, so I'm discovering) – there is no image on the cover, only this sentence: 'I loathe my childhood and all that remains of it…' (The serif lettering is red.) Imagine being the human being capable of writing that. (The background is snowy white now gone grey.) Imagine being so absolute that you can make that verbal gesture. ('…all that remains…') No fondness, no forgiveness. (Hal saying to Falstaff, 'I know thee not, old man.') I immediately start to negotiate with Sartre: 'All – you really mean *all*?' (Jesus saying, 'Who is my mother? and who are my brothers?) 'Aren't you a little fond of some of the patisseries you used to eat? The sherberts and fondants?' (Michael Corleone saying, 'I know it was you, Fredo.') And when I fail to get any concession out of Sartre ('Quand j'ecris "tout", j'intends "tout"') I start to argue with myself. 'He's exaggerating – this is an aspiration to absolute loathing, not absolute loathing itself, because absolute loathing would make no such statement.' (King Lear saying, 'Never, never, never, never, never.') 'The absolutely loathed childhood would not be recalled even to be dismissed. It would already have been subject to liquidation. Nothing signals a passionate desire for acceptance more than a passionate denunciation.' (The Buddha saying, 'There is no wisdom, no ignorance, no illusion or cessation of illusion, no decay or death, no end to decay, no cessation of suffering.')

What if Flipper were to think so contemptuously of his childhood, for which we are responsible?

Freitag 25 August

Valedictory morning. Goodbye to Leigh, she heading for work, as if for the last time. I'm driving up to Ampthill to see Mum, collect my trunk. Will have to go carefully. Sometimes in the last few weeks I've thought myself more prepared for Flipper's death than his life – his wriggling little presence. (Janice and Dave and Marnie.) Perhaps it happens and then never becomes banal. Turned Mozart's Requiem off before the M1. Drove very carefully. Perhaps the thing of parenthood is an enforced permanent sublime. Unavoidable repetitious epiphanies. That being intellectual-speak for Love.

Samstag 26 August

Mum has never told me – keep Mum – that she, or how *much* she wants to live to see and hold Flipper. It's not the kind of thing she would say – meaning, she'd never say anything to make an already emotional situation worse. And as her son I've never said anything to her to try to encourage her to live longer – not more than, 'I hope you're feeling a bit better today.' Mum always feels a bit better today, it's just over the course of a month that she gets worse. If there were no months, only todays, she would live in a steady state of having slept well and feeling a bit better thank you. Her self-control is terrifying. When she hugs me, at hello and goodbye, I know she wants to hold on longer and pull tighter, pull me into being younger and capable of being comforted, but she lets go as soon as she thinks the hug has lasted its usual length. It's only when I rehug her, without breaking the first hug, that she accepts this as a statement of my need – my reasonable need not to let go – then she will tighten her arms around me again as if to say, 'Ah, I understand,' or 'If that is the case,' or 'Alright, then, let's doublecheck'. Even sitting where I am, writing this, I can remember very precisely those very precise – the last very precise hug. Mum, behind and beneath everything, is a scientist, and her quantities are always very carefully measured out, and her qualities – her outcomes – are calibrated as accurately as possible. Green is not green but celadine, leek, verdigris, emerald. Each hug is not only itself but also a specimen of a hug. Which makes it sound like a kind of distancing, and I won't deny that I know from observation there are other hugs from other mothers that say, 'There is nothing in the world but us, and we are beyond time.' Infinite, operatic hugs. My mother's hugs are more like botanical drawings, all the more beautiful for being anatomical, all the more intimate for being labelled – labelled with 'Goodbye, my lovely boy,' or 'Be brave, for my sake' or 'Yes, I do hope I live to see him, too.'

Sonntag 27 August

I find myself wondering how much life I have left – and so, how many days of Flipper's life I'll be alive for. What's the sum total? Is there an out-of-control truck heading towards me, yellow, loaded, and all the way from the Hook of Holland? Or just an average infarct? Which one of the two two-thirds is in the post for me – arrest or cancer? Or is it the one in-between, basic old age (plus dementia)? When I think about death generally, I am able to kid myself into acceptance. Here/not here – okay. Doable. But as soon as I have a health scare, and there's a specific, I'm like, 'Okay, anything but X – that's not how I want it to be.' (And I seem to become American when faced with the Grand Canyon of Decease.) We're all tourists in recreational vehicles. Every year, while visiting some site of outstanding natural beauty, we get out and walk over the grave of our future anniversary. But we don't shiver. If we knew we were going to die on *this one date*, everything in the world'd be magnified – before it began to crumple away from us. I don't know how my mother sees a red rose or a documentary about wildebeest or Van Gogh. She doesn't strike me as heightened, numinous. Even if she were, I think she'd keep it to herself. She told me once, years ago, about an experience she'd had. I can't remember where she said she was – not driving, not put in danger by it. Nothing in particular was happening, and then she noticed a pinprick of burning gold in the centre of her vision. By the time she'd taken it in, the pinprick was already bigger – (not her words these) now a spangle, a cigarette end, a blowtorch seen head on, always unvaryingly bright and golden. She watched it, couldn't help watching it, as the disc of it waxed and waxed until it encompassed her vision. Without squinting or flinching, she found herself staring into a beautiful spinning golden sun. I remember she emphasized how beautiful it was. I don't know if it stopped for her, but I think it began to shrink – at the same steady rate – almost as soon as it had reached its glorious maximum. While she was still taking in the fact of it, it was reducing itself down to blowtorch, cigarette, pinprick, nothing. Like the scientist she is, Mum described it to me as a visual quirk – not as her precious vision of the angels' hierarchy or of *gloria in excelsis*. It was very beautiful, she said.

Montag 28 August

Trying to find the right – correct – best – appropriate – apposite – apt – best – absolutely right – *mot juste* (never) – fitting? Trying to find the fitting word is like reaching – delving – reaching into a bag to feel about and fetch out the right thingie by texture alone. Thingie, object. Cut *feel about and*. Sticky wooden pencil stub, brass 2p coin, metal penknife corkscrew attachment, plastic comb, manky glasses case, blister pack (Ibuprofen), blister pack (Rennie), metal AA battery, cloth wallet – wallet! Or, eyeliner, vinyl Oyster card wallet, mascara pencil, pleasingly rough screwed-up dried-out wet-wipe, waxy tampon box, soft tangle of EarPod wire, plastic rape alarm, asthma inhaler – no, that's the rape alarm again, meaningfully ridgy edge of key, snakeskin (fake) purse – purse! I wish this bag simile was all there was to it, and would do, but while it gives a sense of hunting and rejecting, it misses rhythm, stress pattern, vowel music and consonant percussion, etymology, allusion, allusion-avoidance, appearance, class implications, avoidance of or overriding of avoidance of repetition, and most of all exact meaning. It also misses out that the thingie might be in someone else's bag – perhaps Oxford University Press's, or the Urban Dictionary's, or your Facebook friends', or maybe you have to make it yourself out of bits of other words. I've taken apart the decision-making process, which is nothing like taken-apart – it's feeling a feeling and judging a judgement. This? No. This? No… This? Maybe. This? Yes. Next. Hang on. Maybe the maybe was better than the yes. Then this? No – maybe. This? etc. I don't like 'trying' and 'fitting' together in the same phrase (trying clothes on in the fitting room; it's fitting this is very trying). Trying to find the right word is like reaching into a bag to find the right thingie by texture alone. Check the rhythm of 'find the right thingie by texture alone'. Ride a Cock Horsey to Banbury Cross. So, change it to 'find by texture alone the right thing'. Change it back. This is what I do all day long. This is what I spend all day doing. This – doing this – is how I spend my days. This is all I do all day. This is what I do all day. This is what I once did all day.

Dienstag 29 August

On Tuesdays, it's usually the binmen. Today it was the heaviosity of a cloudburst I heard first of all, before the shouting and plastic banging, before the grind of the bin lorry. It is still raining, with extra drops falling between the common drops. I think about my papers, in boxes in the cellar, and what life would be like if they were flooded, pulped. Then it's not even piles of drafts and proofs that appear to me, it's the notebooks and diaries I keep with me on the first floor. Almost thirty years' worth of things worth noting. With them, the anxiety is of fire. But who, apart from me, would care? I am terrified they, not any published books, are the best I've seen and thought and felt and somehow got down on paper – paper that remains paper in one vulnerable place. And now I hear a siren outside, through the microsplashes, through the accumulation of threat. It's raining tiny flames. And I know because it's the lesson I most often teach myself, that none of this lasts. And that this is okay. If I persuade an archive to accept my papers, I might delay their destruction – I was going to write 'their death'. My death. I might seek to preserve the vanity of the illusion of my significance for fifty or a hundred years. But there is no safety in human institutions or digitisations. The power will fail and the basement will be breached, eventually. For a while people will remember 'God Save the King' and 'Happy Birthday to You'. Children will chant folk songs like 'A Pizza Hut A Pizza Hut Kentucky Fried Chicken and A Pizza Hut'. I'll be gone – I, and anything I've written, will be gone long before the campfire times. What will be lost is what can't be summarized or hummed. Nomads need no novels.

Mittwoch 30 August

I don't write much about my day-to-day reading in here. It has an effect on me, of course, and sometimes – for good or bad reasons – it makes me despair. Very often, I want to be the writer of something I've read (say, Muriel Spark) – and I go away and, a short while later, or months or years, I write something *as* Muriel Spark. Privately, I'll know that the story or poem is hers – her rhythm, her sensibility. If it hadn't been for reading her, I couldn't have written as I did. But, to become a story, her original impulse and subsequent distastes have to pass through me and my colourblindness, my paranoias, my Ampthill. What she were trying to do was probably less to do with the shapes of sentences than exorcising an uncle or midwifing a kink. If it's plain witchcraft I encountered, in her words, it'll become piebald, lopsided, quiescent or sacrificial in my account of it. (Although I will admit tribute, if ever anyone asks.) I am milder, usually. Her carnival will become my sesshin, and my sewing will be patterned upon her orgy. Of course, I'll think her full of realness, with a mainline to idiolect and unprocessed cheese. When I admire, it's always crush – but wanting to *be* rather than to *be with*. If I had *her* hair, and her coat, and could be vicious because I am gorgeous, how would I angle my head as I entered the syntax of melancholy? If I had grown up running down the corridors of *his* life, would I be plural in my honeycomb heart and hive-like in the tessellations of my verbs? If I were as secure in the unity of my identity as him, and had such bad teeth, and bad breath, could I then monologue as whitely in the spotlight of memoir? Would I want to? No.

Donnerstag 31 August

Am I going back into a previous period – not time-travelling but imitating myself as I once was? I mean, if I write what I'm thinking of writing, which is a page about page numbering. Isn't it a bit of a re-do of that day I wrote about hyphens at the end of lines? And I'm not sure I'm as into doing this as I was into finally getting that down, three decades after being told about it. Walter's friend Karl, once he discovered breaking words halfway through with hyphens, at the end of a reporter's notepad line, and resuming them the line below, began to produce page after page – for the pleasure and power. As a boy of a similar age, I did not have a similar feeling about page numbers, which I began to add – as I'd been told to do so – at the bottom left of each verso page, and the bottom right of each recto. Yes, I felt proud and delighted and accomplished whenever I added another one – Look, I've written a fourteen-page novel! – but I soon became superstitious about them. I would not number a page until I had completely completed it; that is, I had not only reached the last line but had reached a point where I couldn't see myself having to make another mark on it. If there was any doubt of this, I didn't feel the page deserved to become the next number up. (I don't know if page numbers are cardinal or ordinal. Are they being counted or put in a specific order?) And although I only ever did one draft of anything, unless a teacher forced me to rewrite, I was always anxious about whether or not I need to add a bit – an adjective or another sentence with a vivid verb. (I very rarely crossed out, because that would be losing written words.) Even today, I will not put a number on a page before the lines are as filled as they're going to get – maybe not written to the end of the last, but completed enough that if I died it would at least make sense. Because the superstition, of course, is that to number pages on which you haven't written is to die and leave them blank. You, by adding a 6 or a 121, are not only being hubristic, you're also advertising your hubris. You are taking a bow before curtain up, before the play has even been written. If I were to number an empty page, I would listen to my heart, expecting not to hear it.

Freitag 1 September

Can't get it together today. Water birth tour, King's. Rain all the way there, on the bus. Our previous visit to the Maternity Ward, the room we went around gave off no sense of having witnessed important and extreme human events. It had no patina of loss or sheen of joy. Like other hospital spaces, it was designed to be wipe-free. It was just a room. There was no atmosphere of grandeur or even of specialness about it. Some of the equipment, the gas and air pipe, was specific – but it could have been in any ward. The water birthing room felt different. The consultant showing us around told us a baby had been born in there less than an hour before. Yet I'd felt as soon as I walked in, 'Something could happen here.' I don't think this was to do with the very large bath, which takes 40 minutes to fill. There were thirty people going around. When we entered the room, the lights were dimmed. They can cycle through different colours. 'Disco lights,' a midwife called them.

Samstag 2 September

Rain. I am forgetting what's happening. Do a grab-bag entry, rounding up everything in my head. I still miss Ziggy – his ginger nobility and gentleness. Not like scrapper Mouse the Cat. I still miss the Buffy glass that Mouse broke even though I didn't think it was part of the desk set-up – not at the time. Lèxi gave it to us. Buffy had become completely transparent, but her background hadn't faded. Leigh's flu got worse, and yesterday I went home by train – as it seemed Mum was going to continue her gradual fading, rather than cut to black. I couldn't concentrate on the train. Read a little *Great Expectations*, listened to a lecture on Hume and Kant. I phoned Leigh, who was in a miserable state – made even more miserable by the paper she has to finish by Tuesday. This morning Mum was very tired. I didn't stay long. Confirmed I had found the right recording of her chosen guitar music. ('Recuerdos De La Alhambra', Francisco Tárrega, played by John Williams.) I'm stilling trying to find the singer she wants for the 'Fear no more the heat o' the sun.' It's hard to bear, imagining hearing these next time through the crematorium's PA system. I asked if Mum wanted to go over her un-eulogy. No, a headshake. I read the cards on the windowsill from Caroline (Jessup) and Nanny (Rome).

Sonntag 3 September

One thing that's always with me at the desk is tinnitus. My ting-a-ling. I rarely hear it *hear it* unless I listen for it – listen out, listen in. It is a glittery, glistering sound; flittering-blistering, like something coming to the boil that shouldn't be boiled, because it's sentient though made of silver. A tiny man in a tiny orchestra playing a tiny triangle, on a loop, forever-until-I-die. Unless I'm unlucky and it becomes Einstürzende Neubauten, industrial; mutates and escalates to a Beethoven-level clangour of anger and fire-station alarm. I prefer the current pernickety mosquito of aluminium, the pre-cold sore tingle of annoying half-sound. Trinkle-trankle. Tinkle-tinkle. Maybe it is aluminum, not aluminium, and maybe it is bottle-top, not single silver bell. Hi-hat unclosed, washy cymbal, but also with Philip Glass needlepoint – Chipmunk's version of the orchestra stab of the Psycho shower scene. Or I think that I can hear the electrons bouncing through the wires of the house, like sperm up a fallopian tube. It is a presence, an opalescent presence. Tinnitus, tinnitus, its' – it's – it's a million billion trillion wristwatches ticking increasingly unceasingly, unpleasantly incessantly, infernally eternally. Yes, bitingly and bitterly/ it ticks on unremittingly/ within me quite exclusively/ as if to find a use for me/ that may be just traducing me/ or somehow introducing me/ to tingling jingles, chiming rhymes/ a-tisket a-tasket/ it won't cease if I ask it/ but loves to live repetitive/ so snickety pernickety/ invisible and risible/ tick-ticking like a – like a little flea/ as near as ear, as inner ear/ as inner ear and inner ear/ and all they hear is all they hear/ is tinnitus and tinnitus/ it is… it is… it is in us…/ in us it is, is tinnitus/ (as tick and tock as ceiling mice/ as stock a schtick as Doctor Suess)/ It sits kitteny/ it licks stickily/ it's Tintin's sins, isn't it?/ It's nuns' tits, it is./ It's Titus Stintsun's sinus stunts, int it?/ It's nits in tu-tus sittin' in situ in Inuit's tin units, innit?/ Flittingly a little flea/ fits flippers on its little feet/ then fleets its flatfoot flippantly/ in flippin' Little Italy./ Metal-peddler Petal/ copped a proper copper kettle/ up in Popocatépetl/ yup, to settle debts in Settle.

Montag 4 September

I spent a whole morning on that, yesterday. On tinnitusness. Don't know why. (Later: Flipper.) Patter songs. Pitter-patter of little songs.

I have been trying not to remember our grief after the third. Even at the time, I think I was quite concentrated upon not filling myself up with images. The surface of the hardboard reminds me of the beach sand where we buried the small remains. But they weren't really remains, because they were the left-behind not of something but of something that had failed to come to be. A failure without fault, and a non-existence that deserved our continued love. We hoped for a baby girl called May or Muriel or a boy called William or John. I hated the idea our world would become an unbearable place. We talked through what if. We discussed adopting an unwanted girl from China. And there were things we no longer did, because we couldn't. We couldn't watch *E.R.* Leigh couldn't stand seeing children in peril. I didn't want to see other people's happy endings, other fictional people's fictional happy endings, but neither did I watch horror movies. We couldn't be young. Even though we hadn't become parents, we were definitely no longer children – looking up, blaming, gaining power from lack of empathy. And we cried and and we cried and we cried more violently than I've ever cried. We climbed-clawed through one another. We slipped handholds, and did not go upwards. We hit where we'd bruised. The breathing. The taste of spinal fluid behind our teeth. We jarred. We did not arrive where we were trying to get. We fell, became a knot of hurt. I was glad when we got rid of that sofa – it had become desolate. Yet we still sleep on the same mattress, with the same small bloodstain. And I am very afraid this all might happen again, and worse, as it has happened and is happening to other people. The Miscarriage Association. It becomes lyrical – the beach, China – but it starts out as a form of absolute ugliness. I don't want that again. I want my damaged beauty.

Dienstag 5 September

Another scan this morning, probably the last one. Some worries beforehand, about the heartbeat. All fine – breathe – all fine. It is almost routine. Equilibrium as hubris. But I am not as anxious about this one as the early ones. There is some logic to this: we are nearer to a good end. But to hurt most the worst would come at the most unexpected time. Flipper looks remarkably like a baby.

Afternoon, yoga birth rehearsal at Brockwell Lido, with Una. Was enjoyable. It's still a very strange group – eight or nine pregnant women, most with their partners. So many potentialities.

Leigh calm. Calmer than me.

Mittwoch 6 September

When I'm lying on the lawn looking at the swifts in the sky, I see my floaters; also, sometimes, when I'm driving on the motorway to see Mum, and the windscreen is dry, and nothing is happening – no scary wall-of-freight, no undertaking psychos, no brake lights ahead. I don't see my floaters when I look at a page almost exactly 12 inches from my pupil. Searching for them just now, in between the lines of the diary, it's as if my vision is unflawed. But if I gaze at a distant and featureless blue, my eyesight becomes jellyfish in an underpopulated aquarium; or, more exactly, several chummy bacteria beneath the lenses of a microscope; or, with more grandeur, star-collapses seen by the Hubble. They are gummily transparent, asymmetric, and when I blink they jerk diagonally down and to the left, but, within a moment, they have travelled back to front and centre. I know they're not moving – it's my eyes lazing in some way I can't control. For a while I had an even more distinctive shape: a Mandelbrot set breaking up in a bath of acid. Over the years, that has fallen apart and reconstituted as something that looks more like an ampersand &. That's how I make it out – a mathematician, given my eyes, might see a delta function δ and a typesetter, a silcrow §. Like visual tinnitus, I was worried for a time that the presence of floaters would send me distracted. How could I concentrate with constant annoyances? When I was driving, their diagonal flicking made me carsick, and when I was looking at the sky the swifts were ruined. But, like most constant and little-varying things, the mind knows to tell the brain to ignore them – they're not potential dangers. Floaters are not sabre-tooth tigers.

There was a young foetus called Flipper/ who'd bound his Dad up like a kipper/ 'Be born in one piece/ or all hope will cease/ for Flipper rhymes with calliper.'

Donnerstag 7 September

Such long and dense rain, curdling on leaves, that branches fall off trees, and then trees fall down.

We're in limbo. I'm reluctant to work on the novel, knowing I might be interrupted for months. When will Leigh's waters break? Will they break at all? Imagine, Flipper born underwater in his own balloon. Them having to pop it. I've never seen a photograph of that. The waters breaking feels like it really will be the point of no return. But return has been an illusion for eight months – there was only, and still is, the possibility of a human or the possibility of a human loss. Thoughts of Janice and Dave and Marnie. We've been in touch, but they still don't feel like meeting up. Perhaps in December.

I ordered an exact replacement pencil sharpener – black, tank-ish. It is coming from America and costs >squeak<.

Freitag 8 September

Dinner at Holly and Nirpal's. Not much happened during the day – the cot arrived and I put it together with an Allen key and an attitude of patient lovingkindness (with the occasional 'fuck you you fucker'), feeling useful for once. Also at the dinner were a married couple I won't name. Now I don't know why, perhaps I shouldn't be writing this down when I'm drunk, but I remembered halfway through why I'd heard of this couple before – thought not met them. Nirpal had started talking about Leesa, daughter number one, nine years-old – but then Holly changed the subject; and I flashed on it: this couple were a local legend, in a very bad way. They had gone on family holiday in the South of France, or one of their parents had a house there – I imagine a sunny, paved driveway, quite wide, or maybe gravel. And for some reason, a confusion, the father piles into the car – estate – and reverses, and reverses over one of his three children – I think it was a younger daughter; she died. (Maybe there was a panic; he felt he had to go somewhere.) She liked to hide under the front wheels of the car. This was six or seven years ago. I think they moved, after it happened. But the story followed them. And the thing was, over dinner, I knew the mother could sense exactly when I'd remembered this. The father kept on the rest of the evening (he was quite boring; I think he'd retreated into being boring, as a grief-response), but between me and the mother it was incredibly tense from then on. Leigh already remembered – I asked her on the walk home. Holly and she knew they weren't mentioning anything to do with the dead daughter. Then I blundered in, and became aware, and instantly the mother became aware of my awareness. She had purple triangles beneath her eyes but her nails weren't bitten. The kitten had chewed a sock to bits, when we got back. Empty house, no children. Yet. It was one of my favourite red and black stripey socks. I am not unfeeling.

Samstag 9 September

Put formally, I am afraid of having to mourn for my mother and also my child – but I'm also anxious about mourning and celebrating on the same day. I would be doubly wrong. Mum could die the moment Flipper is born. Where should I be? Where would I prefer to be, if I could be at the wrong place by mistake? He asks himself where his greater duty lies. He decides it is with his mother, as she is unique, and there is always the chance he will father another child. But I will only have one first child, and I will have missed its birth – out of duty. Out of being in the wrong right place. My internal monologue is this: *Please, no – please, please no – please, God, no – God, please no – no, no God – please, no-God, no – please, Whatever, please.* As I said yesterday, I try not to go near this. This bullying grief. Don't hit me again. Get off Leigh. We are shy – pain-shy. What's it like to have no mother? I remember when I was, say, ten years old, accidentally discovering a holiday friend had a dead parent – I felt angry at them for not carrying a sign to warn me that they were other. A black veil. How could they swim in a Dordogne pool or play table tennis with no mum? How was it possible that I'd mistaken them for normal, like me? What they had suffered was cruel to everyone else, all of us still-loved children, because we had to find some perverted kind of acceptance – when all I wanted to blurt out was, 'Why aren't you dead, too?' How can anyone continue to live when the cause of their life has ceased existing? It's unfair on me that you're such a weirdo. I don't want anyone to force me to feel guilty for just being normal. This is the conservative impulse, the seed. No-one could be more normal than I am. Take your difference and your suffering far away from me, because they're making everyone feel bad. Where are the security guards? You're bumming everyone out, man. Anathema and shibboleth, leper and excommunicate. Can't you see the world would be a better place if you and your kind didn't exist in it? Can't you do us the favour of disappearing before we are forced to eliminate you? Delete the poor, juice the unproductive, shame the compassionate, and all in justification of a higher justice: what's right – not what's good, what's *right*.

Sonntag 10 September

Rain so thick it curdled on leaves, and branches fell from trees, and trees fell.

Leigh's jaw aches, from being clenched when she forgets to unclench it. Mine, too. She made a venison stew today that went wrong, curdled. A few days ago, she made a stollen that failed to rise. She is trying to be organized about Christmas. Yes, Christmas. These setbacks annoy and depress her.

This afternoon, for quite a while, Flipper didn't move, so Leigh had a bath to get him going. She wanted me out of the house. I went to the British Library and ended up reading essayists, Johnson, Hazlitt, Pritchett, Wyndham Lewis. After dinner I finished painting the radiator in the second bedroom – five coats in all. Leigh's dad is coming tomorrow to put a new radiator up in the kitchen. Nesting. While he's here, I'll be quick-visiting Mum.

I don't think I've thought enough about Leigh becoming a mother, and what that will mean to her. Instead, I've been thinking about it through thinking of my Mum. We talked about it this afternoon.

[Marginal note in pencil sharpened with blue pencil sharpener:

Things having a trajectory towards their use: the buggy, the changing mat, the clothes in the drawer. I wake up and Leigh puts my hand on her belly. The movements below could be a child under a duvet. An egg-shaped bump which constantly appears is probably a knobbly elbow.]

It's only a house. Eventually, someone else will buy it, move in and pull up all the carpets. They'll see the gaps between the floorboards and know the place was *built*, and that it can and should be rebuilt. It needs improvement. By then, we'll be somewhere else. But for now this house is ours – unless uniformed men kick down the door and tell us to leave. We have been reassigned, they say, we are not told to who or what. Five minutes, that is all we are given to clear out – a suitcase, another, a rucksack. Mouse has run out into the garden and away over one of the walls. I spend two minutes trying to find him. From my desk, I grab my pens, this, my laptop, hard drive, phone charger, Keats' *Poems*, woodface, a metal water bottle, spare glasses, what else? – one minute. Upstairs, I grab some clothes, a second pair of boots, a photo album, and then we are standing on the opposite side of the road. We watch as all the front windows of our house are opened, even that one we'd thought was painted shut forever. The rest of our possessions begin to be thrown onto the gravel area behind our front wall. Where foxes shit. There is my first guitar. There is our ladle, our television. The neighbours come out of their houses and begin to pick up whatever takes their fancy. Passersby join in. We watch. We are ignored. The soldiers or police start to pass items out the front door, where a queue forms to take potluck. We would have expected that neighbour to like that Anglepoise lamp, but she turns and throws it on the ground pile. She rejoins the queue. I did not save the rhinoceros and the Mercedes, and already I regret it. Where will my emblem be? Our plates are all broken, though they were chipped anyway. We whisper to one another. We try to think of what we *haven't* seen ejected from what used to be our house, back when we were planning an evening in bed. I haven't seen some of the pictures, the two Auerbach etchings; Leigh hasn't seen her Japanese prints. Is it possible one of the soldiers does art valuations? It is now dark and will soon become cold. We have watched enough to know what happens. Our neighbours ghost us. If we move towards the house, a rifle pushes us back. This is no longer our territory. We must find a diminished life elsewhere, and try to think of something other than rage and revenge.

Montag 11 September

I have to be in two places, and I can only be in one.

When I'm with Leigh, I feel that Mum's going to die without me there; when I'm with Mum, I sense Leigh getting anxious – and I think about a sudden set of contractions set off by this, and me not back in time for the birth.

I go to see Mum. She says she's fine. 'I'll be here for a while yet,' she says. Then she says, 'Long enough,' and I wonder what she means.

I think I know what she means, but we've never spoken about it explicitly. Had the talk. But towards the end of my visit, she said, 'You should be where you should be,' she said. I got the feeling she was sending me away.

Maybe when she's gone into the hospice, things will be clearer; someone will be able to tell me a likely date. I have no idea how it happens. I suppose it depends how fit you are.

Mum seemed okay, for the time she was awake. She offered to make me a cup of tea when I arrived, but that would have been it for the afternoon. 'Zonko,' as she says. So, I made the tea. For some reason, Dad had to go out. Even with him there, the space of the house feels different, knowing that she'll be absent from it; imaginary echoiness.

New radiator in the kitchen done. I didn't even see Leigh's dad or get to say thanks.

Dienstag 12 September

Leigh will be induced this Friday.

We went in to see a Registrar at King's this morning. Of course he was young, brown haired. We thought we were going to talk about whether she could have a waterbirth. But he was concerned about slightly increased chances of stillbirth over term. He recommended Leigh, because of her age, and history, be induced at 38 weeks. 'If you were to ask me what I'd do…' As far as I was concerned, he'd already said, 'unexplained stillbirth' three times – after that I was likely to agree to them delivering the baby wearing clown costumes, if it might lower the risk. He then did a sweep – said he could touch the baby's head. This happened behind a drawn curtain. Leigh asked, loudly, 'Has he got a lot of hair?' She's heard that heartburn equals hairy baby. Her cervix has opened a little. Induction might take a day or two. Lexi is coming for tea. She will come and stay over at the weekend.

Later: Leigh told Lexi she was terrified, although the word she used was afraid. 'Of what?' Lexi asked. I expected Leigh to say, 'Of dying during delivery.' But she said, 'Of never having another interesting thought for the rest of my life.'

I am still thinking about running over one of your children in a car – the sound it must have made, the sounds you would make afterwards.

My brother called to say Mum was much worse today. 'I can't see how she can last much longer at home,' she said. 'She can't do anything.' A nurse said the end can come very quickly, once it starts to come. Should I go today?

Mittwoch 13 September

Mum has gone into the hospice, outside Bedford. Today's the day I have to reach behind the big black printer and bring out my fan – to sit on the lid of the printer and to fan. (Mouse comes for a visit. He's much bigger than January, when – just like now – he used to stand on the page and demand I run my fingers through the snow white of his gorget, his ruff. Nowadays, when he lies at the end of the garden, front paws crossed with white dots at the tip of teach, he looks as if he's got a napkin stuffed in his collar.) The heat has hit 28 degrees; I'm wearing long black shorts and the membrane of a green T-shirt with holes under the arms (from overuse, not design). (Mouse has huffed off. I think he senses something is about to change.) My legs are bare, with my right instep tucked under my left thigh. It soon gets sweaty. I reach for the fan, put it in place, plug it in and switch it on. In half a minute, it is churring, and Mouse is curiously back. What is it? What is it? He stares at the aluminium blades in their clamshell-shape steel cage. I wonder, are his eyes fast enough not to see a blur? The thing should have three speeds – 0 1 2 3 – but the plastic slider snapped years ago; neither does it turn side to side, aiming its cool turbulence through a wider arc. That gizmo broke, too. My guess is that it always runs on 3. I find it wearying, the constant breeze – like a propellor plane sat running outside an aerodrome, never taking flight, just sat running. (The fan's brand is Aeromeister.) Like Jim Ballard, it dreams of the freedom that waits above the clouds and the indulgences of acceleration and loop-looping. Even though its power-to-weight ratio is laughable, it still claims ingenious-ingenuous kinship with Chinooks and Apaches and drones. Climb aboard and we'll take to the skies! I don't feel windswept with off-camera heroism. It's like having your face licked by a moist dog for hour after hour. But a day or two a year it's better than the alternative of clarty sweat and airlessness. Maybe I can work./ Phoned Mum. Spoke for three minutes. She says she likes it there, they're very caring, doesn't want to go home.

I wish I didn't start so many sentences with I. I wish I wasn't forced to start so many sentences with I. I'll sometimes be writing an email to someone – perhaps even one of commiseration after someone has died (too many some- words) – and I'll look back after the first four sentences, and see that all of them begin with I. I suppose this is hard to avoid: I am saying what I feel, detailing I's specific response – and to begin sentences with you ('You must be feeling…' 'You needn't regret…') seems somehow intrusive, aggressive. (Too many ands.) I anyway don't like the word 'I' – it would be better if the single letter for self-referring-to-self was squigglier, rather than a Doric column. I should be – I could be replaced by Q or &. (I'm not going to do it here; it'd be affected.) 'I&I' is an elegant solution – 'I and I say…' Impossible for me to use I&I, though. I must avoid blackwishing. (I've written this before, haven't I? I say the same thing elsewhere, but have forgotten it.) I was writing a letter last week, to Sinéad, and found myself I, I, I, I-ing – but when I tried to vary sentence beginnings, it became insincere, and I had to start it again. In copying it out, the original phrasings felt insincere, too. 'I wish there were something more I could do.' 'I know he knew he was loved – especially that he was loved by you.' 'I am glad the end was peaceful.' I know I will soon be receiving these letters – this kind of letter – she not he – soon-ish. I hope I am not hyper-critical of them. I expect they'll just make me cry, and wish my mother was still alive, so they didn't have to be written. I wouldn't have had an I, or a chance to dislike it or write it, if it hadn't been for her. I can't repay that. I know she was a lovely Mum – she was interested in what we did, me and my brother. I remember she could enter our worlds without destroying them: gift. (I hope Leigh gets the chance to be like that. In a few days.)

Donnerstag 14 September

I went to the hospice (alone, Leigh too tired/tense) and found Evan and Julie already there. Lovely people. My favourite of Mum's friends. His yacking laugh; her singing speech. We spoke while Mum slept. It wasn't a big conversation, but – given the circumstances – it was tender. Julie knew Mum during the dufflecoat days.

After a longish silence, Evan asked Mum, 'What are you thinking of?' And she said, 'Whether I can reach the things on my table.'

Just typed up some words Mum dictated to me, after Evan and Julie left; words to be read at her funeral. Very hard to take them down. She's quite hard on herself – said she was a lazy person, which isn't true at all. She also told me what music she wants, and which recordings. Brahms. Bernstein. It all seems to be sorted, in her head. Music from America, Germany, England, Spain. I tried to be very present while I was with her in the small room but was aware Leigh could have spontaneously gone into labour. Something could have gone wrong. Because it was just us, Mum didn't bother having her wig on, and her head was like a baby's. The ink-blue veins. But she can hardly drink any more. Orange juice, which she loves, is too thick. Down to water. And after water, there isn't anything else.

Drove straight home. Leigh's small suitcase has been packed for two weeks.

The new replacement black tank-ish pencil sharpener has arrived. I don't have time to use it.

Bath. You know this is a retrospective luxury – your future self is envying you. So, you stay in longer than you really want.

Spending lots of time in hospitals and hospices, makes you realize how nice the non-medical, non-dying world – the world outside – can be, on an average day. To choose a direction and walk in it for a while, without a walking frame or a nurse to your side. What an absolute privilege. To have objects around you that aren't wipe-clean but are personal, beloved, well-used. Things never to be taken for granted and yet always taken for granted. We think we're normal, because we're so blithe. When people are old or ill or disabled or a bit shouty, we put them where the walkers don't have to see or hear them. The children of Turney School in their special minibus. When I'm at my desk, I can hear them shrieking in the playground.

Tomorrow, Leigh is induced.

Freitag 15 September

To hospital. Waited. 4.32 pm. Leigh induced, then back home. Fed Mouse, who seems to sense something. Tea and waiting.

Samstag 16 September

7:11 – Long night. Contractions and more contractions.

10:06 – Phone calls. 'No, nothing yet.' Mum okay but asleep.

11:11 – Lexi arrives. All in black.

12:15 – Pain. Hospital. Walk up and down the stairs in the hospital. Home.

17:48 – Big contractions. Walk in the park. Oh Jesus fuck. Hospital again.

19:56 – Home again. Brother calls. Mum hasn't woken up but is fine.

23:11 – Off to hospital again. This time?

Sonntag 17 September

Montag 18 September

Delivery suite. People shouting 'Push!' Eight or nine of them. Shouting, really shouting. Lexi calm. Hairy crowning head – very hairy. Black hair. 7:58 pm.

A BABY!

John. I luff him. He's operatic; I'm singing. No need to worry about that. Delicious bonds. I'm crying. Texted my brother who told Mum and Dad, separately. He's not sure if Mum took it in. He'll tell her again tomorrow. I walked all the way home from the hospital, over Denmark Hill and into Herne Hill at about 2am.

Leigh's still in the Maternity Unit. She's not meant to phone from there, because the phone signal interferes with the monitoring equipment (they say). She just sent me a text: *John is sleeping*. My son is sleeping, no longer in the offing.

I got to the hospital just after 8 am. Leigh exhausted and tearful. 'I can't feed him,' she said. Slowly, we got ourselves back together. Nights in maternity are pretty tough – although the people in the adjacent beds were quiet while I was there. Routines: food, pharmacist with medication, questions about meals later in the day – all puddings with custard (catering is done in Wales), different shifts of midwives introducing themselves, blood pressure, paediatrician to look over the baby. My brother came. He was surprisingly understanding about breastfeeding. Leigh is expressing, colostrum is coming. She worries none is going down. John very mucus-y; bubble-mouthed and pukey. We phoned Dad, who held the phone up for Mum. I don't know if she heard anything. John was sleeping, but he made some noises. 'She knows,' said Dad. 'She isn't making much sign, but I know she knows.' After that, it was just crying. 'It's not fair,' he said. 'She's too young.' In the room she was in. We promised to come up soon; I wish we could go tomorrow, but we can't flee the hospital. What if we went today? Got in the car right now, to dash – in case. 'I don't think anything's going to happen quickly,' my brother said. 'But she's fading.' I hated leaving Leigh in the maternity ward, but there's an end to visiting. I walked home over the hill, as I did after the birth. Watching television felt so strange. Who are these people? Sitting at the desk to write this. I stroke the surface of the desk, and wonder how Flipper is. Leigh just texted to say he's okay. We're not sure if she's allowed to use the mobile in the hospital, but she's doing it anyway. 'He is so small,' she said. 'So so small.'

I've decided to keep the beard, for the moment.

Dienstag 19 September

Leigh less exhausted. A better night with better feeds. She even managed to sleep for a couple of hour and a halves. (One of the midwives later told us we could leave John at the desk, to be babysat, if Leigh really needed some rest.) John slept much of the day – so much so that Leigh began to worry about it. In the afternoon, she crashed. Holly came to visit, and my brother, again. He said I should go and see Mum as soon as I can. It is unlikely there will be a conversation. 'She's not really talking,' he said. 'But she's still in the room with you. It's not like a coma.' Leigh was lying, semi-sleeping on the bed. I whispered details of the induction, ventouse, stitches and breastfeeding to Holly. My brother said he couldn't remember Lizzie doing anything in the hospital but cry – she had a very sore ventoused head. (Ended up caesarean anyhow.) So very special to look at John. Sinéad's email said, 'He looks so saintly.' She unerringly makes the right comment. I decided to make a quick trip to see Mum, although I wasn't sure about the driving. So tired Leigh was worried I might crash. I kept to the slow lane. It was one of those dream drives up the M1, where there's no snags around Hemel Hempstead or Luton. Straight to the hospice rather than home, that felt weird. Like I was being unfaithful to something. When I think of Mum, I still think of her at home. SatNav found the hospice. Dad wasn't there, just Mum, sleeping. What does it mean to visit someone and they don't wake up? I stayed an hour and a half, drank two cups of coffee, left when I thought I'd fall asleep driving. Back ten o'clock. 'How is she?' asked Leigh. 'How is he?' I asked her.

Mittwoch 20 September

Leigh lower again today – wanting to go home. (I have to take John to see Mum. She has to see him. I hardly want to mention it. Leigh knows – says she wants to come.) When we ask, going home seems likely so we start to plan, and I to organize. I cancel visits from Evan and Julie, and Holly – Leigh too exhausted. I try to get her to sleep as much as possible. She commented that when people say it's very difficult, you don't really understand what they mean. John sleeps, Leigh dozes, but her section of the maternity ward was much louder – a Nigerian family & many friends (& their phones), an Australian woman whose baby cried and cried. Leigh distressed. Clearly home would be the right place. It also seemed best if Leigh's parents came to help out. We needed back-up. They said they could be here at six. I went and got the car, bought formula: Leigh is topping up breastfeeds with it. We were told her drugs weren't ready but that I would come back and collect them later. Leigh showered. I wrote a story. All packed up. It took two trips to the car. John out into the cold November air in the car-seat – stripey red trousers, the red jumper Leigh knitted, snowsuit which avalanches him. Car-seat in and off! Had got David Bowie's 'Kooks' ready to play. Willyoo stay an' I luvva story? Written for *his* son, Zowie, I think. (Zowie now Duncan.) The idea of Bob Dylan as father occurs to me. *John Wesley Harding* about parent's view of the world, not rebellious teen (like 'Subterranean Homesick Blues'). Home, across the threshold. A moment I'd also anticipated.

Donnerstag 21 September

My brother rang at seven and said we should come now, if we could. So, we had to get in the car, disorientated as we were. Leigh's parents saw us off. They'd made a packed lunch, even. Driving back from the hospital was terrifying enough. This is really what cars are like – metal beasts yearning for impact; Robo-wars. And everyone on the street a psychopath. John is so small, so very small – I hated the idea of driving with him on the motorway. Leigh sat in the back with him and told me to be careful. We got there safely around eleven a.m.

It happened. The scene. But Mum was completely unconscious – or seemed to be. There's a photograph – I took some photographs, not knowing if it was ghoulish or not. Some proof for grown-up John, I suppose. We cried – we all cried; except Mum, who was very calm. Her breathing wasn't calm but her face was calm. Leigh's going back home, but I'm going to stay up here; for Dad, for the end. I have a deadline on a story for a competition, and I have my laptop with me.

Break.

Knackered, after driving Leigh home and then coming back on the train. Not that she's likely to need the car. No bad word from my brother at the hospice whilst I travelled. I was planning to eat with Dad then go there. But he phoned as I was cooking spaghetti, 'Come now,' he said. I took a couple of bananas from the bowl. Dad didn't want to come. He said he's said goodbye already.

Freitag 22 September

Long day.

Samstag 23 September

Mum died.

Sonntag 24 September

Sitting with Mum in the hospice. They made her nice. Made some notes.

Some of these days are going to be blank.

Montag 25 September

I came home yesterday evening. Last night was okay. Leigh said the ones when I was away were harder. Boo – he's become Boo since I was here – is beside me in the study (9:20 am), sleeping after a Five-Act feed. I never thought we'd get here. One week old already, and only a decade has passed.

Breastfeeding is not going well.

Looking round the house, when we were thinking of buying it, I remember standing in the middle of the second bedroom and thinking, *Will we...?* And going into the bathroom, and seeing the possibility of him or her in the tub (even before we'd decided to buy).

Mouse looks at the baby like an alien looking at a painting.

My brother is doing the death duties: taking the certificate from the hospice, registering at the Registry Office. I wish I could do some of it. He says it's fine. Dad can't do it. Dad's not fine.

Dienstag 26 September

Sleeps he. The hair-whorl on the top of his head, satellite photo of a hurricane. A more snatched, fragmentary world-view – but with greater detail. Smiles don't mean but frowns are factual. When your fingernails could cut your baby, you cut your fingernails. His breathing sounds like daddy mouse in the next room inflating a li-lo with a footpump. Leigh talking to Lexie about the birth. Most of her memories, she says, are non-visual – because her eyes were closed most of the time. Except for the moment, near the end, when she opened them to see a tableau reflected in the dark window. Nine people shouting 'Push!'

Mittwoch 27 September

First thing this morning, a Five-Act feed. A tragedy. I feel appallingly terrible when I hand Boo over to Leigh – after that moment, useful-useless, I might as well drop through a trapdoor and out of the whole production (not even to come back at the curtain call as a Who-was-he?). I suppose I still have some lines: 'Maybe give it another try on the other side' or 'Why don't you wait a bit?' Leigh finds me more than annoying, and I try only to give support, not advice, even if it's advice I've heard her get from health visitors or at the breastfeeding clinic. But leaving the room where this failure – she sees it this way – where this grief is happening, that seems – that's not what a good father would do. They would be silently present. They would not ask, 'Did Boo feed? Did Boo take something? Is he getting enough? Is he losing weight?' This afternoon, when she saw us going for a walk, and made the mistake of asking how things were going, the next-door neighbour heard Leigh's account and said we should just give up and bottlefeed him. She meant both of us, because I *could* be part of that – I could play a major role in us becoming second-rate parents. As she spoke, I wanted to push her away. It's difficult enough without people voicing what you've been secretly fantasizing. Forbidden thoughts. No, we'll keep going – Leigh will keep going, keep falling through her own infinite series of trapdoors. Failed, failed, failed.

I drive up and back, to see Dad and visit Mum. She's now in the funeral home. She's in a wicker coffin, wearing her hiking gear – hiking boots, soft green and fuchsia jumper. That's what she wanted to be cremated in. She was very clear on that, as about everything else. Funeral music. Her words.

Donnerstag 28 September

Okay night. John/Boo feeding six or seven times. I am now in my study, where Boo sleeps in the Moses basket, emitting little grunts. I think he might be waking. He looks more like a human being, but that's perhaps because I'm getting used to him. He seems more finished. At this stage, they look so highly etched – each hair distinct and important, Holbein-like. He has long, wrinkly fingers and dry-skin palms. Dad made the pianist comment. Yesterday, when he was crying, I put on Mozart's Piano Sonata in D minor, adagio, and he went to sleep immediately. I did it partly as a joke, to prove the sentimentalists wrong. He looks a bit like Henry James. Perhaps we should call him James instead of John. Or Jack. He looks more like Jack than John. I like this baby stage, when they dress all in white. My throat is bad. I sang to John, to Jack, to Boo, at 2am, and lots of notes were missing. My study is too stuffy.

Freitag 29 September

Unreasonable crying – week two. All of us cry unreasonably. As anticipated, far far away from the books in the bookcase. Not individually – any of them could be picked up and read on any page; collectively, from the culture of them – of reading them regularly, serially. (This noted in the car-park queue at King's, attending the breastfeeding clinic.) A day of gently grey clouds, New Yorkish. A piano trio on the radio. (10:47 am.) I stand at the window holding Boo, hoping someone will see us and wave. Two firemen walk past, relaxed-looking. They don't look up.

I always mean to note down the day the ants swarm – sand up from the cracks in the pavement, and long-winged beasties in the gutter. But I always forget. I think it was about the start of August this year. Maybe the last week of July. I saw them on the way to the corner shop to buy oatmilk. Why I need to note this now, I don't know – images from a former life.

Walter has given up skydiving and taken up serious trout-fishing. He has also moved out of his mother's and up to Scotland, to be closer to the best beats.

When I first touched my son, I first understood the meaning of *flesh of my flesh* or *my own flesh and blood* – and I cannot even begin to think of how intense this feeling of holding one's own, one's ownmost own, must have been for his mother.

Now starts the craft of the father.

The new replacement black pencil sharpener works perfectly, and is the right shape and colour. But the pig has just escaped into the walled garden.

Samstag 30 September

Back to Dad's.

Sonntag 1 Oktober

Just heard from Holly that the mother from the dinner party, the one whose husband reversed the car over her daughter – she killed herself. She jumped in front of a train at Denmark Hill. So terrible.

Home. Leigh hands over Boo, a bottle, and goes straight to bed.

Montag 2 Oktober

Today is the first day of Winter term. Some lovely emails from colleagues, since they heard. I'm feeling guilty about not being with them, not teaching. But also a sullen sense of liberty, released into something unknown. I won't get any work done this Study Leave. Every hope I held lies in my arms. Immersed in this one moment. I look to my right, at the bookshelves in my room, and the books on them, and think – and sometimes say aloud, 'Someday, I will get back to you.' Then I have to go off and do something, like put a wash on, or disinfect some bottles. It's not as if I'm breastfeeding; it's not as if I'm a woman in 1890, or 1790, or any time. But God am I kerflumped, banjaxed, shagattered, kiboshed. I think there are some words still in my head, even if they're not getting onto the page. This page. This doesn't count. Used to count but doesn't now. I think about sleep, and people tell me this is the easy bit. 'Wait until they are four months old... Wait until colic... Wait until the terrible twos.' And I think, 'At least if they're going through the terrible twos, they've made it alive to two. We have no guarantee. What if we fuck up? What if we do something obviously wrong? Or he has an allergic reaction to something we just couldn't have predicted?'

Funeral arranged for Saturday 7th – Bedford Crematorium. I spend my free time looking up the email addresses of Mum's friends.

Dienstag 3 Oktober

Cocooning.

Mittwoch 4 Oktober

I realize other people might pity me. I don't want them to.

Donnerstag 5 Oktober

I told Leigh, at least twice, but I haven't written it here – my mum
bottlefed me. I'm a bottle baby, and I'm doing alright.

Freitag 6 Oktober

It's very wearing, being grateful all the time. I wonder, has it ever been a murder motive? So easy to turn smile-smile-smile into resentment.

Samstag 7 Oktober

Mum's Funeral. Bedford Crematorium.

Her music.

'Recuerdos de la Alhambra' by Francisco Tárrega (3 mins 54 secs) played by John Williams.

'Dirge for Fidele' by Vaughan Williams (3 mins 50 secs).
   'Nothing ill come near thee.'

'Ihr habt nun Traurigkeit' from 'Ein deutsches Requiem' by Brahms (8 mins 16 secs) played by Herbert von Karajan and the Berliner Philharmoniker.
   'As one whom his mother comforteth,
   so will I comfort you.'

'Make Our Garden Grow' from *Candide* by Leonard Bernstein (4mins 01 secs).
   'PANGLOSS
   Any questions?'

Sonntag 8 Oktober

These are Mum's Words

> I've been very contented because I've never had great ambition. I've been given a very good time of birth, place of birth; I've had a very lovely family. I think I'm a fairly lazy person, actually. I've never overexerted myself to achieve the highest. I've had a modicum of intelligence, which I've used. It's been lovely to make friends with likeminded people; I've never needed a lot of friends, but those I have are treasured. I've always rather wished I were gregarious and outgoing, like other people seem to be. But I think that I was more fulfilled enjoying my smaller circle. I want to say something about David: He was *right*. We *fit*. We were very compatible. I feel content and very lucky, in the ending, because I know how it'll come, more or less.

Montag 9 Oktober

The Booster Boo, in his decadence, *louche* as well as *débonnaire*. Folds in his arms and legs. His torso, the shape of a six-sided beetle shell. Going milk-mad, milk-drunk. Floppy headed before sleep; whizzy headed when aiming for the nipple. He grabbed his first object today, the black and white stripey smiley-faced toy my brother bought us. He pulled one of its limbs towards him and put it in his mouth – that'll be his hobby for the next two years, tasting the world. And most of the time we'll be trying to stop him. It's easy to see him as an indefatigable fact, rather than a vulnerable animal. Bereaved parents on the news: they are dealing with the removal of a sine qua non; a given quality of their universe has been removed. How can that beauty be gone? The Damascene Child. The Possum of Posset.

I am split in two.

Dienstag 10 Oktober

If I were instantly transported – teleported, in fact – to the surface of the moon, I would (like any normal person) freak out, panic, suffocate and die. But say I'd been warned in advance, given an hour or a year to prepare, then I could have got myself ready to see and sense it. After the whoosh or zoom or nothing. I don't know what I'd learn from the weird drop in temperature or from the complete absence of airflow. The new place might smell of dry ashes or water that has been frozen, defrosted, frozen, defrosted. But it would be the light I would try completely to experience – the light of a far-reflective place come close enough to circumvent. In the clearest distances, I would see raptor details. The shadows would be manifest, as if they had volume as well as tone. (My ears would hear – would hear my tinnitus, my struggling heart and my desperate blood.) (I would ignore my hearing, as much as possible.) Perhaps there would be time for me to look at the earth against the blackest ever black and the untwinkliest ever stars. Maybe I would make of it – this distinct world – my last glance, after I fell down. But before then, well before then, I would want to pick up moondust and grey my palms and fingers with it, as if I were a gymnast. Then I would pogo once, to see what the slow fall was like. And then, with my unconstricted chest telling me just how little time I had left, I would attempt a somersault, undertake a somerset. What matter if I didn't make it? I wouldn't be ridiculous or triumphant if it turned out to be a double or a one-and-a-halfer. There would be no-one there to watch me scuff up the dust, overflip, land on my hands, fall hissing on my back. But then, what if I were instantly teleported home, with no warning, after expecting for a year to die in a place I had always adored-from-afar, my heart had always hoped for? Would I be able to write this, or anything like this? When the sensations were recent and the observations real, would I care? I know what this is about. Of course, I know what this was about. In my mother's final minute, after her final year, she was instantly teleported to the moon. I watched her – grey, pogo, somersault, fall hissing.

Mittwoch 11 Oktober

New fathers are aquaria into which all stare to see what strange creatures swim. It is like looking into a honeymoon or a divorce. There
are amorphous, gliding squid but also wittily quick fish.

What am I most afraid of, now Boo is born (apart from Boo dying)?

Donnerstag 12 Oktober

Birdsong inside the bottle of formula, birdsong from the teat and the airbubbles; larks, regular.

Neck-cheese of a milk-mad infant child.

I look at him swaddled and think, 'When I did that (swaddling), I didn't really *do* it – it was past tense even as I was performing it. I was beyond its doing.'

Freitag 13 Oktober

More communicative vocalizations. Leigh is worried that if she doesn't breastfeed him, he won't know and love her. The other NCT mums who *do* breastfeed tell her they are going to introduce the bottle, too. He fights to digest. Neck is strong, pushing back when sat on my lap for feeding – as if we wanted to do a backwards roll. Now he grabs, not quite randomly. I imagine I can remember myself, as a baby, feeding whilst asleep – the knowledge all you have to do is keep swallowing and the milk will keep coming. Leigh roughs his hair up, I smooth it down. I also give him a centre parting, side parting, mohican and Tintin.

Samstag 14 Oktober

Dinner out. We weren't sure we could manage it, but we tried. Holly asked how I was. I started talking it through, the end, and I just started to weep as I've never done – I just fucking fountained and spewed all of it out. Shouldn't write it. The end. All came out. I said it. The only thing I've ever seen that was 'like' my mother's death was *The Exorcist* – or moments in other horror films when what you thought was safely dead suddenly lunges out to grab the living. I held my mother's thin, sinewy hand. Her right hand. I was not going to let go. My brother, at my mother's dying breath – the horror-movie one – thumped back against the wall. If he could have crashed through it, and into the next room, I'm sure he would have done. He was completely fucking jumpscared whilst I held on. I am proud I held on. I am a little disgustingly vain that I managed to. Sometimes, in arguments in my head, I bring this out to win. 'You don't know anything about anything until you've held someone's hand as they're dying.' Rubbish. Conceit. I was there in my father's stead. I don't know if he could have done it. Nothing to think you're special for. Millions of people have gone through the same, some a large number of times. They don't speak much about it. Their children make horror movies. When my mother was a child, a relative of theirs came to live with them, and to die of cancer. My mother heard them screaming. It was terrifying. I was terrified. I shook at the kitchen table, as I told Nirpal and Holly. After my mother was dead, I said, the nurse who'd kept up a commentary, reassuring my mother that we were there, naming us – in the minutes afterwards, she apologized for not warning us about that final breath, which has a technical name. 'There wasn't time,' she said. I had looked into my mother's mouth. I had seen her teeth, which did not look good. I had been breathed upon. I had felt the breath from my mother's mouth, which did not smell good. Her last breath was one I was there to inhale. We shouldn't have gone to dinner, but I feel better. I feel worse for writing this. I will write more.

Curled up, her head on the pillow, she looked like an extra from a sci-fi movie about a depersonalized society. (There's usually at least one shaven-headed woman in each fascist dystopia.) *THX 1138*. The mother, the dying mother, the main character says goodbye to, before going on the run and finding a way to free the slaves. I got up quietly to leave, but she heard me. 'You're very understanding,' she said – I think she said. And I think I understood what she meant – that my father and her friends came and talked and tried to cheer her up. But what she most wanted was people to show they didn't want anything from her, not any more, not anything she didn't have the energy to give. With some of them, she must have pretended to fall asleep, even when she felt strong enough to stay awake, just to stop them talking. I am not criticizing her friends. They were expressing their love. But an expression of love is an awful demand. It drains a lot of limited battery power. We don't have an English etiquette for sitting in silence for 20 minutes. It is hard to say, but we both of us felt, my brother and I, how Mum relaxed when my father was persuaded to go home. He was too much – much too much. His endearments were too clumsy. 'Look at you,' he said. 'Look at you.' He was boyish and we were ashamed. He was boyishly inept and made us ashamed of him. My mother did not need to hear, 'Look at the state of you!' She needed to know someone was there who would go away quite soon but who would also come back quite soon. She was happy to listen to us talk among ourselves, and not take part. It was the fact of the talk, the subject didn't matter. Her children, alive. This was her family, the family she had made with my father, and these counting down hours were the last time it would be complete. It was the death of the Litts. 'Dad!' my brother would say, after he had said, 'Just look at her!' or 'It's so cruel' – as if Mum couldn't hear, wasn't there, was already a dead body. I think I had to have a word outside the room, to remind him that – before he spoke – he should think about how Mum would hear what he was saying. You had to suppose Mum had loved this boyish ineptitude in him. It meant her superiority – her emotional superiority – was never under any threat. He would never see or understand any more than she did. He was useful to her, but what was profounder in her was between her and her children, and was relentlessly unspoken. The room breathed out when Dad went home because we knew that – now he was gone – we could manage. We understood the nurses' harmonies. There weren't going to be any more wrong notes that night – not until Dad came galumphing back in the morning, blundering in with fearful tears. 'It's not fair.' (It was not fair. It was pointless to say it.) But I think I was able to just sit because I did not have those things to say. My brother reacted by becoming like my mother, by saying what she knew my mother would say. This isn't difficult for him. Being my mother is my brother's vocation. If there was a joke to be made, he would make it – as long as it wasn't inappropriate. We did laugh. But my father needed guidance, calming; he needed, gently but firmly, gently but firmly, to be told to stop doing what he was doing and to do it another way – then, meekly, immediately, he would do that new thing as if it was what he'd done all along. It feels disloyal, but if it comes in the head it goes on the page: my father suffered from too little emotional intelligence, my mother from too much. (It's a wonder they stayed married.) All the openness was on his side, all the forbearance on hers. When he left the room to go home and sleep, the room became as it should be – we were able to organize it for my mother's final comfort. When the nurses came to wash her, we knew we could leave. At one point, they advised us that some people do want to die alone – they were ashamed or embarrassed that anyone is there. Perhaps they know their bowels are going to relax, and they're too decorous to allow that to happen. And so, in suffering, beneath painkillers, they live on and on – exhausting their relations, prolonging their own days and nights and days and nights. At one point, they advised us to leave my mum alone, to die that way if she wished. Making decisions like this made me feel fully, undeniably adult. But I only felt that completely after she'd died, with me holding her hand. So we did, we left her alone for – I think – an hour. It was difficult to do so. My brother went home and smoked. I read in the Quiet Room. And when we went back in, my mother was just as she'd been when we went out – only one hour closer to a fairly close death. We could only assume, because by then she'd stopped speaking, that she did not want to die on her own. We took that as a statement, one of her last, and did not try it again. The nurses didn't advise it again. We trusted them; they knew their business. I think of them sometimes, the people in hospices, all the different kinds of leavers and stayers, when I'm doing something completely unlike what they're doing. When I am diving into a swimming pool or buying a good cup of coffee. I hear the air-pump that kept the bedsore-avoiding mattress aloft, a soft and infuriating grinding every hour of the day. After my mother died, that was what I was gladdest to get away from – the grinding. My dad was not there when mum died – I think we were all glad of that. My brother and I were able to make it calm, do the night shift. Earlier, I had played mother classical music on headphones, hoping she might die to a Mozart aria – but the headphones annoyed and I think pained her. So when she died we had the television on, and although I think my brother turned it off, what was showing was Gordon Ramsey's Kitchen Nightmares, the American version. Not what I would have chosen; not, I think, what mum would have wanted – although she did watch it sometimes. By this time, after several days of nights in the room with the air-pump, my idea of a good death had changed. I had been aiming for a tableau – the whole family there, no-one to miss out and always afterwards regret it. Now I just wanted one of us to be there, so she wasn't alone. I had aimed for a high culture ending, choral music. Now whatever might distract the people around the bed was fine. I wanted us all to say our final words just before the final moment. Now I knew we'd all said all the words we had several times. There was no more to say. We were exhausted with trying to find new things, or new ways to say the old ones. I really bloody wanted my mother to die, and soon. She'd lived three days beyond the point she would have wanted to live. There is no ethical dilemma. I could identify the moment she would have felt her life was not worth living – it was when she failed to take a final sip of water. Beyond this, it was thirst, exhaustion, dehydration, awareness of suffering of those around you you love but no longer have the capacity to feel empathy for. A day or two earlier, she drank orange juice with joy. Before that, she smiled as she sucked a polo.

[INSERTED PAGES:]

● ●

Now, I would have pressed a button, I would have signed a form,
I would have – I did consider – lifting and holding down a pillow.
Finally, it was a good death, it's just that – I've learned – good
deaths are also utterly appalling.

● ●

Sonntag 15 Oktober

Anyone's body can deviate extravagantly from good health into jerky *katastrophé*, like, moment-to-moment. Over pretty quickly, right? Screens torment us with x-rated youth's zestiness.

Was up in the night, three times.

Montag 16 Oktober

He does preacher hands, coral-fish lips, lopsided smiles, he gurns like an old wino (both have no teeth); he goes zonko like a smack addict – pure blank; he starts to cry during feeds, when the bottle isn't in his mouth; far less Lord Snooty and His Pals – far less the Buddha; he looks up after a milk-rush with huge self-possession. 'So, *you* are the feeder?' his eyes say. 'I associate you with milk.' It is an economy of lactation. Scabby babby.

Dienstag 17 Oktober

Registering Births and Death, same waiting room. Cheery ring-tone of the bereaved man's mobile. Registrar comes in and asks, 'Mr. Stravinsky?' He gets up and goes. When it's our turn, I ask the Registrar. He says he does births, deaths and marriages all jumbled up on the one day. He was a little quiz show host. 'You came in here with nothing, and you're going to leave with nothing.' Quiz show host or Victorian preacher. 'We come into this world with nothing, and it is with nothing we will depart therefrom.' Not strictly true, if we marry we leave to rejoin or to wait for the potential of a partner for all eternity. Theologically. Spotty face. He craps as we change his nappy – yellow poo shunted out very matter-of-factly.

Mittwoch 18 Oktober

Wants to be held. Wakes up if put down in the Moses basket. Sleeps better between us in bed. We shouldn't but we do.

A month since Boo was born.

Donnerstag 19 Oktober

What have I done – by drinking milk? And spreading butter, pouring cream, eating and loving cheese. As a conscious adult, I have
paid money directly and indirectly to an industry that, in order to
make its product, inseminates heifers, separates heifers and calves,
slaughters calves and overfeeds heifers, then industrially extracts the
food intended for the calves. The heifers are not indifferent to their
calves. (Reports of the sounds they produce and the behaviours they
exhibit.) If nothing else, they are made to go through a vast hormonal
preparation on disappointment. Drive past a green field in the coun-
tryside, dotted with white and black, and that's what you're seeing:
grief. We have the words orphan and widow, but we have no word
for a mother who has lost her child and doesn't know if it is alive
or dead. An unmother, a post-mother – neither coinage is accurate
nor carries any heft. If we all stopped drinking milk, there would
be no cows in the fields, and there would be no reason for many of
the fields. So goes the argument. Some of the cows are intended as
beef. If all schoolchildren, every year, were given a guided tour of a
farm and then an abattoir, would we still have so many green fields
with black and white in them? I could drink black tea. The children
tell their parents they love animals. Have I ever seen such pride and
love as Roger Robson wrestler/farmer among his Belted Galloways?
Isn't it better to live only your prime? Shouldn't everything die at its
ripest? After generations – so many even since my mother gave me
boiled milk when I couldn't sleep – aren't the heifers used to it? Milk
is what cows are for. As one whom his mother comforteth, so will
I comfort you. In fifty years, will cows be viewed as slaves?

My mother, in 1968, wasn't producing enough milk, so the doctor
advised her to bottlefeed me condensed milk with an egg cracked
and whisked into it.

Leigh: 'I can't believe we made him. Where did you come from, little
bright one?'

Freitag 20 Oktober

The pad of my little finger seems to fit the fontanelle in Boo's skull. It's as though, because I'm his father, there's a correspondence between the two. Leigh doesn't like me touching there, because she thinks I'll press too hard; I won't, I will only touch like so, so I feel the pulse. It would be a very dull observation to say Newborn babies are fascinating, but it might be worth saying that we find lots of other things fascinating because they're like babies. I'm sure this is true of kittens and lemurs, but also robots and moons – anything that seems unusually self-contained, and that makes us feel we've lost our sense of scale or of what is and isn't a person. When I look at Boo, I want to be smaller, so that he would look bigger to me. When he's lying next to me in bed, I sometimes close the higher of my two eyes and observe him from an inch above the sheets. So close I can hear my eyelashes scrape against cotton. He becomes a giant sleeping beneath a hill or a vast god-statue that will soon come to life. In relation to some things, a miracle or an earwig, he is already very big, but compared to a car driving past at forty miles an hour or a fighting dog being exercised in the park, he is too terribly small. Touching his fontanelle makes me feel, for a short while, that we are both the appropriate size. I am the approximate shape of a father and he has the conventional dimensions of a son. I'm still very aware what's beneath his thickening flesh – I first saw him as a floating skeleton, light gray on black, and his soft bones sometimes seem brightly visible. That's why his toothlessness, when he yawns, is so shocking; his spine is beautifully complete, like an ironic smile, and yet we need to keep him alive so he can become fully articulated. What if he dies in America?

Samstag 21 Oktober

His eloquently unmeaning gestures. If there's nothing new under the sun, write moonlit. Gradual mummification and acquisition of dadness, daditude.

Sonntag 22 Oktober

I do a lot of thinking about the 57 varieties of death. There are accidental ones for the Booster Boo, followed by and bringing about
deliberate ones for me. I drop him down the stairs: I swim far out
to sea. I don't call 999 when he blanches white: I stab myself in the
heart with a carving knife, or I get Leigh to stab me in the heart — and
she might want to use something more painful than a carving knife;
perhaps a corkscrew or a vegetable peeler. There is nothing I could
do to make up for killing my son. Leigh might blind me with forks
and castrate me with craft scissors (we already have craft scissors)
and finish me off with the griddle — people would still sympathize
with her, and feel sick when they thought of me. How could you?
It was a mistake. But you should have known. I know I should have
known — I know now. Please give me another chance. Please let me
have another baby. I'll do better this time. No, you smothered your
firstborn as you slept — and it is still completely your fault. No-one
could be more guilty than you — except the mother. The mother's
terrors are worse than yours, and you will never know them. If you
ask what they are, you'll be subject to chaff and then flak. Why do you
want to know? I want to tell you you're a good mother, and that I will
forgive you however horribly you fuck up. No, you won't — because
then I'll be the worst thing: the unnatural mother.

I cannot kill   what I brought to birth —
for a mortal, for a mother,   one death is all-death.
We pray for imperfection,   seeking asymmetry,
needing nothing   close to complete.
All we can ask   the Gods to grant us
is modest obscurity   in a humble house.
Let us be little,   bless us with boredom.

Montag 23 Oktober

I see the bodies of young mothers, how they have adapted. I see
them alongside Leigh. There isn't any use for willowy and gamine is
gone. Instead, there are broadened ankles that can support columns
of bone supporting one or more extra humans. Arms have become
weightier, necks widened and gained a line. Veins surfaced. A future
iteration of their child has already done some colouring in on their
cheeks – cloudy scribbles. Women who have never gone phew or
wiped their foreheads do so now. They've gained silvery beauties on
the sides of their bellies – waxing moon on sand ridges. Love-snails
have left trails in parallel around the corners of their breasts, which
will soon no longer have corners. Their upper body flesh is forgiving,
impact-resistant. (Often it's anger, keeping them going.) (After being
kneaded, the resting dough tightens like a testicle in the sea.) Here
are gingerbread mums, dark rye, strong white. Yes, they are yeasty,
although often too they smell of cheese. (I am among them at clinics.)
This one may be camembert in the sun, and this one may have the
sorrow of roquefort. They are aware that yesterday's glass of dry white
wine can mean today's souring – of milk, of mood. Oh their poor
poor nipples – smarting from the last use whilst already beginning the
one after next, somehow. Endless need. Did that happen? Were we in
the park, and now are we back, and have we come again? Fluids pass
remorselessly through them, but they also feel all solids as temporary
stiffnesses. Soon enough everything will return to milk. Just milk.
I stand to the side, guiltily unchanged. I'm less fit than I was a month
ago – have eaten too much cake and sugared my tea. But I haven't met
with a climacteric. This tiredness in my lungs feels middle-aged; if
I needed to, I could run to the Post Office Tower, I could punch the
stranger. 'Get off,' I could say, and do the protecting. Mothers give life
and leave fathers only fantasies of saving lives. If that happens, we'll
be equal. (He dreams of dragging his son from the sea.) The bodies of
young mothers tell me I am insufficient. Leigh's body tells me I might
as well be in prison, or New Zealand, or 1594. I wish I could send my
strength into her, but it's the wrong kind of strength – it's even the
wrong kind of wrong.

Dienstag 24 Oktober

A week ago, Leigh said she'd fallen in love with Jack. She said Jack, not John, not Boo. Today she says she's just starting to enjoy it. In bed, his first proper smile – same place as the first kick I felt. He's very spotty at the moment; acne-red on his earlobes. Less pukey, though he just brought a whole feed back up on my trousers. He does like going to sleep, except whilst being held. Euphemisms for death seem to do for his slumber, putting him down, will he go? he's well off…

Plenty of chance to listen to music whilst bottle-feeding. I'm not so patient of dull CDs, and will get rid of them, even if recently bought.

Intellect resolves; beauty absolves.

O/h (young woman to two friends in Escape Bar): 'It was never meant to be a long-term relationship.'

Mittwoch 25 Oktober

Ignorances, mine.

My mother's death was one of the most ordinary events I have ever witnessed. It took place in the same place as did the birth of my child, you could smell that. All essential and ordinary events take place in this place. I call it the Blood Room, because blood is what it smells of. It also smells of piss and shit, but most power-fully it smells of blood. Marriage is an extraordinary event, and does not take place in the Blood Room. Sex, particularly loss of virginity for girls, is the third ordinary event to take place in the Blood Room. The fourth and only other event is violence. Torture always makes the Blood Room. The boxing ring is the Blood Room made theatrical. There are cousin rooms, though. The consumptive made their lungs into a Blood Room. Sometimes, the drinking of Guinness brings certain pubs close. The bullfight, the corrida is a tribute to the Blood Room, and the Spanish, of all European people, live with the stench of the Blood Room almost constantly in their nostrils. The Swedish can forget it almost entirely, for all but a few minutes of their lives. The Delivery Suite, the Hospital or Hospice Room, the Bedroom, the Sports Arena – these are all very ordinary places. In the Delivery Suite, the husband smells what is far up inside his wife – the husband breathes in the back of the womb. He (who may be a she) aspirates Guinness and whiskey, red wine and vodka. Vodka is like the smell of blood distilled, with all the blood-like specifics reduced to transparency. Vampires are a pop cultural attempt to be constantly Spanish. The woman who has, through the fragrance of her womb, reconsecrated the Blood Room, does her best to forget – the baby with white clothes, clean walls, milk cascades – the baby must inhabit the anti-blood room, the dry and desiccated room. Opera is the ritual of turning a theatre bloody. And all of this, as I say, is the most ordinary thing – it is the human that unites us. Perform a caesarean section, the Blood Room has still imposed its threshold. Allow death by lethal injection, there will be a flash or two of the room as the mouth falls open and makes a cave. We know we are inside the Blood Room when we, and it, are aghast. As it overwhelms us, overwombs us, it is a ghastly circumference. For a few seconds, as the baby's buttocks then slippery legs were drawn out, her womb was completely aghast. Our baby was born, and I was awed at what we had done but was even more so aghast at the opening I had witnessed. The meat weeps blood. The torture chamber expresses the torturer's nostalgia for – his holiday in – his own birth. All of this is not intended to glorify the Blood Room (although it is the origin of glory). We do well, when we are cultured, to get away from it – to get as far away from it into fashion, clothes, make-up, skiing, video, screens, children. The restaurant, serving bloody steaks, is not as close to it as the kitchen, but the abattoir is only a parody, with meaningless blood. The abattoir can serve as a reminder. Humans are capable of being Swedish vegans. Flamenco is Blood Room music. I respect the Spanish. The English are criticized for their sangfroid, but for sangfroid blood at least has to be present. The stiff upper lip of the clitoris. Death averages us out. At the hospices, the nurses knew I was just the same as them. They'd been through it. I'd been through it. I was as worthy of compassion as they were. I realized why they might want to work there, because someone has to preside over and maintain the ordinariness of ordinary events. To become adult is to become ordinary; childhood is effortlessly extraordinary, adolescence is effortfully extraordinary; pre-adulthood is the willed continuation of adolescence or the willed return to childhood. Then death makes us ordinary, and we are thankful and full of mourning. We recognize how ordinary our birth was, and we feel less alone. We have sex with one another, alone, both entirely alone. For years, we are able to forget, or for years we seek out satisfying reminders – Catholicism, for example, the religion of blood. Chocolate is blood food, more even than a bloody steak. Opera bloods us, as does fox-hunting, the bullfight, boxing, self-cutting, getting drunk, anal sex, zazen.

It is a great chasmal echoing place, the Blood Room. When you first enter it feels homely, because fleshly – and you yourself are made of flesh, or meat, so how can it be alien to you? But it is alien, because this Blood Room is about the making or unmaking of Meat, not the continuation of Meat in its hobbies and pastimes, tastes and aversions. You are not a living creature, with a future, you are sperm in the womb. You, my child, don't touch the fucking sides. All you are is

Donnerstag 26 Oktober

His foot – not particularly his right foot or his left foot, but either; the utter wow of it – why the world doesn't just stop to admire it. Why conflicts in Afghanistan, Palestine, Nagorno-Karabakh – why they don't pause hostilities to wonder at the beauty of this little limb that hasn't even been used for crawling? I don't believe in miracles – or I didn't believe in the miraculous – until I saw feet – calves – knees – thighs – willy – tummy – hands – arms – shoulders – neck – chin – mouth – nose – eyes – eyebrows! actual eyebrows! – skull – fontanelle – hair. (In reverse order.) And all of them together, so far at least, functioning without flaw. He's on my lap, in the crook of my left arm, asleep for – hang on – ten minutes. The Moses' basket is behind me, with tight white fitted sheet and flanimal. Like spending the day in the T-shirt you slept in. No, I still don't believe in the miraculous, I just have no idea how something so complete and apt can happen. Yes, yes, evolution – but look, it's a foot! Like a cartoon foot, or one given to baby John the Baptist by Leonardo da Vinci. The weight of it feels absolutely right when it pushes against my palm. This is what Leigh has made, inside her body; and my part, all those anxious months ago, seems comic. (Semi-colon.) This is the former Flipper's flipper, that raised an arc across the bellysphere! This will (I hope) run in school sports days, and feel the cold in the sea. It will climb stairs, dance, step on pebbles, get blistered and heal. Already it has been tickled – and if you run your fingernail from heel up to toes, Ex-Flipper stiffens like a kipper. When this happens, his face makes an expression of alarmed delight. How very dare you?! (I don't often use question mark and exclamation mark, side by side, but Ex-Flipper uses them all the time. They are his mode at the moment – camp, invested.) What?! and also What!? and This?!? What-y what what?! And I am watching all this thinking, 'Foot!?' He's waking, with wet mouth and inner rumbles, but miraculously I was able to write these words this whole page whilst he slept. (Tiny cosy shiny rosy.)

Freitag 27 Oktober

Black tea this morning, with a teaspoon of honey, in an attempt to get away from milk. Stop using milk. I made it in the usual big white teapot, but am drinking it out of a small white porcelain teacup. A smaller-than-usual white mug, I should say – since it has no saucer. This is what tea tastes like – he sips – which isn't much. Acrid, like sucking coal. Maybe I should stop with teabag tea, too? When I drink black tea, I think of 19th century Russians with samovars and of Jean Roberts. I can make small life-changes, aimed at reducing my consumption of non-necessities; and I can come to realize that things I think of as necessary are anything but. If I wasn't addicted to caffeine, and habituated to hot drinks, this could be a glass of tap water. How would that be? I think of generation after generation of writers, smoking, scribbling, smoking, scribbling – pen in one hand, cigarette in the other. It was their dialectic of ash and ink, of vocabulary and nicotine. Typists had to pause – pick the fag up, take a drag, put it back in the ashtray (maybe with a tap, maybe not); either that or have it dangle from their lower lip. Patricia Highsmith. Albert Camus. Carson McCullers. Charles Bukowski. Reporter in a movie filing urgent copy. All their words were first seen through a grey veil. I have never written and smoked at the same time – or, to put it more extremely – I have never written smokingly. But I have friends – Lexi and David – who keep smoking, and taking up smoking when they've quit, because it's the only way they can continue to write. Both of them are dialecticians, too; anything mono- is false to them. I worry about the non-smokingness of contemporary fiction, and other forms of writing, but fiction most of all. If it's too healthy, if it's all about productive routines rather than destructive habits – if it's all gym membership and detox, then it's not like people. As a society, he said, we're still smokin', and writers always consume the world. I worry, but it's generally better not to die of cancer than to die of cancer – if you can manage to. The black tea has given me a headrush, even though I've only drunk two-thirds, or maybe it's the honey. It's made me a bit speedy. I feel like I'm riding pillion on a superbike. I feel like I've smoked the first cigarette too quickly.

Samstag 28 Oktober

Watching TV with Dad. I feel sad. I feel very sad. That was antici-pated; I knew that, afterwards, I'd feel sad, along with relieved, angry, bewildered, bored. I wasn't wrong about any of those. But this sadness feels like sadness of a different order. When I try and find its edge, I can't. It's not just a rug I'm standing on; it's the floor beneath the rug and the dirt beneath the floor; it's the dust particles coming off it through the air above it. (There's only one speech for this, and it's from the dying breaths of Lear. 'Why should a dog, a horse, a rat, have life,/ And thou have no breath at all?') I don't feel sad *about* – it's not that 'I feel sad about' my Mum's death; everything around me seems made down to the atoms of sad stuff. Among the saddest-seeming is the stuff other people receive as fun or up. The colours on television, the window displays in shops, the songs at the top of the charts – I see now that they aren't missing the point. Watching TV with Dad, I see it's all aimed at people who are drunk and grieving. That's why every-thing is about faces displaying contrasting emotions: the competition winner beside the runner-up; the angry protestors facing the calm police; the cats in the cages and the cats in the rescue home. (Dad isn't drunk. I thought he might drink more but it's still only the two or three glasses per evening.) Every other advert makes him cry. People treating other people well make him cry – especially if they say they're proud of one another. Sporting achievement slays him – the bronze medal. He is much sadder than I am. Occasionally, he'll say, 'She died too young' or 'It's just so unfair'. We might be watching dogs having operations, or a report on the Nasdaq. Because they watched a lot of television together, almost everything on television reminds Dad of Mum. Even so, TV is his best distraction. On the screen, he sees the sadness from the outside, with perspective and shading, with movement. When the TV is off, he's in the sadness and is the sadness, like slices of mandarin in orange jelly.

This is a bit like that page I wrote a couple of weeks ago and ripped up. Should I tear this out and rip it up, too?

Sonntag 29 Oktober

Drove home from Dad's in the morning.

Furry teeth can, I feel, be useful in bringing urgency to the work. If one of your anxieties is that you can feel the rot, you are more likely to be – have I written this before? Has someone else written this? I had the thought, in the form of a sentence, a couple of days ago – wheeling Boo through the park. I didn't write it down, forgot it, then remembered it yesterday (I think), while brushing my teeth. Before I brushed them, they were a little fuzzy. Afterwards, I made a note, but today, writing it, I am starting to think that I've already said the same thing in this diary, or something very similar (about the slight pressure of wanting to go to the loo being useful) or that I've read one or both of these statements in someone else's essay or blog. My sense is, I read the needing-to-go-pee thing but that I've made up the one about tooth decay. Which still leaves my sentence as derivative, if – perhaps – an observation that's worth making. After getting up, writing for a bit, having breakfast, returning to the desk and continuing through the morning: that's when furry teeth happen. I know Auden wrote about peeing (in the sink), but the statement isn't his. It might be an American writer. This sense – this being loomed over by precedence, comes more and more often; because it's me. I am repeating myself. In a diary, it doesn't matter; for a reader, it'll just be early signs of senility. What makes me anxious is that I might be doing it in fiction, and I'm sure I'm doing it when I teach. Giving the same writing advice I gave ten or fifteen years ago does, I suppose, it has stood the test or stayed the course. When I'm tired, I'm more self-repetitive; I also am clumsier. I am tired – did I already say that? I am so fucking tired. I am shagattered. Instead of writing this, I could have been napping alongside Leigh and Boo, who are side by side in our bed: she, long; he, long too, but mini. He stretches out, arms above his head as if celebrating. This, I've been told, is a good sign – a non-foetal baby is one that feels a right to its place in the world. Sounds dangerous.

Montag 30 Oktober

Dad had a fall, not serious but serious enough, and had to go into hospital by ambulance. This was yesterday afternoon. They are happy to discharge him tomorrow or the next day, but he can't look after himself yet, needs lifting out of chairs, so we're going to have to find a nursing home where he can stay for a week or ten days. 'Until he's on his feet again.' Would he have fallen if Mum was still alive? Has her death made him careless? It's made him unsteady in every way. Forty-five years of female guidance. I don't think he was drunk. He was in the downstairs loo. I don't think he's drinking. Luckily he has a call button round his neck, and pressed it. (Mrs. Hope knows help is coming.) He's just wobbly getting up, and diabetic, so he's slowly losing contact with his purple feet.

Just phoned my brother – I found somewhere in Bedford. They have a room that's just come free. 'We know what that means,' said my brother. 'Sadly,' he added. I will go up and take him tomorrow, or stay over and take him the day after – if the doctors want to keep him in one more night. I doubt they will; he's not exactly interesting to them. You start to see the world-shattering god as the nurses see him, just another old man – more charming than average – who forgets to drink enough water. Because his generation don't like water. ('Fishes pee in it.')

Dienstag 31 Oktober

This grab-bag is full of sweeties. Some shaped like skulls, some like vampires, some like plump pumpkins.

I made some notes, whilst sitting by Mum, I won't copy them out. I won't type them up.

Walter didn't do anything notable this month. He went fishing. Next month, he'll be sixty-seven.

Mouse has become a little less manic since Boo arrived.

When was the last time I went for a swim?

Mittwoch 1 November – *All Saints*

Heart-attack is not-cancer, and cancer is not-dementia. Of the three biggies, Mum would have chosen cancer. It allowed her to organize her finances, say her goodbyes, and die where it was no inconvenience to Dad or the emergency services. Imagine the embarrassment of dying at the bridge club, or the Citizens Advice Bureau! Dropping Dad off at the nursing home was awful. They welcomed us with some formalities about direct debits, then they showed us through into what they called the Atrium. It was a long conservatory which seemed, at first glance, pleasant enough. Old people sat to left and right, looking inwards. Dad – moving behind a walking frame – was taken to a free armchair, and I was fetched an upright chair to sit close to him. Even as we settled ourselves, a small man opposite was shouting every few seconds to Rosemary! (I guess his wife) in the next room. (When I asked, on the way out, I was told Rosemary! was too far gone to recognize him. He wasn't going to stop shouting, though – in hope she would come through to join him. The fact she ignored him made him angry.) But I remember most of all the man to Dad's left, Alfred. He didn't say anything to us when we sat down, just spat gently in the direction we were sitting – not because he hated us, but just because he always spat a little off to his right. This was the reason no-one had been sitting in that chair. I think one of the carers noticed, and realized they weren't making a good impression, because they came and suggested we move to a chair in the house. 'The quiz is about to start,' she said. 'General knowledge.' It was eleven o'clock. The prize was a chocolate bar, and Dad – type 2 diabetes – easily won. In fact, he called out every single answer ('Cairo!' 'George Harrison!' 'Focaccia.') before anyone else could speak. I wanted to say, 'Hold on, Dad. They're going to hate you if you just waltz in and start winning the quiz every Tuesday.' I had to leave him there, with the shouters and the spitters. He said he was fine. He said he would go up to his room soon, and have a nap. I had left his small travelling case on the bed.

Donnerstag 2 November – *All Souls*

I miss milk in my morning tea – and I had milky tea a couple of days ago, at the care home. Until you taste it really taste it, milk tastes like water, just like water tastes of nothing. Then, when you make an effort, you find there's an opening into plainness, whiteness, smooth-ness. Milk tastes as it looks, as cider does and whiskey doesn't. Whiskey should be blacker, redder, and should have gold streaks in it. (Also, maybe red wines taste white and white wines red.) The warmer milk gets, the fuller of savour it is – foetid milk, from the back window of the car after a long journey, is bilious and farty. Goats' cheese is its cousin, not its second cousin twice removed. But boiled milk had cracked the sugar-clouds and is choirs of strong comfort (by long association) – is chocolate without cocoa and honey plus spine. After drinking hot milk, I feel braver and more able to face the nightly battle of rough dreams. (Nothing ill come near thee!) (As one whom his mother comforteth, so will I comfort you.) Milk puts its white arms around me, as it sings, and tells me – not directly, only through the singing – that if I cry, I won't hear the words properly. If I keep crying, I may miss something very important – a statement – in its plainness and thereness. Although everything in and about the embrace is love, I could still miss this love if I don't show I am shhh. The hot milk needs to know that I am not here but there there. If she is to perform comfort, I need to perform being comforted. I don't want to be a bad boy, because I am her brave boy. Hasn't she given me everything? Haven't I drunk her blood direct from her, before I understood – years later – that it was milk? As if there's a difference. At the time, I was gulping time – more time and more time – blood-time – I needed more time to gulp more time – if I didn't gulp, I couldn't gulp – time would squirt too fast through time – time in my seeing and up my breathing – there was there – there was time there – I would choke on time – and pukely-puke up time – if I didn't gulp I wasn't a gulper, and all I was was the pulse in my throat – the time-blood-milk-pulse – the glug of the gulp a gulper glugs.

Freitag 3 November

I am shagattered. Did I say that already? I said that already. I think I need to say it again, because it's the chorus. Of my life. Of the song of my life. Right now. I'm so tired. Are you tired? Me, reading this – me, in the grown-up future, are you even more tired? When you remember this period, you won't remember this period, because you'll have been too tired to form memories. Here's a memory for you: Jack suddenly becoming Flipper again, at two in the morning, so that I saw him as if he were still inside the womb. Another memory: His head wobbling as he gets ready to latch on to the nipple, but then he doesn't latch on; and Leigh cries, feels failed as a mother, and weeps. He'll take a bottle with expressed breast milk – that's where we're at. Bone-tired. I am too tired to think of synonyms for tired. Even writing the word synonym is exhausting. Why bother? Books are for people who have slept or for people who can't get to sleep. I'm writing this now Leigh's mum has come to take over for a while, so we can sleep. I'm catching up on words. I am mimicking myself of a week ago but also anticipating where I'll be in a week's time. This is an interim of non-slog. Someone else is putting the crusty babygros and the fitted sheets and the muslins and our posseted-on clothes in the washing machine. I remember falling asleep with Boo on my chest, last Saturday or Sunday, and not worrying he would fall off because I knew I wouldn't move; I would be corpse-still until he grizzled and woke me. I was as secure as the mattress in his cot. Does the Booster Boo make me happier than writing? I don't know. He makes me very afraid that no decent writing will happen from now on, because I'm prepared to call another human being the Booster Boo. Is all that's left of me mush? Maybe I'll write better because I've become so vulnerable. Maybe I'll write worse, because I've become so vulnerable. Happiness, or greatness? Jack, or writing? Och, we know it's non-binary, this world. Don't make me choose. You snooze you lose.

Samstag 4 November

Dad seemed older when I went to visit this morning. He said he wanted to go home. But the doctors have said he needs at least another week. In the night, he said, women with dementia scream for the police. Some make choking sounds. 'It's really like they're dying,' Dad said. He kept trying to stand up, for me to take him home. I told him I couldn't. I explained why. Then he would try to stand up again. Drove home.

Sonntag 5 November *– Guy Fawkes – Bonfire Night – Fireworks*

2.44 am. It is enough for me that Jack is alive and safe with Leigh safe and alive to look after him and enjoy him, even if I were to be dead before the end of the next sentence. Short sentence. 2.57 am. All the reassurance I need is that the worst is still to happen, and if we're careful enough (carrying him up and down the stairs), and I'm superstitious enough, it might never happen. Sleep. 7.12 am. Here, I was going to list three possibilities that are different kinds of worst, but I don't even want to write the words. (They were fast death, slow death and very slow death.) 7.55 am. Years before there was any chance of me becoming a father – in Prague, in Bermondsey – I would think of these things, and how I didn't understand how the bereaved, the left-behind, didn't implode. Often, they do – not as black holes, but as consumers, alcoholics, non-participants. I am scared to even begin thinking of their pain. All of that love and all of that effort and all for nothing. Back from the chemist. 11.00 am. But it – their child – was never nothing. Since he was born, I have been asking myself whether Flipper's and John's and Boo's and Jack's lives would've been worth-while, even if they were to end within the month? Short month. 11.21 am. Is coming to sensation and consciousness of any sort – is warmth, dampness, blur, 11.31 am, dazzle, lullaby and cuddle and milk and sleep with dreams – and panic and weeping – are these, in themselves, with no aftermath – are these good? 4.42 pm. To feel your fist being coaxed through a snug cotton sleeve, and to sense poppers neatly clicking from your down-there to your up-here. 6.11 pm. To be lifted high-high and away from cramp and terror, and have the inner hurt burped out of you. 8.13 pm. To hear the hum of Mum, the future language you will never reach but which you can be sure adores you. 8.22 pm. But there are orphans who are only rarely picked up, 11.11 pm, and never with commitment. 1.54 am. Are their sensory lives, if over in a fortnight, better than continuing to be mineral?

Montag 6 November

Is unloved life, in the earliest moments, still a good? Sometimes I imagine a form of reincarnation that is this: in an infinite universe, every part of it at some time is every other part of it. In this iteration, I am myself, but in a multitude of others I am Leigh, Mouse, Boo but also each other object, animal, person that ever existed or will ever exist. I am this atom and then the next, but also this consciousness and this totality. This means that whatever I inflict, I also suffer; anything that is stolen from me, I also steal. (Without causal link or satisfaction – but there is absolute balance.) Similarly, I repeatedly experience every form of existence. On earth, I am virus, mica, oxygen (I spend a lot of time being oxygen) and stag beetle; elsewhere, I am whatever is possible there. So what of the human example, the infant born in a field to a shamed girl, a mother who lives only long enough to pull her baby from between her bloody legs and up onto her ribcage? That baby will, in its short life, know mainly distress and hunger. (I am saying neither he nor they nor she, because either seems punitive. But take it as a tender 'it'.) The warmth of what it lies upon will cool. Perhaps there are breezes across its back. It will cry and cry until it stops – a high, loud, full-body bleating of unanswered alarm. Like a dog miaowing. Although it won't know it is making noise, it will have that power. It may also be able to open and close its mouth, in quest of the nipple. Is this abandonment-to-being worthwhile, even so? It will hear the air, and the push of flesh against ear even if it doesn't hear birdsong or the barking of foxes. Through its eyelids will come light that it would have later known as red, pink, violet, purple, perhaps even green. If its eyes opened, it might see the blur of night. Its own tongue and its own drying spittle will be the only tastes it tastes, but they are tastes. I want to pick it up, the thought experiment, although there is no-one around; I can't bear him or them or her not being rescued by a shepherd or the guilty father. There is absolute balance. In an infinite number of iterations, they remain abandoned, and in an equally infinite number they are discovered.

Dienstag 7 November

If I start this entry further down the page, I won't have to write as much to reach the bottom.

Leigh, feeling 'baggy'.

Bill the plumber arrived and started work. We can use Holly and Nirpal's bathroom, while we don't have ours. Bill has an autistic son. Bill smashes tiles that we kept clean.

I suppose this adds up to a sort of self-portrait – desk as inky-stained mirror. If there's swank, it's because I'm swanky. Vanity, vain. I wish I wasn't as I am (but you know that already).

remembered rapture

Mittwoch 8 November

I feel guilty that I haven't changed completely. I'm angry with myself. I'm raging. I'm silently raging. Still, I want to write above anything else. Even now, I need to get away from people in order to be alone. Boo, I already realize, is going to count as 'other people'. His birth didn't change my essential selfishness. Am I already a bad father? (In this humid house, right now, change means nappies – reusable ones we keep in a white plastic bin, then put out once a week to be washed and returned.) But I think it's a good father who doesn't place the responsibility for their entire life upon their child. Leigh feels the same, I know; she wants to get back to her research whenever that's possible. I can hear the washing-machine running, puke and poo coming off babygros. Thank fuck we don't have to wash each by hand. I stood in my room, looking at my books, holding Boo against me, and said – to my books – I think I said it aloud, 'One day, I will get back to you.' And, oh, they seemed so far away. I just am too exhausted to think of a way of describing how far away they seemed. Later: They seemed way way away, off and over the sea from me, on a far shore, where adults live – that's the best I can do, after a cup of tea and some seed cake at 10 am – tribes of adults who lie on their backs all day long, using their single enormous feet as umbrellas, so they can read contemporary fiction in hardback. Boo grizzled or didn't. At that moment, I felt very intimate with my books. I knew they were as much part of me as Boo was or the sea was or yearning was. In writing this, I remember how much I wanted Boo to be born, and that's there – all the time – in the smell of his head. The *smells* of his head, because they are many: the sometimes-wrinkled brow smells skin-sweet but the fontanelle is sweeter, more like honeyed almonds, and behind his ears is friendly armpit, and where his skull meets his neck is slightly sulphuric. It's all a heroin version of scalp. He changes moment by instant. A red blotch can travel across his temple and down his cheek as you watch, like a Space Invader or a spaceship in Conway's Life. Time has gone weird, though: I keep waking up the day before yesterday with two weeks having passed since I checked what day it is. Or was. Or shall be. The days are made of cake. The cakes are made of spaceship.

Donnerstag 9 November

By now I have to say I like – I *love* the physical act of writing; it comforts me. (I phoned Dad. He is glad he's going home tomorrow.) At other times, pursuing other occupations, I feel as if I am presently dying – I feel aware of the dying on which my living is based. Worst of all for this, shoving the skull right up in my face, is shopping. I know that for some people, shopping has the opposite effect (and so shopping is their writing). When they are trying on clothes or choosing a saucepan, they feel they're doing the very thing life is about: improving. In that dress, they will be a different, better, more beautiful person – and they will meet more interesting, desirable people when transformed by the wearing of it. (It fits!) With that saucepan, they will cook just like a TV cook. If I'm forced to take the number 3 to Oxford Street and make these kind of choices, I feel I'm using something of myself up – something more than the hours they consume, these this or thats. I'll happily put in an equal number of desk-hours changing a character's appearance and soul, or having them make a drumkit from pots and pans. Food and clothes – these are essentials, not frivolous, and things I will always associate with Mum. (I will also associate drinking a glass of water and taking a deep breath with her.) Her cooking tasted good because (I realized a few years ago) she put cream in her goulash and butter in her risotto and generous seasoning in everything. I saw the skull come through her face when she stopped shopping – when she went into the hospice and knew she'd never have to visit Tescos again. Clothes were important to her, but I think she was very unsatisfied with how she looked in them, and even more unsatisfied with her preoccupation with appearance. Vanity. Apart from a Breton jumper, jeans shirt and Scholl sandals (on holiday in France), the most stylish thing she wears in any photograph is her wedding dress. It is white silk, ankle length, not fitted but shapely, with no visible seams. Today it would be more suitable for a Chief Bridesmaid. It is absolutely simple, chic – and with it she wears a white pillbox hat and a veil like floating petals. I can imagine this dress making Audrey Hepburn appear very Audrey Hepburn. Mum never felt particularly beautiful.

Freitag 10 November

Bill has made good, loud progress with the bathroom. It should be finished by the end of next week. Right now, it looks like a cave with plastic pipes. His son has been fine with him working away.

I took Dad home. He didn't cry with relief; he wanted the TV turned on. I was very close to crying.

'Rosemary!'

Samstag 11 November – *Remembrance Day*

Thinks: I'll be up at two, or one thirty, tomorrow morning – bottle diagonally down into the mouth of 'a growing boy'. Phrase has come to mean something, since I've seen a weight-double in seven weeks, and Boo's fast-forward complexion. Crusts and spots move round it like clouds seen from a satellite. Above his eyebrows down to under his chin. The yellow scurf on the front of his ears has now retreated behind. White flakes appear in minutes. You can see the trampoline buh-dum of his fontanelle, a Rorschach-shaped inlet where the horn of a rhino-like monster's head would be. (On the back of a dirty lorry, white finger-cleanings where the door must be opened – messy, vagina-shaped, like Jackson Pollock's 'The Deep'.) Boo smiles at his mother. He doesn't just look at her, he looks *to* her.

Sonntag 12 November

One thing isn't one thing – I can't keep them stable as dry goods, as discrete entities. If they don't slide into one another (most of them do), then I do their sliding for them. There are obvious relationships, as sensible and traceable as power lines between pylons (though try following these from nuclear generator to urban conurbation: what a tale of trespass and prosecution, of private lands and government reserves). There may even be ley-lines of mythic implication. But there are also non-identical twinnings, there are unmorphed units linked to flamboyant switches, there are circuits schizzing with sweet polar energies, there are jellies full of atomic kindship with alloys and hairballs. Constantly, it spasms – the interlinkages that are more like yoghurt than physics, more like charisma than logic. (I'm not saying it's a good thing.) Perpetually non-nothing turns itself inside-out. No personal property. It is very hard to notate this when it's a nine- or eleven-dimensional visual score. Trying to try hard isn't going to make it any easier, and nor will acid or schizophrenia. There are no short cuts to the metamorphic sublime. Mis-spell Nietzsche. Proteus Unbound. It is burgeoning, all of the yeastiness of us, and it is consuming sugars. We can no longer afford our own meanings. We can no longer afford our own meaningfulness. We can no longer afford our own meaningfulnesses. Soon enough it will be fungus on every gun-emplacement, leakage dripping into irradiated silos, moss thrilling through concrete, bacterial Vegas and Havana.

Back to the fun of fundays.

Boo's hair has gone spontaneously into a mohican.

Montag 13 November

Boo pukes two feeds in a row; world darkens, slightly.

Dienstag 14 November

Bad night last night. Didn't get to sleep until around three. Boo refusing to sleep. I had him for quite a while, walking up and down, singing in my croaky voice. (Cold I've had since he was born.)

I should remember I had bad nights before – 16 June. It wasn't all sleep.

Becoming a father changes clarinet to oboe, grandfatherdom oboe to bassoon.

Leigh having an evening bath. Not me.

Mittwoch 15 November

Writing with my right hand, Boo on my right shoulder. If we do one thing a day (lunch today, film yesterday) it means I find it difficult to work. I have to look after the Booster whilst Leigh expresses. I can hear the sucker grinding away downstairs. Boo doesn't like sleeping unless he's on one of us. This situation will improve. This situation will improve.

[Written in the margin in pencil sharpened with the black pencil sharpener (new):

'You're not depressed,' says imaginary Mum. 'You're just a bit glum – buck your ideas up. Spit-spot – that's the spirit.' I don't know if my mother ever quoted Mary Poppins at me.]

Donnerstag 16 November

Weariness is with me at the desk, or perhaps just average knack-eredness – and maybe also sometimes depression; but the fact I put *maybe* convinces me it isn't. Not really. 'Depression can be mild,' and I suppose there's no reason I don't have the wash of it over me. Yes, I do have thoughts of suicide. No, I don't have a suicide plan. Ideation. Well, I know I wouldn't jump in front of a train – because of the driver – or off a cliff – because of the palaver. Recently the idea has been of swimming straight out to sea, then straight down, then opening my mouth and letting the happiness in. I am tired. Jack wakes, sleeps, wakes, pretends to sleep, wakes. I've never been this tired. My tired is tired of being tired. My tired is tired, but still wants me to talk about being tired to anyone who'll listen – usually other new parents who are too tired to listen. They wear their favourite jumpers and touch their eyelids more often than usual. 'I'm exhausted,' we say – competing to find a new way to put it (but too tired to do so). 'I'm just utterly fucked,' one Dad said. 'I almost drowned—' said another. 'Fell asleep in the bath.' 'You had a *bath*?' we said. 'When did you have time to have a bath? I've been flannel-washing since August.' I just took a break, to rest my head on this lovely, comfortable page. I might have ink on me now; my head had sunk down before the word August dried. My so-called depression isn't David Foster Wallace's black spider (corner-hiding, needle-armed, lethal). What do we think of DFW now? Poor man./ When you hang yourself so the person you love most will be the one to find you. Bad man./ When you are so panicked the meds no longer work, because you came off them to go onto better ones that turned out worse. Poor man./ When you once threw a woman from a moving automobile. Non-man./ When you're writing *The Pale King*, and *The Pale King* isn't working – because you're a pseudo-Buddhist, and fascinated with boredom, labour, blankness, but you can't make these fly narratively (and your last book was *Infinite Jest*). The Man./ So you write for a while about infinity, but end up back in the slough of yourself. Again. Poor man./ He doesn't need anyone's forgiveness. His own final act would have made him shake his head, touch his cheek, touch his bandana sweat. Dead man./ Tax return. Hanged man.

Some people, it should be said, did notice my awfulness, and tried to save me from it. (I seem to have been joined by regret at the desk.) Immediately after Oxford, I went to my parents' house in the very very far South of France. They referred to it as a château. It was three sides of a courtyard, with towers to left and right as you drove in. When I got there the house was occupied by builders working for Titus, the rogue whose project it was. Apart from my parents' bit, there were five or six more units, including one for the live-in caretaker. Owning part of a château was the height of my parents' affluence. There was Titus, Walter, and Walter's wife, Ally, and their toddler, and Noy, and Dave. Walter was the one who attempted to save me from myself. He was burly, bald but gave a sense of having a cross-dressing alter ego. He owned a 2CV. One evening, I had gone into the village – about two miles from the house. Walter, alone, picked me up. How I was – my coldness, my deadness – had obviously struck him, and pissed him off. For some reason of his own, kindness or aggression, he confronted me with it as soon as he drove off. I can't remember his exact words. I think, like Henry James' Strether, he told me I had to *live* – that I was young but wasn't alive. What I do remember exactly is what Walter did, in his 2CV. When we were out of the village, and I wasn't responding: he began to weave the steering wheel and swerve the car, zigzaggly. Then he turned off the headlights. My deadpan became more absolute. I sat like a dowager. I sat like May of Tek at a funeral service for a beloved servant. Walter was doing his Lawrentian best to prompt me into fear, passion, life. He didn't know what he was against – boarding school, me vs. my parents, the shared house in Oxford where for the final four months I probably said twenty words to my housemates. My carapace would take years to be corroded away, from the inside (with thought) and from the outside (with love). Chekhov's 'The Man in a Shell'. Walter was trying to sledgehammer it open. I wish he had, but it was impossible. In the 2CV, I was profoundly embarrassed – for him. That he was doing something so obvious as begging me to *live*. E.M. Forster, *A Room with a View*. 'Such an undeconstructed concept,' I thought, 'Life.' And I remember what

Samstag 18 November

he did in his despair, after he'd stopped zigzagging the car and turned the headlights back on – his despair at my sangfroid. Walter stopped the 2CV in the middle of the Southern French road and roughly kissed me on the lips. No attempt at tongue, not that I remember, just a kiss – the kiss of life. Walter was married. Walter and Linda had a toddler. Walter was involved with human emotions and rebuilding a house. Perhaps he was a plasterer or a painter; I don't think he was a brickie. The kiss failed – or its effects only started to come through months after I was out of the 2CV. I didn't flinch. I made it as if it hadn't happened. Perhaps Walter was wise enough to know that this scene, forced, embarrassingly like a scene from a coming-of-age novel, would only mean anything – change anything – years later. But I get the sense he gave up on me immediately. In the following days, there wasn't even any awkwardness between us. He must have told Linda, who wore dresses with dots on and put up with an incredibly male house – where they chopped the heads off champagne bottles with a machete, off the balcony, over the lawn (my parents were still finding corks ringed with glass two years later), and where they plotted to liberate Nelson's battle standard from a small French church and bring it in glory back to Bath. I wonder, did Walter expect me to kiss him back – to show warmth, and prove I wasn't entirely a cold fish? Truth is, I was a cold fish – drained of blood, slices of cucumber for armour. And today – today what? – I admit I can see myself doing exactly what Walter did to me, to some het-up version of myself who needed kissing. Because my carapace was a horrid, appalling thing – but it was also expensive and well constructed. Walter was against death, explicitly; he was fighting my death-in-life. I get the feeling that if I'd been a Spaniard or a Cuban, no-one would have permitted me to go as far as I had into the psychic deepfreeze – but maybe I am accepting a touristic or E.M. Forster view of countries with warmer climates and (heavens) hotter blood. E.M. Forster, *A Passage to India*. We have no India, no Italy. I imagine a flirtatious grandmother forcing me to dance, or an uncle taking me to a brothel. Not that

Sonntag 19 November

there aren't Hispanic *otaku* or Cuban bedroom-dwellers. I, as me, would have hated being forced to be embodied, and communal, and funky. Earlier, as a thirteen-year-old, not yet entirely gone over to The Smiths, maybe I would have shyly welcomed a detour back into mental health. The world in general would still have been equally wrong, but I might have moved along my line within it more – if not more gracefully, then less gracelessly. Walter was my one-man South. But it took the ignorance of Prague to give me the outlet – not physical, but the possibility of an emendation word by word.

Why am I thinking this now, and feeling it urgent enough to write? Perhaps because we had sex again, a couple of nights ago. It was lovely but very different. It was different but very lovely. Not conception sex; completion sex. Woolly.

Montag 20 November

My cardy. I never did my woolly cardigan, writing about what I wore when I wrote lots. (Back in the before-times.) Good to have bare arms to write — left elbow on the desk or opposite page; right arm free to rub desk-surface with skin, not nubby fabric. The cardigan looks home-made, used to belong to my dad, might have been knitted by Mum for him — I can't ask her any more, and I don't want to ask him because he'll start crying. The pattern is grey with a double row of blood red squares (dried on paper blood) alternating with a single row of sky-sea blue-green (colour of my eyes, with added grey). The squares have a lightly criss-cross butterflyness to them. Everywhere it can be frayed or mothed, the cardy is. But I love it: it was round me when the good words came and when they didn't, when I spilled the coffee and everything else I could manage.

I should mention that Bill finished the bathroom today, which is a relief. It's not a good idea to have a baby and a plumber at the same time.

Dienstag 21 November

But I do make something, even if it's to my own distaste – I try to make a new thing every day.

I am leaving the rest of the page blank.

Mittwoch 22 November

'Oh God, I always really fancied you, I just never – you know – got up the nerve to actually tell you.' Isn't this the *worst* thing anyone can say? Especially when they're just married, or seven months pregnant. But I suspect something like this is what obituaries are for, in my case. 'We always rated him, we just never felt moved to buy and read and talk about and review his books. And now we're really really sorry.' (It can never flourish 'til its stock is in the ground.) I'll never be such a good writer, and such a fine chap, as on the day my death is announced. Until then – unless I am taken hostage and released – I will never know how loved and admired I am. All those editors who really fancied me, and those publishers too nervous to tell me what they feel. 'Brilliant writer, terrible sales.' A shake of the sad head; a tut at the bean counters. 'If only he'd been a bit more popular, he'd have been a lot more popular.' The problem – my problem – the problem of me – is that I have never written the same book three times in a row. (J.G. Ballard. Sarah Waters.) 'You just never knew what you were going to get when you opened the packet – and though I admire that, the reading public need a bit of a chance to settle down and catch up.' Years ago, Lawrence Norfolk advised me to write a series like *A Dance to the Music of Time*, or at least a trilogy. 'They'll never get you otherwise,' he said. Oh, I think they get me – they get me alright. 'He wrote too many books. It's not good to give people the sense that if they miss this one there'll be another along in a minute.' If only I could have been like Donna Tartt and fucked glamorously off for a decade between novels. Worked on my collapse. Crafted my anorexia and my other absences. 'I'm afraid to say we all rather took him for granted.' (Donna Tartt is not anorexic.) Sadly, I've forgotten the things I wanted to drop into interviews about previous novels – all the subterranean links are rotting away. If someone started to dig, there's a lot they would find. Out of print. I will never be Donna Tartt. A shake of the red hat. No-one fancied me – I was never distant enough for them not to tell me what they thought.

Donnerstag 23 November

I've never been all that good at living, and I was really crap at being young. I mean, at being twenty-five; at nine-years-old, and ten, I was master of many important life-skills: tree-climbing, fire-lighting, running fast over gorse. I knew what to do in case of a German invasion. I enjoyed testing myself, preparing. If there was an assault course, I was round it twice. (Mouse has caught a moth, and is having fun with it. I have to end that. Moth didn't survive. It wasn't super-special, just carpet brown and a miracle.) But then I grew out of War, and Space – and once Girls became paramount, I never had much fun having fun. Because I was performing in hopes they'd like me, love me. I never really enjoyed fun. By sixteen, seventeen, I'd started to fear death so much – fear dying before I'd done something to justify living – that every hour became Happiness, or Greatness? (Life, or Theatre?) Yes, I got drunk, snogged, smoked pot, took acid (once). Later, for about a fortnight, I was promiscuous, and slept with anyone who'd have me (three people, it turned out). But there was always a sense drenching me, steeping me, that the water of life was art not sex or any other kind of fun. People found me cold. (Walter.) I was a sorbet, ice run through with the wrong kind of sweetness – a sorbet of remorse. (All sorbets have always tasted to me of remorse, even the raspberry ones.) It was impossible for this pear-shaped body just to be pleasured flesh, and for me not to watch myself watching myself. If he's good at anything, I'd like Boo to be good at incarnation. We joke about the Berlin Philharmonic, Leigh and I, but I'd also like him to happen upon his true vocation, and for it not to be out-of-date or futuristic. Having a calling that is the echo of your own moment, with time running backwards so you seem ahead of it – that's the luckiest anyone can be. At twenty, the need to be elsewhere, working, made me undesirable. How could people have me if I was already had? Already seven years married to a desk.

I ain't got no home in this world any more.

Freitag 24 November

Wrote some more novel.

Samstag 25 November

To Dad's. My brother there. We sprinkled some of Mum's ashes around the flower beds. (Make their garden grow.) The rest of her is in a big off-white jar on the windowsill in Dad's bedroom – behind it is a framed photograph of her I've never seen before. She's sipping a chocolate milkshake through a straw, and looking mischievous and holiday-happy. We had some champagne, toasted Mum, then had some tea.

When Dad had gone upstairs for a nap, I told my brother about a strange recent conversation with him. He said he'd spotted Mum, flitting – he says she flits from room to room. I told my brother he insisted he'd spoken to Mum, and that she had told him he was 'doing well'. 'No, that wasn't Mum,' my brother said. 'That definitely wasn't Mum. If she had the chance to speak to him, she'd give him a bollocking. "You're not looking after yourself properly, David."' We laughed. Mum would not be chuffed with Dad. And she'd let him know it.

Sonntag 26 November

Page missing.

Montag 27 November

Page missing.

Dienstag 28 November

I wrote yesterday about my father. Cut it out.

He smoked, she didn't; she died, he didn't.

Mittwoch 29 November

I wrote something like this: How can I avoid becoming my father? Is there any way my back – bent now over this page – won't soon be as bowed as his? Can I remember to be polite, and ask people more than one question about themselves?

Of what am I most afraid? That was the question I brought to the desk this morning, though I only thought of it halfway down the stairs from taking Leigh her tea. But now I see it on the page beneath yesterday's, and one answers the other: I am most afraid of becoming my father, but what may allow me to avoid this is my terror of becoming him, and my awareness of my terror of becoming him. Becoming what? Becoming unobservent, inexpressive, non-productive, selfish – I want to continue to be useful, even if only in my limited literary way. (Not a doctor.) Maybe I owe my father my vocation, because I early on began to notice that he wasn't noticing things my mother and I noticed. About the mood of the room just above the rug, about the consensus of the birds singing in the pines in the park. Details too small for a giant like him to perceive, just as he couldn't thread a needle or pick up a pin from a marble floor. However, this means I was always trying to be his countertype. In the flat above the antiques shop, I took to taking my mother's side. Wanting to be in her voicing of the world, which stayed warm with me and didn't speak from the corners of the ceiling, which didn't have a chin that gave me shin pie and made me scream – wanting the kind of vocation she would share in a whisper, not sell in a speak. Along came my brother, and home was permanently won for femininity. Go away – go away, we were just playing. We were just playing an L.P. of Carmen, of the Carnival of the Animals, of Peter and the Wolf. We were just playing botany, and saving spiders rather than killing them – look at their eight hairy legs, but those aren't hairs. I don't think my father noticed he was an interruption.

Donnerstag 30 November

It's not as if there's always a subject. Sometimes there's just grief and routine alongside ambition and curiosity. (Sometimes, more accurately, there's the grief of routine and the ambition to maintain curiosity.) I admit, it is a curious ambition, to maintain a routine of your grief – like smoking, like consciously remaining a smoker, now, into early middle age – a smoker who still rolls their own cigarettes (from Mellow Virginia in Rizzlas). From childhood, I remember some smokers who smelled delicious, and you wanted to be near the baking of their Russian Honey Cake, whereas others – slaves to the same brand of tobacco – were like heatwave urinals that made everyone gag. However, there are also in-between people who reek of charisma – and that charisma may include pee-pee among its notes of pepper, accomplishment, bacon, plus sperm or menstrual blood, or both. At a certain point in my youthful yearning, around the time I wanted to do nothing but stay in my bedroom listening to Cocteau Twins on my Akai stereo, my parents would take me out to antiques emporia or English Heritage properties, and I would smell someone who would totally overwhelm my subjectivity – that's my way of putting it now. Back then, I'd just have said (if forced) that I wanted to *be* them – wherever they lived, I wanted to live there, whatever they did or didn't do, I wanted that as my occupation, and whoever loved them, I wanted to intoxicate them, too. If that had miraculously happened, and I had never gone back to my records and my village, I wouldn't have mourned. As I inhaled their hormonal routines of boudoir and attic, lawn and library, they – becoming like them, becoming them – became my ambition. All of them always seemed self-complete, and of course I never spoke to any of the so so fragrant, redolent ones. The heirs. The Parisians. The virtuosi. I was beneath their curiosity, beyond the pale of their civilization. But that was what made me adore them. I was extraneous. For them, je n'existe pas. Les plusieurs. L'inconséquent. If they had known I'd one day make myself into a writer, perhaps they'd have flinched. How could something so ordinary – like the smell of a match lit five minutes ago or the infinitive of the verb to be – even begin to aspire to a fabulous subject? It's not as if there's always a subject.

Freitag 1 December

Strange how little I've thought about teaching, and students, since – since Mum died or since Boo was born. I can't tell which. I was thinking about teaching during the Summer, thinking it wasn't going to happen.

A student (Felix) made an official complaint against me. He is questioning the mark his dissertation got. He claims I was biased against him. Because he is a man.

I know what Walter would do to him.

Story about a cat-owner. The cat starts speaking to them, but only says one thing, and only says it twice. The cat looks up at them and says, 'They'll never believe you.' 'What?' they say. 'They'll never believe you,' says the cat, and never speaks again.

Samstag 2 December

Again and again I try to teach myself patience, and again and again I become angry at how angry I've become – over the slightest thing at the most trivial time. Like a man, like a human man, like a humanly human man, I swear at the constant physical betrayals of the world. It seems designed for nothing more than to humiliate me – me, who it should augment and flatter! Important, dignified and universally admired moi! Ich, who am the ultimate point and cause of every last atom of it! You fucking fucker. When the floor becomes a trip hazard, because I am paying more attention to how three words sound, one after the other. (Nearly never not.) When I have a sneezing fit whilst carrying two cups of coffee up the stairs. You bastard. When I chip a nail trying to lock my bike or bang my head getting into the back of a New York taxi – because the brim of my baseball hat is hiding the frame of the door. Cunting cunt. Sometimes I laugh at my own rage, before it makes me punch the desk. What a silly billy. But more often there's no outside to it – the thing that I'm in, the annoying agitated self, is inescapable. I want to be able to order time to skip back to before the accident. I want political decisions – on a larger scale – not to be so obviously disastrous. (The British people seem to like disaster. They are so much in love with the idea of a new war, a second Blitz, a fresh Dunkirk. Any chance to get angry at the French or make threats towards the Germans.) And so, I sit on my zafu and continue sitting even when I feel sitting is the most annoying thing I've ever done. I could rip out of my body and just spasm into HULK SMASH! But I continue sitting, and sit this out, sit tight, sit on it, and I see there's still a wall in front of me, and a body in front of that wall, and the wall gives as much of a shit about the body as the body does about the wall.

Sonntag 3 December

My self-image and my disposition in respect of that image – *what I think of me* – is that I am generally well liked and, I suppose, that this goodwill depends on me being generally (to everyone I encounter) pleasant, polite and inoffensive. Hello to the person behind the till, and goodbye, too. Exactly – as near as I'm able – how my mother would wish me to be. Thank you and please and your hair looks nice and how are you feeling today? If I think someone hates me or thinks I'm a cunt, I find it hard to continue my gesture. Man interrupted. Leigh says, when we talk about it, 'Imagine how anodyne you'd have to be, never to offend anyone.' And I think that I have often in recent years aimed for anodyne – 'I have been more timorous of exciting animosity than desirous of provoking animated devotion.' (Translation: I would prefer not to be known than not to be liked.) That's not what I said back to Leigh, not in those words in this century; that's what I said in 1787. In this century and kitchen, I said, 'I know I want everyone to like me, and I know this is a weakness.' But there is more than enough hatred in the world; it seems the one thing that can be created from nothing. Compassion consumes patience, empathy, humour – saying to someone, 'No, that's not what I meant' (even though it was). The fuel for hatred is hatred, and it's the kindling also, and the spark, and the desire to light a fire and get warm by burning something or someone down. Even at the desk, I feel inhibited by the idea that what I write is being anticipated with disgust. There are muggers, around the next corner, and they don't want to steal my phone, they just want to kick me. You fucking cunt. Look at you, already on fire, and you don't even know it yet. I want to be empty – I want to walk past them as my broken outline, without detail, easy to miss. Anyone who has been bullied will choose invisibility for their superpower. They will stretch themselves out, as thin as they can go, in order to do their best not to be locatable or kickable in one spot. But the rule of the whole thing, the thing of the world, is violence – violence done as eloquence or violence taken as harm. It's clobberin' time. It's always clobberin' time.

The password to my laptop is d!sregarded*

Montag 4 December

People have told me that, after a while – they differ in how long – I will go back to remembering Mum as she was before she got ill, before she got spectre-thin and bald and went into the hospice. They don't say, but they also mean, I will forget how she was when she died (quite a few people know we were there, me and my brother). I don't think I will ever forget that. It was too horribly real. It was the realest thing, even though it was mediated by horror movies and – well, mainly horror movies. I don't think high art prepared me for the death-rattle. Sibelius 5th Symphony, last movement, maybe. The final breath and then, when you think she's restful, the full stop, and that's surely it, we're safe, and after a sublime minute of calm, the harsh gasp and the tight grasp, and you're looking into an open mouth that's hissing the smell of tooth decay through a horse's teeth – and you want to be full of love but really you've never been more appalled. (My mother the war.) You've never been more disgusted, and guilty about it already, but you held hands – you did manage to hold hands right to and through the end. And you and your brother didn't say 'Fucking hell – what the fuck was that?' even though it's what both of you were thinking. 'Why did no-one fucking tell me it's a horror movie ending, false ending, false false ending?' You leave the death room as fast as you can. You get out and go and drive through the Bedfordshire night. And you switch on the radio to hear some deejay being upbeat, and you think 'How can you? How can you when *that's* the end?' Then they play a song, and you realize, *that* being the end explains a lot of why the deejay is how the deejay is, and why the song even exists. The song sounds different. Like everything, the song is suddenly saturated, squeeze it and it'll weep, piss itself, rain wetness on the song below. You never realized how spongey everything is. My mother has been sucked up into trees, flowers, clouds, headlights, indicators, stop signs, cakes, spatulas, caster sugar, teeth, wigs, rings and into the words for all these things. (She taught me most of these words.) It's even worse for Dad, which is why everything makes him cry – in the days after you tell him. He can't pick up a tea-towel without looking at it and saying, 'She was so young – it's so unfair.' And he wasn't even there when she died.

Dienstag 5 December

Writing this (I'm continuing from yesterday) isn't making me feel any better. Mouse hasn't visited for a few days. I don't think he's being tactful. Perhaps I smell different.

There was a woman in the room with us, when Mum died – I realize I left her out when I wrote that yesterday. She was a bit naff, with her death-spiel, saying things like, 'Your children are here, Helen, and they love you very much,' but I was glad she was there, otherwise that wouldn't have been said – not in that way. Mum became weary with being told we loved her. I didn't like hearing a stranger use her name so often – the celebrant at the funeral did that, too. The woman was a nurse from the hospice, and she did tell us a few things to expect. That the bowels sometimes loosen. But afterwards she apologized for not having warned us of the death-rattle – it has another name, Latin, beginning with s. 'Sometimes they stop breathing for quite a long time.' 'Sometimes they.' They, plural; they, from being present many times at many deaths – this one not memorable. 'I'm sorry it shocked you.' My brother was sprayed against the fucking far wall – if he could have gone back through the bricks, he would've done. Away from here, away from her. The Mummy. My father must never know this. We told him it was a good, peaceful death. We had learned. That's what a good, peaceful death looks and sounds and smells like. She wasn't in pain, she wasn't Keats in the coffin-room hanging over the Spanish Steps, but she seemed to keep going beyond all reason. Her heart, so strong and fit, bucked on – spasming her through minute after hour after day and night and day of continued, unnecessary life. That fucking inflatable mattress churning the whole time. It's not morally difficult. I could tell you the minute she'd have wanted it ended. She was so healthy it made her final internal collapse slow-motion. I wished she'd been a lifelong smoker. End it quicker. S for Singultus. Such a strong, bucking heart in a starving, cancer-haunted body. She squeezed the blood out of my hand; she squeezed it white. And I turn from that to Boo, and I find him an unbearable consolation.

Mittwoch 6 December

I wrote a couple of months ago about my Mum's advice to me, before I went up to Oxford. I didn't write about losing my virginity – which I try not to think about, too much – to someone I didn't love. Even when she was dying, but still well enough, I didn't bring this subject up with Mum. Maybe she would have liked to know whether I'd followed what she advised, or disobeyed. We weren't beyond that, even in the hospice. Just she and I, plus the wheezing mattress. I don't think we broke into some field free of embarrassment – people do, don't they? Sons are able to ask, 'What were you thinking when – ?' Daughters are able to bring up taboos, laugh about them. The deathbed as sexual liberation. Of course, I told Mum I loved her every time I saw her – even when I could see similar declarations from other people were extremely wearying to her. I mean, they caused her to flop from the effort of responding. She wanted it just to be in the room, the love, but known and unspoken. Anyway, I think that's what she wanted. And so, I never told her about Lynn, nor about the fact I didn't tell Lynn I was a virgin until afterwards – when it hadn't gone swimmingly, when it had only barely involved penetration (perhaps) – and how Lynn cried, without speaking, and how the room suddenly became the saddest room I'd ever been in. And how, perhaps even on returning to my room, after walking Lynn back to the room of the friend who'd invited her to the party the night before – perhaps that same early morning I wrote my first short story, called 'Happiness,' which said exactly what had happened and what had not happened. I've never been able to write that story well enough. I sometimes think that everything I've done since was an attempt to become a good enough writer to write it. Lyn was over a decade older than me – which seems a lot now. Beautiful. Beautiful heart-shaped face. Absolutely black hair, pale skin of the English winter – or maybe she was Scottish. Wouldn't that be wonderful? Her generosity – the fact she liked me well enough to undress in front of me. But I should have told her, not styled it out. Even if I didn't at the time, I sort of love her now. You have to love someone if you're together with them for so long, for decades, in a room that sad.

Donnerstag 7 December

The student (Felix) has withdrawn his complaint. Once he realized he was still going to get a distinction, despite not getting over 70 for his dissertation, he calmed down. One day, he will ask me to give him a reference, and I will give it.

Freitag 8 December

Since December last year, I have changed – been changed; I am – am I? – less certain, fuller of different brands of terror. I'm fuzzier. It is no longer clear to me, in almost any circumstance, whether I am doing the right thing. (Pick up, put down?) (Leave room, go in?) I have less self-confidence because, I think, it seems – 'it seems' rather than 'I think' – I have less self. That reads badly. The self has less time to be selfish. One of the NCT mothers said, 'I don't know who I am anymore.' She was about to cry. Cry gently and easily, like a person who has done a lot of crying. Cry like we all cry now, unembarrassed, being around a lot of crying. She was talking to another one of the mothers, Farha (it was Farha, at Farha's house) – I overheard, because I had tuned out of the fathers' conversation. They had been talking about finessing their burping techniques. Tea and cake and comparison. This was a couple of days ago, maybe three. Jumpers with snot stains on the shoulders. The smell of warm yoghurt-not-yoghurt and antiseptic and occasionally the sonic boom of a poo. These are the smells of all our homes. 'I'm just a feeding machine,' said Farha, who runs part of a plant-importing business. 'I'm just a breast.' She had started to whisper by the third sentence, and might have said, 'I'm just depressed.' It's harder for people whose jobs were social. They're suddenly at home all the time whereas I'm still at home all the time, it's just that all the time is now very little time for anything but keeping Boo alive and comfortable. We fear nappy rash, and the bad nights that follow. We think about those who have been sleep-deprived as a form of torture. I like my hands – I just spent a minute looking at them. I'm grateful they are capable of doing the fiddly nappy stuff. This evening we will watch television and try to be ordinary. Because of the long slide to Christmas, the screen is full of sparkles and often sounds like synthesized bells – this is not only during the adverts, which we no longer turn down and talk over. We sit and accept them. I part-love this fug, and the moments I am abandoned and grayfolded within it. But I would like to be on the ramparts of a hill fort – a frosty morning, a sword in my hand, my watch about to begin – I would like to know crisp, medieval senses again. Cut through to the world which still has thorns.

Samstag 9 December

I will use a pen I never use to say what I never say. A red pen, only every intended for correction, not for joyful disquisition, wrongheaded splurge. (Boo slept for four hours. I have energy today!) It is a privilege to witness the end. Just because the human story is concluding, there's no reason the funeral rites need be any less spiffy than the christening. At least, we secretly feel, we're here for one of the main bits – not 1740 to 1750 or 9000 to 8000 BCE or the million decades when the earth was doing nothing but cool. Each of us makes his own negative contribution to extraction. When you're in a hole, stop digging. We know we're naughty, leaving the charger on overnight – sipping oil through plastic straws. Nothing smells more like first love than gasoline evaporating from noonday blacktop; it gives you the headache and the high and the hope. I am a driver just like you. We rev at the lights, we overtake one another on the straights, we brake too late for the apex and corner on two wheels. There will be a crash. As Ballard knew, that's what cars are for – carmageddon – demolition derby – the wrecking ball. Here we witness the interpenetration of sternum and steering column, the tremulous juncture of injection-molded aluminium and moist pudenda. We are not unaroused.

DANGEROUS BEND AHEAD – SPEED UP.

Societies are immoderate; socialized humans are greedy. We were doomed the moment we synthesized fun. *I could give up everything but...* We are desperate to total it and get back to geological time. Let's leave our multicoloured stripe in the fossil record, the Legocene, and after that the nuclear smear of half-life aeons. Perhaps some other. What rococo creatures this fizzy planet will pupate! What sub-tigers and gray post-fetishwear carapaces of crawl! All unrecorded.

Sonntag 10 December

Today, as some other days, around one in three, I feel I have the wrong head on. This head might be good for smashing some cunt's nose, or eye-socket, or cheekbone, but it's useless for doing what I need it to do – which is, right now, coming up with examples of things my dur-brain might be good for. Why am I fantasizing violence? Headbutt of a butthead. I just saw Boo in his Moses basket. I just put my fingers under his nose to check he was breathing, because he was breathing so lightly. Why am I raging? It must be because the skull beneath this skin, this head I hold, feels as if it wants to go heavily forwards, and end up somewhere significant. I gotta fuckan do fucken somethin before I fuckin die. You're in my fuckin way. Isn't all writing gatecrashing someone else's mind? Especially writing music. Yesterday I was thinking – while holding the small boo – Beethoven is a bully. At any given moment, he doesn't let you feel anything but what he wants you to feel. He stands on a podium and conducts your scored soul. Bach, by contrast, allows you to walk openly through the architecture or knot garden that he envisaged from the start as *for others*. It's the difference between being alone in an unlocked cathedral or deserted alameda and waiting in a cell for the torturer to have you fetched. But Beethoven comes after Bach – and we've been trying ever since to be either more or less of an artist than him. Maybe, in its brutality, I have on my Beethoven-head, and know that with it I am about to do bone-damage, and so am Beethoven regretting the shattered civilization of Bach. You can sense, very often, that Beethoven is already nostalgic for what he is in the process of destroying, of obliterating. Praeludium: Everyone – gentlemen, ladies, everyone – if you want to, if you care to look through this doorway that I am nodding and gesturing towards as a possibility, if you pop your head in first and then follow if you feel like it – here is grief or exultation or stoicism or the horn. Here is a powerful emotion you are free to choose not to share.

We are all of us, even God, incomplete.

Montag 11 December

'My exhaustion is an ocean; my panic is oceanic.' I woke up with this phrase, having dreamed it (including semi-colon), and it was *all* I had to bring to the desk. Much too rubbish for a poem, but not without trashy truth. The different waves of tiredness I'm feeling go from tsunami to gentle undulations in the sunlight over rippled sand – where being a floppy being is an entire pleasure. I'm on paternity leave; all I have to do this morning is buy some wipes from the chemist. But then, Oh God, there's the shattering of self against high cliffs of *I just can't do this*. Three a.m. this morning after wakes at nine thirty (we were in bed by nine) and ten thirty and twelve and two fifteen. Cleaning up puke from the kitchen floor, and myself, with Boo as perky as a meerkat – London outside, snoring under orange skies. Then comes the morning, with a trip up north to the cranial fucking osteopath – who does nothing that seems to make any difference (I can see her fingers moving, as if the back of Boo's head were a clavichord). And driving there and getting everything into the car in the first place – clothes bag, spare clothes bag, nappies and changing kit, buggy base, expressing gear, wipes and muslins, a book to not read while we're waiting (if he sleeps). So much stuff to do so many things. If we were on the savannah in Africa-before-it-became-Africa, he'd just shit on the ground as we held him away from us. He'd breastfeed or die. We'd carry him under our non-spear arm or on our backs. Prehistorically, we could do without these things we use once and throw away – these exhausting things. In between landfalls of crash and smash, there are all the moods of seafaring waves. I am lifted with joy but sink in despair; I surge with hope and lurch into troughs of terror; I twist into turbulence then relax into long smooth calms – interrupted by the feeding of gannets. When I look out across myself and the wide future of myself, all I see is all waves behind waves following waves chasing waves – all the way to the dim horizon – and each wave has its glint and its shadow. A fin, too – there might be a fin far out and a shark and a death and blood splurged through the blue water. Jack's blood. The wave might crest over the cranium of a gigantic octopus – the beast of absolute collapse, the behemoth of utter submersion! The tentacles!

Dienstag 12 December

The tentacles! I could be suckered and clung to and dragged down into a washy-weedy heroin unconsciousness of fatherhood. Underwater, I would find I could breathe the watery element. My merman concerns would be entirely practical. Have we got enough seaweed to clean Boo's bottom if he does five poos today? Should we stop letting Boo sleep between us on the sea-bed, in case the currents of my dreams roll me onto him, and he suffocates? But then, we surface into sunlight, and there are the dolphin moments, when Boo is still Flipper at his absolute Flippermost. I've tried to write this well; it has gone on for more than a page; it has tired me out even more.

Later. For the first time, I looked back at that photograph of Mum with Boo. On the day they met. I don't even know what I think of it – should we keep it? Is it grotesque? She looks awake, because her eyes are partly open. Looking down at him, although I don't think she was. If anyone looks dead, it's sleeping Boo.

Mittwoch 13 December

Contented, exhausted.

Donnerstag 14 December

He looks around at us, at the mobile; he's a curious boy. He's a curiously curious boy. Mouse fascinates him, when he comes close. I wouldn't be surprised if Boo's first word was 'Mouse' – confusion right from the start.

We take him into town, Covent Garden, to meet Janice and Dave and their two girls. I feel abysmal, showing them Boo. But they are doing what they can not to make it difficult, or painful. Christmas things are being sold around us – grotesque wooden trees covered in baubles, chocolate nuts. We hug when we meet. Of course we cry. They say Jack is lovely. They are so generous. It'll be different, next time. We planned to have coffee, but we all have hot chocolate instead. Boo sleeps, because it's quite chilly.

Freitag 15 December

'What do you think your legacy will be?'

'I've thought about this a lot. I woke at around six thirty this morning, and I thought about it until eight o'clock – when the alarm went off. I knew you were likely to ask me that question, because I'm getting old-ish and it's quite useful to have the answer recorded, for the obit, for when I die, for if I'm newsworthy enough for an obit. I thought about various ways of answering, as I lay under the sheets, and I was oppressed by imagining other writers who have answered the question more wittily or charmingly or movingly than I'll be able to. It would be easy but lazy to say, "That's for other people to decide." The answer is – my considered answer is, "I think it's a deliberately impossible question." It's designed to put the person being asked in a very extreme situation, so that you and your viewers can watch them fail to cope. False modesty will come across just as badly as deep vanity. A joke could seem pretentious, and a curated aphorism extremely silly. "What do you think your legacy will be?" I would like to say, "Nothing – absolutely nothing, because nothing anyone does will endure." But some things people do last for more than a century, and in human terms that's a lot of time. It's false to say Sappho or the Buddha or Shakespeare or Euclid left no legacy. And now it seems I'm comparing myself to Shakespeare and Sappho. Alright, let me do that. I estimate my legacy as less than a millionth of theirs – in reach, in influence, in profundity. The only question is, how much less than a millionth? But that's also saying nothing, nothing interesting. Instead, I'd like to use my remaining time to say this: I was born into a culture which, while it formed me, and while I adore much of it, and while I can only speak from within it – I was born of a culture that is almost totally wrong. There are enough vestiges and contradictions within the culture, enough self-questioning, for me to have glimpsed what outside might possibly be like. I will never reach there, because I carry the inside of the culture with me – wherever I am, it is, too. But I can gesture towards another way of being. I can say, "Live towards otherness." That's not the answer you wanted.'

Samstag 16 December

To Dad's, for a quick pre-Christmas visit – without Leigh and Boo. The loneliness of him, the terrible loneliness.

Mum was Dad's life, and now she's dead he's living an afterlife. He suffers it, dislikes it, but he won't do anything to change it. Well, he did buy a painting from the market – along with the marmalade. It's awful and he loves it. He is planning a trip to visit his brother in Australia. He won't go to the local swimming baths; he loves swimming. I am dismayed. We expect the people who have dominated us to be able to at least sort of control themselves. But how annihilating a happy marriage can be. When someone has done and been everything for and to you, you are left alone and baffled. My father wants his hearth and home back. He wants back 1985 and 1978 and most of all 1967. My father stands on the doorstep of the world, looking out, pretending he is considering actually fucking doing something. He hates his walking frame, but will not climb on the exercise bike. He pricks his thumb to test his blood-sugar level, injects his insulin, then eats one of the Wispa bars that were hidden in the drawer with the napkins and tablemats. This is death by daytime television and hot cross bun. I don't want to be critical. Dad is grieving and depressed (but unwilling to consider antidepressants). He is a man of his generation, by which I mean a boy who never had to grow up. ('Look at the state of you – I mean, just look. It's so unfair!') I realize I am extremely angry at him for not being there when Mum died. We even saved him the effort of that. All life is another term and another term at boarding school. No vac. Get some sweets from the Tuck Shop and try to skive off Games. He cries when he mentions his House Master – who stood in for his father after his father died. 'A great man,' he'll say, meaning the House Master, not his father. I talk to my brother about Dad. We know he will not change. It's hopeless; he's hopeless. Still, I bring him cake and cut him a generous slice of it and we lounge around the Common Room trying not to get a detention.

Sonntag 17 December

The mother who knows her daughter will never be as beautiful as she herself was and still is. The six Japanese schoolgirls arriving in Piccadilly Circus, by coach, for a two-week visit (or perhaps just four of them). The glamorous Hollywood film star, 29, riding the Scottish hopper bus to the final stop – then taking the small ferry to the island. The prisoner in solitary confinement who solves a murder by the prison governor in another wing of the jail, and who succeeds in getting the governor arrested, tried and convicted. The autobiography of Judas Iscariot. The lives of Elizabeth I and Margaret Thatcher and Elizabeth II and Princess Margaret done as a double exposure. The squire assumes the armour and identity of one of King Arthur's knights, after his liege master falls into a stream and drowns on his way to rid a village of a dragon. The seven 1970s students who each bet *they* won't be first to step outside the front door of their large shared Georgian house squat, and the collapse into barbarism of the society inside the house, and then the collapse of the house. The medieval monk who suffers from the psychological effects of 24-hour surveillance by an omniscient God. Aliens arrive, take over and – among other things – change Earth's property laws; if you first owned land, you cannot sell it because *it* owns *you*; how this changes the life of one Native American family. The grandson of an SF novelist tries to reclaim vast royalties on a fictional invention of this grandfather's that became a reality and changed the lives of everyone in the world. (These last two, somehow, to fit together in a First Contact *Bleak House*.) The novel about the psychic trauma suffered by the Pevensie children who were once sexy kings and queens in Narnia. *The Good Killer*. The heroic journey of a very old lady to the shops to get her groceries. The model – well, everyone says she should be a model – who is beautiful but *not quite beautiful enough*. The big multi-stranded London novel. The sea-voyage novel. The truly alien alien novel. The Oxford undergraduate novel no-one needs.

All these stories I know I will never write.

Montag 18 December

What will people actually say of me? What? Who? Sorry, who? – I think he's in the day room. You'll have to ask one of the nurses. Someone gave me one of his books for Christmas, years ago, but I really couldn't be doing with it. Bald, very bald, but a big beard. He'll have written about this somewhere – a whole section on what people were going to say about him after he died. I remember he had a nice grey greatcoat that I always envied, though it was far too big for me; and I used to touch it when we were talking. Who? I always meant to get around to reading him, but there were so many other books, and his never seemed to be all that urgent. Was he the one who wrote that memoir called *Scent of Dried Pink Petals* or something? He did quite a witty speech at his retirement. I have some letters from him; I don't think they're worth anything. Arrogant – I knew him for years and I always found him quite pleased with himself. Did he write poetry? I didn't know. Is it any good? He gave me lifts to football when I was twelve; said we didn't have to talk; knew I was embarrassed – I liked him for that. He wrote too much – it's that simple. I always met him at the Lido, and we talked about swimming and Buddhism and coffee. Didn't he write that novel where the red edges of the pages came off on your hands? I broke his glasses once by pulling them off – my parents told me this; I have no memory of it: we were in Southwold. No, I mean he was *around* the same scene, but I never had much to do with him. He used to have the Veggie Special Breakfast with a poached egg, and tea with brown toast. They had such a beautiful baby. Yeah, wrote some of the weirdest shit you're ever gonna read. He always talked over me – I'd be trying to say something really quite personal, and he'd just began telling some unfunny anecdote about himself. We did a few festivals together, when my third novel came out, in Croatia and Slovenia – he didn't speak Serbo-Croat. Who? I liked him – he wasn't my best friend at college, but I don't think either of us particularly made the effort.

Dienstag 19 December

Preparing for Christmas.

Mittwoch 20 December

When all your effort was erring, and all your curious, sincere work turns out to have been a waste – because what you've written is shit, and when you read it back you know it's shit: uncompostable, toxic, irredeemable shit.

That's not true: I always assume I'm misguided, but I know not everything I've done has been worthless. It's just, the frustration of thinking the last months could have been dedicated to something better. Isn't now the time to try to write the big book, the Big London Book? Am I still not ready? Do I need to know what happens to everyone in the crowd? Then I think, 'The Big London Book will inevitably be even shitter – stick to the small desk book – which you've been writing on the side – almost without noticing.' (A siren – I did notice that one.) There are some good qualities to the shit, just as human shit could be part-paracetamol, part-caviar, part-golddust. I have to accept, as I have before, that I've written in order to keep writing and in order to bring me to the point where I could write another thing. It has sometimes taken three drafts of a failed novel to write one short story, or one paragraph in an essay, or one sentence in a notebook. I know I am always wrong to call it a waste; and it's probably not even inefficient. If it's not toxic, then it's mulch, humus, compost; if it's toxic, radioactive, it clears a space around it for mutant lifeforms and kickarse cockroaches. There are areas of attempt, stations of power, that I haven't approached for years. When I think about them, a rabbit runs down a service corridor thick with fungi. Asbestos ceiling tiles fall down into forests of ferns, or bramble-tangles. Rats give birth within split hard drives. I may never live here. They are not project.

Donnerstag 21 December

Contented, exhausted.

Freitag 22 December

The last time she ate chicken. The last time she set off for the shops with a handwritten shopping list. The last time she sang Handel. The last time she prayed – if she ever prayed. The last time she saw anyone called Richard. The last time she wore earrings. The last time she went to a restaurant or had friends for dinner or went to friends' for dinner. The last time she heard my father's voice and understood what it was saying. The last time she did exactly what she wanted to do from the start of the day to the end. The last time she visited a garden centre but didn't buy anything because they didn't have what she wanted. The last time she had toothache. The last time she came off Junction 12 of the M1. The last time she ate lunch at the Battersea Decorative Antiques and Textiles Fair. The last time she said lunch at the Battersea Decorative Antiques and Textiles Fair was much too expensive – especially for exhibitors. The last time she was polite to a difficult customer. The last time she became frosty. The last time she sold something. The last time she said the flowers were lovely. The last time she went to the toilet by herself. The last time she said Buggeration whilst parallel parking. The last time she used Tipp-Ex. The last time she spoke to a man who had been in prison. The last time she put something back on the shelf in Waitrose. The last time she drank champagne. The last time she used a needle to remove a splinter from my thumb, or from any of my fingers. The last time she heard Mozart. The last time she told me to hold still. The last time she put down her sewing basket. The last time she used her lanyard at Cranfield Institute of Technology. The last time she had anything to do with Human Resources at Cranfield Institute of Technology. The last time she wondered if she was still young. The last time she drank from a coffee mug that was designed but not manufactured in Denmark. The last time she put on a dufflecoat after choir practice. The last time she trusted someone she knew she shouldn't. The last time she saw a stalagmite in situ. The last time she saw an iguana on the television. The last time she won a hand of bridge she should have lost. The last time she said the flowers were lovely even though they weren't. The first and last time she visited the Alhambra. The last time she used nail clippers.

Samstag 23 December

Yes, I think something on top of or parallel to the year is coming to its end, at the end of the year. My usual feeling – now no differently repeated – is that I've written *too much* and that, exactly because of this, I *haven't written enough* of the kind of writing I'd write if I wrote less. What this slow-distilled poetry or prose would be, I have no clear idea. It would be better, I think; it would – I feel – not be quite so normal; I hope it would do more than five or six things aptly and at once. Maybe it would look difficult on first glance, but once someone started reading their way in they would start seeing the forest with different eyes – they would see it with the eyes of the forest regarding them. The eyes of the trees and their dead leaves just as much as the eyes of the beasts, regarding them. After an initial bewilderment, their peopled panic would metamorphose into a stippled-dappled pleasure – *esse est percipi*, to be is to be perceived. As if all the eyes of all the wings of all the butterflies in a cloud of butterflies were to wink at one another in iridescent sequence – a cascade of acknowledgement like a peal of bells ringing the extent, the extant. This coruscating chorus of sight and insight would be in no way confusing – it would be like light like light on the curve of a mackerel shoal as it swerves in the swell and brings form to the dark whelm.

No. Stop. I can't write more than this. Another sentence would be too opulently populated, would be too much more of already too much. Like all prose this is trying to do what it does by saying what it can't. Statement, not embodiment. The crowded language of crowds – 'a hundred thousand soldiers advanced through the carnage of the battlefield, each with their own sensations of terror or exaltation, puzzlement or shame'. I, it, can't do multiplicity and simultaneity, it can only say it can't say them. 'A lot of important things were happening to a lot of important things.' And I, king of all I survey, underling of all that surveys me – I am left with an image as overfished as the mackerel – am left with a symbol as kitsch, as near-extinct as the butterfly – the absent ghosts of a billion billion colourless eyeless Monarch Butterflies failing to arrive in Mexico –

It's possible I have finished. If there's anything more to do, it's a landscape – degraded, familiar – that I can see from the desk but can't be startled by; because I'm not in it to jump at a screech owl's screech or be mugged by the reek of a dead badger. There's geological time, and cosmological, and my own death or persistent vegetative state. There's a core of uranium sinking in to the water table and exploding into the fossil record. There's the plastic from 1997 reaching my bloodstream or Flipper's central cortex – a new shampoo's microparticles or polystyrene that hugged office supplies as they arrived. There's everyone's future lodged in a graph describing soil erosion, halfway up. There's the execution of all domestic animals, by order of the King. Horror and shit, there's horror and shit. There's also flyover states insisting on persisting, and those who still believe they can afford to fly over them. There's Hull and Bangladesh and Trinidad and every atoll. There's armies fighting mirror-images. There's no clean water. There's Intelligence deleting all record of the word Artificial. There's the last last broadcast. There's what can only be an impossible residue. There's the fact that water descends and water vapour forms clouds. There's anxiety remaining even when only microbes suffer it – worry about being late, fear of embarrassment during the sales meeting, shame at blood and bleeding, despair over the landscape. There's perfect obedience to beautiful equations that only exist in distantly fading radio signals. There's the archive of loam. There's what – there's the whale on the beach, and the sand worm beneath it. There's Voyager meeting dark matter.

Sonntag 24 December – *Christmas Eve*

When we stand or sit or lie in the presence – or kneel – of a work of art that we know is beyond anything we could make: in extent of meaning, in pungency and radiance, in control of the most minuscule arcane details of craft, in texture and tang, in immediacy, in swing and funk and aura and qualities that still lack names, in fascination and in life. When we confront the obvious fact of our own belatedness and inferiority, we at first despair and then begin to bargain and plot and recalibrate and censor. It would be better to stay with the despair, because it at least has a sublimity of scale – has whelm and chasm. It puts us in our place. And we early on realize that whoever made what's present before or around us had, themselves, to suffer exposure within their own cathedral of lack. (I wish I could call it something other than cathedral, but 'cave' isn't constructed enough, and 'firmament' is too created.) Although they entered with the public through the highest, grandest entrance, we know they – the artists – slunk out through a side door, escaped via the crypt. Already, the obsession of the question had possessed them: *What is there still to be done, when this has been done?* (Cosmos, world, cathedral, me, cathedral, world, cosmos.) Once outside, once departed, some will immediately become thieves, some will spend decades masquerading as alchemists; a few will enter the seminary and train to be monks, and a few of these will succeed in becoming abbots; some others will go to the library and end up, almost by accident, as scribes, historians, bookbinders and librarians; then there are those who turn iconoclast, and preach against all gospels; those who climb up the porches, statues, gargoyles until years later they find somewhere from which to jump; those who run hotfoot to the nearest available body and spend three decades fucking it; some instead who decide to study architecture and follow this into physics, metaphysics and mysticism or mathematics or both; some go insane and are elected to high office and some conscientiously pursue politics all the way to bedlam; some apprentice themselves to stonemasons and woodcarvers; and some return the next day, or the next month, in rough clothes, and begin making small inept sketches, but return the next day, and the next. These last are the worst.

It may be that I am coming to the end. I don't think it likely, but I do admit it's possible. When I wrote the first sentence on this page, I meant writing; now that I read it back, I seem to have been referring to death. That is one of the astounding things about death (Astounding Tales) – how you can name it unwittingly, how you can name it whilst knowing nothing about it. We don't even know that it happens, because verbs may not apply. The happening of the happening is all and only preparation for an event which is not an event, for an experience there is no longer anyone or anything to experience. In this case, it's wrong to say, 'I will die'. After a certain period of time, the thing I've conventionally called I will be what people have repeatedly called dead – parrot-fashion. But at the instant of death, which I know from research and have myself seen is a very woozy moment of heart-death, blood-death, brain-death, consciousness-death – midway through the Janus door, it may be only half-I or minus-I that is in any way present and correct. All died deaths may be absent and incorrect; if so, all deaths are mistaken. I don't mean an afterlife, something more like the action of a verb and how it has built cathedrals and within them chapels of glorious soaring carved tree-like wood and within them stone mausoleums and within them tombs of marble and porphyry and within them coffins of oak and within them boxes of white lead. We would put nothing adoringly around a creature incapable of dying our death for us. (The Christian God is a God simultaneously capable and incapable of being put to death; He is also much easier to make and eat than other Gods.) The verb would be better in its childish, playful form – not to die but to be deaded. 'I deaded you.' 'You didn't.' 'I did, I deaded you. Now be dead.' (A metaphysical poem.) What I meant to say at the beginning of this strange page, before I was engulfed by cathedrals, is that as I've increasingly come to say more and more about less and less, and I've now got close to saying everything about nothing – maybe it'll soon be time for me to stop ending. (No, death isn't nothing but, even more so, death isn't not nothing.)

My brother is with Dad for Christmas. We are at home. Phone call this pm.

I wish Dad had died, not Mum. Shouldn't think it, let alone write it, but I was anticipating Mum-without-Dad not Dad-without-Mum. My father should have gone first – that was the arrangement. We all knew it. She would have been so much better at grief, and life, and life with grief, than he's being. Sadly, then gaily, we would have gone to galleries and concerts. Mum would have remained curious about the world, not just watched TV. Would have taken the hard knock, knuckled under, kept her pecker up. Would have been brought through it by plucky clichés. She would have gardened and played bridge and kept the house. (To give him his due, Dad wishes he had died, not Mum.) Mum would have wanted to come and stay, to help us look after the Boo. In our sitting room, she would have Boo on her lap – as a newborn, as a leveret, as a chunky-chunker with pinched wrists, as a cardigan-wearing wriggler, as a talker, as one of the Grand Old Duke of York's marching men. (Again! Again!) We would drink tea and eat cake, as we do at Dad's, but then we would go for a brisk walk round the park. Away from Leigh, I could ask her advice, and it would be good advice. She would tell me what I was like, when I was Boo's age, because she would remember, because it was important to her (then and now), because seeing Boo doing this or that little thing would bring it back. Dad does not remember little things; I don't think he noticed them at the time. He says he admires me, for being present at the birth, when – for me – he was at home eating steak and kidney pudding. Men weren't welcomed in the delivery rooms of 1968. He faints when he sees blood, and they wouldn't have wanted six foot five of Lancashire crumpling to the lino. He is still crumpling. He wallows and is clumsy. He is a hippopotamus. (I know hippos can be dainty, unlike rhinos.) He is a clumsy hippo. I love him but fucking hell – just be some fucking use, why don't you? They were married almost 50 years. She did everything for him. She systematically and comprehensively de-skilled him. I know nothing.

Dienstag 26 December – *Boxing Day*

What have I done this year? Things have happened to me – big things, perhaps so big that I should let myself off. I have been changed; I have been rendered more vulnerable. Kidnap Boo and I'll do anything you tell me to. Chat shit about my mum and I'll fucking do you. Just me, by myself. Sitting at the desk, I have written about sitting at the desk writing about sitting at the desk – the desk that remains a table. There are, of course, less embodied ways of being a writer than this, and by that I don't mean giving dictation in a float tank. There's the psychic stuff. There's influence; there's possession. But what I set myself to record, Flipper, is where and how my daily writing gets done or doesn't get done. (And writing stands for writing but writing is also everything else – that's what writers think – writing is trying to do anything expressively.) In doing so, I have tried to be honest, and so it is trivial, because I'm often trivial (obsessed with pens, annoyed with spills); I have set myself to stick close to the moment, and stray no more than ten inches from the hardboard. (Put me in the room.) I may have glanced around, or gone into reverie, but I didn't stand up and walk away – as I will do after I finish this. You, Boo, are grizzling; I can hear you. Me, I'm thirsty and my glass is empty. Beneath the desk, on the angled foot-rest, my left foot is resting on my right foot. (I never wrote about the foot-rest!) The nub of one ankle fits into the dip between the tendons of the other. Outside, Mouse just knocked over a teacup full of rainwater – sounded like. My left palm, on my left wrist, ulna-radius, supports my left-tilted skull. I am writing with the black pen in black ink on a white page in a black diary. Life writing. My breathing is even. My beard aches slightly. I have a better pencil-sharpener than I did at the beginning of the year. Our house is subsiding. You, Jack or maybe you're turning back to John, are with Leigh in the bedroom. My father is at home watching television. My mum's ashes surround him – against the walls of his garden.

Mittwoch 27 December

The first time he sneezed. The first time Mouse sniffed his nose. The first time he seemed to see the black and white mobile hanging over his cot. The first time he squeezed my forefinger with his fingers and thumb. The first time he sneezed twice. The first time we took him to a café. The first time someone mistook him for a girl. The first time he visited a hospice. The first time he puked back a whole bottle of expressed breast milk. The first time he made a sound like he was laughing. The first time he took the nipple then didn't take the nipple then sort of half took the nipple then didn't take the nipple. The first time his poo had a white streak in it like Susan Sontag's hair. The first time he became completely freaked out by I have no idea what and cried and cried so much he went white and I undressed him to see if a wasp had got into his babygro and stung him, but it hadn't. The first time he made Leigh weep by not taking the nipple. The first time he seemed to have stopped breathing, so I called the ambulance, and they told me I'd done the right thing, even though he was gurgling contentedly by the time they arrived. The first time I cut his fingernails by biting them. The first time Mouse's sudden appearance startled him and made him cry. The first time he dressed up – was dressed up – for Hallowe'en (as a pumpkin). The first time he filled and overfilled his nappy just after being dressed in his third layer of outdoor clothes. The first time he had his photograph taken in the delivery room. The first time he did a poo that could be classified as nuclear waste. The first time he suffered and suffered and his suffering could not be mitigated. The first time he turned from his back to his front. The first time he suddenly went stiff and we thought something was wrong but then he relaxed and we told each other it was normal. The first time he woke up nine times in the night. The first time he slept through until half five. The first and last time he met my mum.

Donnerstag 28 December

The last time she wore glasses. The last time she won a hand of bridge, or a rubber, or a duplicate tournament. The last time she was 30,000 feet above sea level. The last time she made someone laugh (when she sent the Vicar away, waited until he was out of the room, then grimaced). The last time she knew one of her children was with her. The last time she pushed a swing. The last time she left the Citizens Advice Bureau office. The last time she saw Evan and Julie, saw Paddy and Mary, saw Steven and Caroline. The last time she thought, 'This will be the last time.' The last time she snored. The last time she peeled an orange. The last time she ate a slice of orange. The last time she drank orange juice. The last time she finished a crossword. The last time she asked for the TV to be turned off. The last time she tucked a tissue up her sleeve. The last time she had sex. The last time she indicated left. The last time she remembered the first time she had sex after she was married. The last time she closed her laptop. The last time she bought bread. The last time she sat on a swing and was pushed. The last time she opened the fridge. The last time she left her house. The last time she shaved her legs. The last time she phoned me. The last time she felt it would snow and was right. The last time she was able to get health insurance. The last time she took off her wig. The last time she shook her head. The last time she breathed in. The last time she held a baby. The last time she was in Paris. The last time she signed her name. The last time she read me a bedtime story. The last time she breathed out. The last time she wore her hiking boots whilst alive. The last time she stopped to look down from a peak. The last time she sucked a Polo. The last time she watched Gordon Ramsey's Kitchen Nightmares. The last time she attended a funeral. The last time she made a roux for cauliflower cheese. The last time she saw her father. The last time she greased one baking tray. The last time she wore a dufflecoat or sang in a choir or worried about nuclear war. The last time she created metadata. The last time she had anything to do with the police. The last time she played backgammon. The last time she locked up the house in France. The last time she read *Interiors* magazine.

Freitag 29 December

The first time he drives alone in a car after passing his driving test. The first time he falls off a climbing frame. The first time he asks someone out and they make an excuse so as not to have to say no. This first time he realizes he will never be an astronaut, even if he does get to go into space on a commercial flight. The first time he really looks at a dead moth. The first time he hates a teacher. The first time he falls off his bike. The first time he realizes life is unfair. The first time he's kissed by someone who can really kiss and who really wants to kiss him. The first time he buys drugs. The first time he realizes life is unfair and it's unfair in his favour. The first time he pukes from the window of a moving car. The first time he realizes he's going to die just like the stinky dead bird on the tarmac died. The first time he throws something away and never gets it back. The first time he sees his own child. The first time he eats sand along with sandwich. The first time he thinks seriously about suicide as a thing. The first time he gets lost on the London Underground. The first time he thinks this is the best song ever. The first time he thinks fifty isn't actually that old. The first time he changes lanes at eighty miles an hour (perhaps he'll never do this; perhaps he'll never learn to drive). The first time he knows the waitress is having a bad day. The first time he takes the piss out of the technology his parents used to use. The first time he sees the truth hanging from the door. The first time he knows his boss is undermining him. The first time he realizes life is unfair and it's unfair against him. The first time he sees a cloud shaped like a castle. The first time he sees Manhattan at night. The first time he gets dumped. The first time he draws the whiskers on a cartoon cat. The first time he gets a varicose vein. The first time he's the Tooth Fairy. The first time he's afraid to ask the doctor. The first time he forgets to be the Tooth Fairy. The first time he knows it isn't love, because it doesn't feel like when it was love. The first time he feels he should take more exercise. The first time he opens a fridge. The first time he swears at a computer. The first time he's offered a seat on a bus by someone much younger. The first time he shoplifts. The first time he realizes his parents are serious about the Berlin Philharmonic. We are going to Leigh's mum and dad's.

Samstag 30 December

I read something someone had written, about constantly re-reading their own work-in-progress, and so I feel I should look back at this – this whatever this is… The re-read lasted about three minutes, before I returned again to the present page and started writing these words. I suppose (thinking about it through Werner Herzog, before he suffers whatever his disgrace shall be) this is not the truth of me but the ecstatic truth. It's not a day diary. It's nothing like what's achievable within a year, although I have only been working on it for seven months; it's what's been stolen from my own impossibility. Because I lied to myself about what I was capable of, I found I was capable of more than any reasonable person (including myself) would have expected. The Tour de France. By speaking out of turn, I said unexpected things someone else should have said, neglected to say. Jump off a cliff. If I can confess: I wanted to write the best book that has ever been written about writing – about the physical act of writing and the metaphysical act. Shoot yourself in the head. Of course this is ridiculous. Even if no one will ever read this, I shouldn't write it down. By admitting the greatness of my ambition, I have exploded the scope of my shame. It has been a very lighthouse keeper kind of life.

I wish I didn't look like I look, or act as I act, but I'm okay with how I write – try to write – when I write – when I try to write as I wish I wrote – when the writing tricks itself into becoming vivid, unzombie – when it's all bending curlicue yet utterly direct – when it's force and frond and fern and furze and force – when it's particle and wave and physicist and physicist's lunch, and almost any word at any point in any sentence – airily grounded, dirt-star – time-formed and whereupon – when it's no longer by me – when it bloody gets it down – when it's it.

Sonntag 31 December – *New Year's Eve*

Such a year, this. Such a great-crappy year. To live it again would kill me.

Phoned Dad, but he'd gone to bed early.

Walter texted. He never texts. His phone is always broken. I texted back. 'Happy New Year, you mad old bastard.' He says he's going to learn to scuba dive.

My brother texted, too. 'Will definitely not begin my novel this year. That's a promise. May, however, record a solo album or climb K2.'

Snuck upstairs to write this. Finish off.

What will happen next? We will stay up until midnight with Leigh's parents and Baby Jack. Watch rubbish TV. I would happily go to bed right now. Since arriving here, I have got much more sleep than usual (since Boo was born) – and am almost fully recovered from Christmas, which was hard work.

As is proper, I will go out of the year in Leigh's arms – as long as Boo isn't in them. Or maybe both of us.

WHY BE A GALLEY BUDDY?

At Galley Beggar Press we don't want to compromise on the excellence of the writing we put out, or the physical quality of our books. We've also enjoyed numerous successes and prize nominations since we set up, in 2012. Almost all of our authors have gone on to be longlisted, shortlisted, or the winners of over twenty of the world's most prestigious literary awards.

But publishing for the sake of art is a risky commercial strategy. In order to keep putting out the very best books we can, and to continue to support talented writers, we need your help. The money we receive from our Galley Buddy scheme is an essential part of keeping us going.

By becoming a Galley Buddy, you help us to launch and foster a new generation of writers.

To join today, head to:
https://www.galleybeggar.co.uk/subscribe

GALLEY BEGGAR PRESS

We hope that you've enjoyed *A Writer's Diary*. If you would like to find out more about Toby, along with some of his fellow authors, head to www.galleybeggar.co.uk.

There, you will also find information about our subscription scheme, 'Galley Buddies', which is there to ensure we can continue to put out ambitious and unusual books like *A Writer's Diary*.

Subscribers to Galley Beggar Press:

- Receive limited black cover editions of our future titles (printed in a one-time run of 600).
- Have their names included in a special acknowledgement section at the back of our books.
- Are sent regular updates and invitations to our book launches, talks and other events.
- Enjoy a 20% discount code for the purchase of any of our backlist (as well as for general use throughout our online shop).

FRIENDS OF GALLEY BEGGAR PRESS

Galley Beggar Press would like to thank the following individuals, without the generous support of whom our books would not be possible:

Cameron Adams
Muriel Adams
Kémy Ade
Timothy Ahern
Liz Aiken
Sam Ainsworth
Jez Aitchison
Richard Allen
Lulu Allison
Adrian Alvarez
Anna Andreou
Simon Andrup
Jerome Anello
Natalia Anjaparidze
Kirk Annett
Deborah Arata
Robert Armiger
Kate Armstrong
Sean Arnold
Curt Arnson
Jake Arthur
Xanthe Ashburner
Bethany Ashley
Robert Ashton
Rachel Atkin
Edmund Attrill
Valda Aviks
Jo Ayoubi
Kerim Aytac
Claire Back
Thomas Badyna
Andrew Bailey
Dexter Bailey
Tom Bailey
Edward Baines
Glynis Baker
James Baker
John Balfour
Maggie Balistreri
Christopher Ball
Andrew Ballantyne
Sarah Balstrup
Paul Bangert
Victoria Barkas
Andrea Barlien

Chad Barnes
Kevin Barrett
Matthew Barron
Phil Bartlett
Morgan Baxley
Perry Beadsworth
Rachael Beale
Rebecca Bealey
Lauren Beattie
James Beavis
Rachel Bedder
Georgia Beddoe
Joseph Bell
Angel Belsey
Madeline Bennett
Felicity Bentham
Jean Bergin
Michelle Best
Gary Betts
David Bevan
Allison Beynon
Alison Bianchi
Gavin Bingham
Sandra Birnie
Donna-Louise
  Bishop
Nick Black
Mark Blackburn
Peter Blackett
Matt Blackstock
Kate Bland
Melissa Blaschke
Charlie Bloor
Blue and Kat
Lynne Blundell
David Boddy
Sophie Boden
Rich Boden
John Bogg
Kalina Borisova
Poppy Boutell
Edwina Bowen
Mark Bowles
Michelle Bowles
David Bowman

Joanna Bowman
Alexander Bown
Matthew Boyd
Astrid Bracke
David Bradley
Sean Bradley
David Brady
Debby Brady
Joan Brennan
Andrew J.
  Bremner
Chris Brewer
Amanda Bringans
Erin Britton
Julia Brocking
Dean Brooks
Anthony Brown
Lily Brown
Peter Brown
Sheila Browse
Carrie Brunt
Richard Bryant
Lesley Budge
Daniel Bugg
Laura Bui
Gayle Burgoyne
Tony Burke
Kevin Burrell
Tamsin Bury
Joe Butler
Esther van Buul
Gosia Buzzanca
Sarah Brayshaw
Andrew Bremner
Kester Brewin
Barry Bryne
Barbara Byar
Jorien Caers
Alan Calder
June Caldwell
Matt Callow
Francesca
  Cambridge
Mallen
Gordon Cameron

Mark Campbell
Laura Canning
Annette Capel
Rhian Capener
Andrew Cardus
Ros Carne
Jackie Carpenter
Leona Carpenter
Daniel Carr
Sean Carroll
Shaun Carter
Stuart Carter
Liam Casey
David Caves
Leigh Chambers
Sonia Chander
John Chapman
Richard Chatterton
Christel Chen
Lina Christopoulou
Neal Chuang
Gemma Church
Neil Churchill
Jack Clark
Deborah Ann
  Clarke
Simon Clarke
Douglas Clarke-
  Williams
Rex Cleaver
Steve Clough
Emily Coghill
Steven Coghill
Daniel Cohen
Paul Cole
Faith Coles
John Coles
Emma Coley
Sam Coley
Jonathan Collings
X Collins
Jess Conway
Joe Cooney
Sarah Corbett
Paul Corry

Andy Corsham
Mary Costello
Sally Cott
Nick Coupe
Diarmuid Cowan
Colette Cox
Isabelle Coy-Dibley
Matthew Craig
Anne Craven
Anne-Marie
    Creamer
Alan Crilly
Joanna Crispin
Brenda Croskery
Alasdair Cross
James Cross
Jenny Crossland
Kate Crowcroft
Miles Crowley
Stephen Cuckney
John Cullinane
Damian Cummings
Stephen Cummins
Andrew Cupples
TR Currell
Patrick Curry
Emma Curtis Lake
Chris Cusack
Will Dady
Siddharth Dalal
Jon Dalladay
Rupert Dastur
Maurizio Dattilo
Sally Davenport
Claudia Daventry
Andrew Davies
Julie Davies
Linda Davies
Nickey Davies
Ian Daw
Emilie Day
Emily Day
Toby Day
Sarah Deacon
Ann Debono
Meaghan Delahunt
Rebecca Demaree
Stanislaus Dempsey
Paul Dettmann
Angelica Diehn
Jane Dietrich
Kasper Dijk

Gary Dixon
Turner Docherty
William Dobson
Mark Dolan
Freda Donoghue
Dennis Donothan
Laura Donovan
Kirsty Doole
Oliver Dorostkar
David Douce
Janet Dowling
Kelly Downey
Jamie Downs
Iain Doyle
Alan Duckers
Ian Dudley
Fiona Duffy
Anthony Duncan
Stanka Easton
Matthew Eatough
Nicola Edwards
Lance Ehrman
Jonathan Elkon
Ian Ellison
Thomas Ellmer
Theresa Emig
Stefan Erhardt
Fiona Erskine
Frances Evangelista
Gareth Evans
Kieran Evans
Paul Ewen
Adam Fales
Sarah Farley
Pauline Farrar
Emma Feather
Lori Feathers
Gerard Feehily
Jeremy Felt
Victoria Fendall
Maria Guilliana
    Fenech
Michael Fenton
Edward J. Field
Paul Fielder
Catriona Firth
Becky Fisher
Duncan Fisher
Nicholas Fisher
Caitlin Fitzgerald
Judith Flanders
Mark Flaum

Grace Fletcher-
    Hackwood
Hayley Flockhart
Nicholas Flower
Patrick Foley
James Fourniere
Ceriel Fousert
Kathleen Fox
Richard Fradgley
Matthew Francis
Nigel Francis
Bridget Fraser
Emily Fraser
Charlotte Frears
Emma French
Ruth Frendo
Elizabeth Frye
Gill Fryzer
Graham Fulcher
Paul Fulcher
Jane Fuller
Stephen Furlong
Michael Furness
Richard Furniss
John Gallagher
Timothy Gallimore
Marc Galvin
Annabel Gaskell
Nolan Geoghegan
Pia Ghosh Roy
Phil Gibby
Alison Gibson
Luke Gibson
Jacqueline Gittens
James Goddard
Stephanie Golding
Elizabeth Goldman
Mark Goldthorpe
Morgan
    Golf-French
Sakura Gooneratne
Sara Gore
Nikheel Gorolay
Cathy Goudie
Simon Goudie
Emily Grabham
Becky Greer
Ben Griffiths
Neil Griffiths
Vicki Grimshaw
Christopher
    Gruppet

Sam Gugliani
Robbie Guillory
Drew Gummerson
Dave Gunning
Ian Hagues
Daniel Hahn
Callum Hale-
    Thomson
Nikki Hall
Alice Halliday
Verity Halliday
Peter Halliwell
Emma Hammond
Paul Handley
Rachel Handley
Paul Hanson
Jill Harrison
Greg Harrowing
Alice Harvey
Becky Harvey
Espen Hauglid
Simon
    Hawkesworth
Connor Hayden
Adrian Hayes
Rachel Heath
David
    Hebblethwaite
Richard Hemmings
Peter Hemsworth
Petra Hendrickson
Padraig J.
    Heneghan
Stu Hennigan
Adam Saiz Abo
    Henriksen
Penelope
    Hewett-Brown
Felix Hewison-
    Carter
Simon Higgins
Annette Higgs
Alexander
    Highfield
Jennifer Hill
Daniel Hillman
David Hirons
Ned Hirst
Marcus Hobson
Jamie Hodder-
    Williams
Nicholas Hodges

Stephenjohn Holgate
Turan Holland
Aisling Holling
Ben Holloway
David Holmes
Rene Hooft
Adrian Howe
William Hsieh
Steve Hubbard
Hugh Hudson
Anna Jean Hughes
Emily Hughes
Richard Hughes
Robert Hughes
Jon Hulbert
Kim-ling Humphrey
Joanne Humphries
Raven Hurste
Louise Hussey
LJ Hutchins
Lori Inglis Hall
Grace Iredale
Simon Issatt
Joseph Jackson
Ryan Jackson
Jane Jakeman
Briley James
Hayley James
Helen James
Michael James
Graeme Jarvie
Daniel Jean
Gareth Jelley
Kavita A. Jindal
Rachel John
Alice Jolly
Alex Jones
Bevan Jones
Deborah Jones
Ellen Jones
Jupiter Jones
Rebecca Jones
Amy Jordison
Anna Jordison
Diana Jordison
Atul Joshi
Sapna Joshi
Claire Jost
Rebecca Joy
Benjamin Judge

Gary Kaill
Darren Kane
Thomas Kealy
Andrew Kelly
Emily Kent
Michael Ketchum
Jeffrey Kichen
Ross Kilpatrick
Anna Kime
Fran Kime
Xanath King
Euan Kitson
Clara Knight
Jacqueline Knott
Amy Koheealiee
David Krakauer
Emily Kubisiak
Elisabeth Kumar
Navpreet Kundal
Candida Lacey
Geves Lafosse
Rachel Lalchan
Philip Lane
Dominique Lane-Osherov
I Lang
Kathy Lanzarotti
Kim Laramee
Steven Law
Jo Lawrence
Lorraine Lawrence
Andrew Lawton-Collins
Sue Lawson
Elizabeth Eva Leach
Stephen Leach
Rick Le Coyte
Jessica Leggett
Carley Lee
Liz and Pete Lee
Tracey Lee
Jessica Leggett
Edwin Lerner
Chiara Levorato
Sara Levy
Elizabeth Leyland
Oliver Lewis
Yin Lim
Chris Lintott
Clayton Lister
Amy Lloyd
Lyn Lockwood

Katie Long
Tracey Longworth
Nikyta Loraine
Zoe Lourie
Kathryn Lovell
Lele Lucas
John Lutz
Michael Lynch
Marc Lyth
Paul McAuley
James McCann
Leona McCann
Chris McLaren
Paul McCombs
Emma McConnell
Fabia McDougall
Grace McHale
Sheila McIntosh
Alan McIntyre
Eleanor McIntyre
Sarah McIntyre
Lucie McKnight Hardy
Gerald McWilliams
Ewan MacDonald
Andrea MacLeod
Victoria MacKenzie
Duncan Mackie
Brendan Madden
Joseph Maffey
Anne Maguire
Sean Maguire
Eleanor Maier
Philip Makatrewicz
Sarah Male
Anil Malhotra
Tom Mandall
Joshua Mandel
Venetia Manning
Chiara Margiotta
John Marr
Natalie Marshall
Paul Marshall
Aoife Martin
Harriet Martin
Iain Martin
William Mascioli
Rachel Mason
Rebecca Mastman
Sarah Maxted
Susan Maxwell
Dan Mayers

Stephen Maynard
Sally Mayor
Jason Merrells
Andy Merrills
Tina Meyer
Lindsey Millen
Michael Millington
Ali Millar
Phillipa Mills
Robert Mills
Sally Minogue
Fiona Mitchell
Lindsay Mitchell
Adam Moliver
Ian Mond
Fiona Mongredien
Alexander Monker
Alex Moore
Clare Moore
Gary Moore
Michelle Moorhouse
Jonathan Moreland
Nigel J. Morgan
Harriet Mossop
Carlos Eduardo Morreo
Elizabeth Morris
Jackie Morris
Joanne Morris
Julie Morris
Patrick Morris
Clive Morrison
Catriona Morrison
Donald Morrison
Penny Morrison
Roger Morrison
Jennifer Mulholland
Christian Murphy
Nicole Murphy
Ben Myers
Electra Nanou
Zosha Nash
Linda Nathan
Tim Neighbour
Marie Laure Neulet
Natalie Newman
Amanda Nicholls
Catherine Nicholson
Sophia Nixon

Mariah de Nor

Emma Norman

Sam North

Calum Novak-
Mitchell

Anna Nsubuga

Arif Nurmohamed

Simon Nurse

Rachel Nye

Christopher
O'Brien

James O'Brien

Rodney O'Connor

James O'Leary

Alec Olsen

Siobhaan O'Neill

Valerie O'Riordan

Sam Oborne

Liz O'Sullivan

Kate Packwood

Steven Palter

David Parker

Dave Parry

Simon Parsons

Gary Partington

Debra Patek

Ian Patterson

Adam Paxton

Mark Payne

Stephen Pearsall

Rosie Pendlebury

Jonathan Perks

Davide Perottoni

Connor Perrie

Tom Perrin

Robert Perry

Seetal Petal

Tony Pettigrew

Dan Phillips

Fergus Pickles

Hannah Piekarz

Steven Pilling

Robert Pisani

Ben Plouviez

Louise Pointer

Alex Pointon
Melville

Dimitrios Polemis

Erin Polmear

James Pomar

Dan Pope

Jonathan Pool

Christopher Potter

Lesley Preston

Libby Preston

David Prince

Victoria Proctor

Jill Propst

James Puddephatt

Alan Pulverness

Lisa Quattromini

Leng Leng Quek

Zoe Radley

Jane Rainbow

Sim Ralph

Polly Randall

Lauren Ravazi

Ian Redfern

Sam Reese

Padraid Reidy

Vasco Resende

Amy Reynolds

Caroline Riddell

Mario Riggio

Alison Riley

Thea Marie
Rishovd

Laura Roach

Chris Roberts

Stephen Roberts

Emily Robinsonb

Ada Robinson

Joanna Robinson

Joyce Lillie
Robinson

Neil Robinson

Lizz Roe

Lorraine Rogerson

Kalina Rose

Michael Rowley

Nathan Rowley

Martin Rowsell

Beverly Rudy

Giles Ruffer

Naben Ruthnum

John Rutter

Paul Ryan

Amanda Saint

Floriane Sajdak

Alison Sakai

Himanshu Kamal
Saliya

Bairbre Samh

Robert Sanderson

Benedict Sangster

Steven Savile

Lior Sayada

Liam Scallon

Amy Scarrott

Linde Schaafsma

Robert Scheffel

Benedict Schofield

Jan Schoones

Ros Schwartz

Craig Scott

Nicola Scott

Stephen Robert
Scott

Darren Seeley

Darren Semple

Henry Settle

Elie Sharp

Nicola Shepherd

Emma Shore

Elena Shushakova

Deborah Siddoway

Kate Simpson

Stu Sizer

Ann Slack

Mark Slater

Jay Slayton-Josh

Sarah Slowe

Ben Smith

Catherine Smith

Chris Smith

Hazel Smith

Helen Smith

Ian Smith

Kieron Smith

Nicola Smith

Shannon Smith

Tom Smyth

Haydon Spenceley

Arabella Spencer

Sarah Spitz

S.O. Spitzer

Chiara Spruijt

Levi Stahl

Conor Stait

Ellie Staite

Karl Stange

Daniel Staniforth

Cameron Stark

Phil Starling

Cathryn Steele

Jack Stevens

Zac Stevens

Mark Stevenson

Jow Stewart

Dagmara Stoic

Jamie Stone

Justina Stonyte

Anne Storr

Elizabeth Stott

Julia Stringwell

Andrew Stuart

Daryl Sullivan

Jesse Surridge

Drashti Sutariya

Helen Swain

Ashley Tame

Ewan Tant

Sarah Tapp

Ednyfed Tappy

Justine Taylor

Peter Taylor

Moray Teale

Alan Teder

Gill Thackray

Helen Thain

Darren Theakstone

Cennin Thomas

Sue Thomas

Susannah
Thompson

Julian Thorne

Matthew Thrift

Alexander Tilston
Fleming

Matthew Tilt

Amie Tolson

James Torrance

Eloise Touni

Kate Triggs

Stefani Tuirigangi

Jojo Tulloh

Steve Tuffnell

Devin Tupper

Mike Turner

Neil Turner

Eleanor Updegraff

Geoffrey Urland

Raminta Uselyte

Francesca
Veneziano

Julia Wait

Susan Walby

Chris Walker

Craig Walker
Phoebe Walker
Stephen Walker
Ben Waller
Anna Walsh
Kevin Walsh
Sinead Walsh
Steve Walsh
Christopher
   Walthorne
Zhen Wang
Jerry Ward
Kate Ward
Peter Ward
Rachael Wardell
Guy Ware

Darren Waring
Diane Waring
Emma Warnock
Stephanie Wasek
Daniel Waterfield
Chris Watts
Sarah Webb
Ian Webster
Lucy Webster
Adam Welch
Joanna Wellings
Ian Wells
Karl Ruben Weseth
Jo West-Moore
Wendy Whidden
Robert White

Ben Wilder
Kyra Wilder
Gary Wilks
Claire Willerton
Andrea Willett
G Williams
Sharon Williams
Emma Wilson
Sarah Wiltshire
Kyle Winkler
Bianca Winter
Lucie Winter
Sheena Winter
Astrid Maria
   Wissenburg
Stephen Witkowski

Michael Wohl
Nathan Wood
Sarah Wood
Paul Woodgate
Emma Woolerton
Lorna Wright
Lydia Wynn
Linday Yates
Faye Young
Ian Young
Juliano Zaffino
Vanessa Zampiga
Sylvie Zannier
Rupert Ziziros
Carsten
   Zwaaneveld